To my wife, Valerie, and children, Gabriella, Michael, and Zachary, and my future grandchildren. May these strategic actions help you make an impact when you get to the top.

—JR

To my loving wife, Natasha, and children, Aniyah, Marquis, Jaz, and Amira, and my future descendants. May these strategic actions be a blessing along your journeys, and may you readily accept your greatest responsibility to be good ancestors.

—RANDAL

RANDA

AND JEFF

BLACK FACES IN HIGH PLACES

10 STRATEGIC ACTIONS
FOR BLACK PROFESSIONALS TO REACH THE TOP AND STAY THERE

HarperCollins
LEADERSHIP

An Imprint of HarperCollins

Published by HarperCollins Leadership, an imprint of HarperCollins Focus LLC.

ISBN 978-1-4002-2899-7 (eBook)
ISBN 978-1-4002-2897-3 (TP)

Library of Congress Cataloging-in-Publication Data
Library of Congress Cataloging-in-Publication application
has been submitted.Printed in the United States of America

22 23 24 25 26 LSC 10 9 8 7 6 5 4 3 2 1

CONTENTS

FOREWORD
by Joy Reid

Each day I make my way down hallways that echo with the voices of many others who have made the same journey; except they were mostly white and mostly male. As I make this daily trek, much of the production is, well, in production, as the elements of news change almost semi-instantly. There are always facts to check, guests and videos to vet, and scripts to write and edit. Deadlines come at a rapid-fire pace. There is team call after team call with my producers, propelling me into what feels like a perpetual sprint to make it to the studio.

This is my sanctuary, where I command the attention of millions of people each week. They yearn for not just the facts but also a seasoned interpretation of the day's news. They want perspective. They need pragmatic, candid conversations on complicated multilayered issues. That is what I bring from the vantage point of an underrepresented segment of the viewing and listening population. Unashamedly, I occupy a space that no one else who looks like me holds. I am the first Black woman to serve as a cable television prime-time news anchor, for MSNBC's *The ReidOut*.

I take my seat, adjust my chair, and exercise the ritual of getting settled on my mark. There is a flurry of activity around me as crews check mics, examine graphics, and adjust the lighting. Producers and writers continue to make changes right up until my stage manager counts me down to air. Through all of this, my thoughts are not just on the meticulously written words but also something deeper within. For those around me, this is routine. It happens many times a day, seven days a week. This is the innermost hub of a network news operation, where sometimes days of work, shooting, editing, laboring over verbs and nouns and tense boil down to this. This is when we will reveal to the world what we know and the people who caused this information to become news. For me, there is so much riding on what will flow from my mouth and into the minds of millions of people. My investment is not just in crafting the written word but also in the image on the screen—my image. Many other Black faces have preceded my coming, including Max Robinson, Carole Simpson, Ed Bradley, Mal Goode, Bernard Shaw, and Gwen Ifill, to name a few. What I have learned from the presence of these stalwart predecessors is that when the red light comes on: say something!

As the only Black woman currently hosting a national news program bearing her name, I am keenly aware of the power of the written and spoken word. I know the feeling of being a "Black face in a high place." I know that what I do and what I say will come with an added layer of scrutiny by an audience and industry still adjusting to my presence. Despite that, I never waver from my core existence as a Black daughter, a Black mother, a Black woman. Every day I'm in this job, I'm very conscious of the responsibility to make that collective voice heard. It's unique to do that as a Black woman. Like many other Black faces in high places, I remain faithful to the life experiences that ultimately put me here. I yield to the lessons learned from others, and now this book will assist you in doing the same.

In 2010, Drs. Randal Pinkett and Jeffrey Robinson captured in *Black Faces in White Places* what millions of African Americans and I experience every day—the sometimes-uncomfortable position of being the only Black face in a white place. By the same name, their book documented this rarely discussed phenomenon and provided a workbook of strategies to exist, perform, and excel in such an environment.

Now Drs. Pinkett and Robinson have created a platform for further discussion and discovery in this book, *Black Faces in High Places*. Interestingly, it documents how to make it to the top of your industry or field, the challenge of staying in high places, and the social responsibility of being "the" voice in the room when issues related to social justice and racial equity are brought to the forefront. This was typified by the murder of George Floyd.

Who can forget the outpouring of emotion and the numerous protests across the globe, crying out that Black Lives Matter? Who can forget the words of his daughter, Gianna Floyd, when she simply said, *"My daddy changed the world!"*? Who can forget the moment when the verdict was read in the courtroom during the trial of convicted former Minneapolis police officer Derek Chauvin who was sentenced to twenty-two and a half years in prison?

George Floyd indeed changed the world. His tragic death caused those in business, government, nonprofits, academia, philanthropy, and media to reexamine their images, investments, priorities, and policies. And the movement around him, much like the election of President Barack Obama and so many other seminal national events with a Black body at the center of the story, produced a furious backlash. And—as is often the case for Black faces in high places—we were the ones people turned to for perspective and direction on exactly what to do. In fact, even when we are not called upon, we choose to raise our voices. As persons of power, we have both the unique opportunity and the humbling responsibility to shape the current and future actions of organizations spanning every sector and to do so in a way that can empower Black people. The tentacles of these institutions can create jobs, affect public policy, redirect funds, seed fairer laws and regulations, and ultimately improve the conditions in our communities.

Drs. Pinkett and Robinson tackle these issues and more by dissecting the lives of those who have been there or are there. Their interviews with global figures, corporate magnates, industry trailblazers, civic leaders, entrepreneurial pioneers, and beyond delve into that which is unseen and unheard. Their stories are relatable in an era of Black professionals striving to make it to the top while also being socially responsible and helping to pave the way for those who shall come.

This book gives a thoughtful approach to a complex topic with ten strategic actions to reach the top, stay there, and create lasting change. I applaud these Black men who have dedicated their lives to empowering others and improving society as they give rise to voices yet unheard.

INTRODUCTION

Any African American in this society that sees significant success has an added burden. And a lot of times America is very quick to embrace a Michael Jordan or an Oprah Winfrey or a Barack Obama so long as it's understood that you don't get too controversial around broader issues of social justice.
— BARACK OBAMA

Memorial Day 2020 is a day that will forever be memorialized.

On May 25, 2020, George Floyd walked into Cup Foods, a market at the corner of 38th Street and Chicago Avenue in South Minneapolis, Minnesota. According to the store owner, Mahmoud "Mike" Abumayyaleh, Floyd was a regular customer with whom he always got along with very well. He referred to him as a "big teddy bear" who would come in a few times each week to purchase cell phone credits. Unfortunately, Abumayyaleh wasn't working that evening, and instead, younger employees with less familiarity with Floyd and far less experience had been assigned to the evening shift.

Floyd entered the store with a man and a woman. The man attempted to make a purchase with a twenty-dollar bill, which a teenage clerk suspected was counterfeit and immediately returned to him. Floyd returned approximately ten minutes later and purchased cigarettes—also with a twenty-dollar bill—only this time the seventeen-year-old's suspicions were not raised until after Floyd had left the store. (In an interview later, Abumayyaleh stated that Floyd was likely unaware of whether the bill was counterfeit.) Following store protocol to notify police about fake money, the employee called 911 to report the incident.

At 8:08 p.m., police officers Thomas K. Lane (white) and J. Alexander Kueng (African American) arrived to find Floyd in the passenger seat of a car outside the store. Lane pointed his gun at Floyd and reholstered it once Floyd put his hands on the steering wheel. After ordering Floyd out of the car, Lane handcuffed him.

At 8:14 p.m., Lane and Kueng unsuccessfully attempted to place Floyd into the back seat of their police car. Officers Derek Chauvin (white) and Tou Thao (Asian American) then arrived on the scene, and all four officers were unsuccessful in getting Floyd into the back seat of the same vehicle.

At 8:19 p.m., Chauvin forced Floyd to the ground while he was still handcuffed. Lane restrained Floyd's legs, while Kueng applied pressure to Floyd's back, while Thao engaged with bystanders, while Chauvin put his knee on Floyd's neck *for nine minutes and twenty-nine seconds.* Among Floyd's desperate last words were the following (excerpted from the chilling transcripts of Minneapolis police body camera footage):

"I didn't do nothing wrong."

"I'm not a bad guy!"

"I'm scared, man."

"Mama, mama, mama, mama."

"Tell my kids I love them. I'm dead."

"I can't breathe. Ah! I'll probably die this way."

"I'm going to die."

"I'm about to die."

At approximately 8:28 p.m., Chauvin removed his knee from Floyd's neck. Motionless, Floyd was placed on a stretcher and ambulanced to Hennepin County Medical Center where he was pronounced dead approximately one hour later.

Derek Chauvin murdered George Floyd.

As these fateful events unfolded, a teenage Black girl, Darnella Frazier, was walking her nine-year-old cousin to Cup Foods, only to witness Floyd begging for his life. The seventeen-year-old high school junior wisely and courageously recorded ten minutes and nine seconds of video footage as Chauvin's knee inhumanely, yet nonchalantly, remained on Floyd's neck, despite his dying pleas for mercy. Frazier's video would capture Floyd's final moments from the street to the stretcher. "It was the most awful thing she's ever seen," her lawyer stated later.

On May 26, 2020, at 1:46 a.m., Frazier posted her video to Facebook with the comments, "They killed him right in front of cup foods over south on 38th and Chicago!! No type of sympathy. #POLICE-BRUTALITY." With more than fifty-four thousand shares, Frazier's video went viral. In a subsequent Facebook post, Frazier wrote: "My video went worldwide for everyone to see and know." This led to outrage and an outpouring of emotion and rally cries for change. It sparked global protests and uprisings in the midst of a COVID-19 pandemic. And it prompted calls for social justice and racial equity that were long overdue.

Meanwhile, as countless hearts mourned the murder of George Floyd, countless eyes were placed squarely upon Black faces in high places—prominent African Americans in positions of leadership and power—such as Thasunda Duckett, CEO of Chase Consumer Bank at JPMorgan Chase; Rosalind Brewer, chief operating officer of Starbucks; Mark Mason, chief financial officer at Citigroup; Robert F. Smith, founder, chairman, and CEO of Vista Equity Partners; and Ken Frazier, chairman, and CEO of Merck. Each one of them found themselves at a crossroads as the world watched—wondering and waiting to see how they would respond to this tragedy.

• • •

As the hours and days ensued, some Black leaders debated whether to weigh in. Others had family and friends encouraging them to speak up. A few experienced demands that they release a statement. Most were inundated, if not overwhelmed, by colleagues who were curious to hear their perspective. All felt a mix of emotions ranging from despair to sadness to anger to disgust.

"Yes, it's painful and my tears are real," said Duckett in a LinkedIn post. "It's 2020 and enough is enough. We can no longer be silent." Mason published a blog to the company's website, writing: "I have debated whether I should speak out. But after some emotional conversations with my family earlier this week, I realized I had to. In fact, we all need to." Brewer spoke openly about being "nervous and scared" for all the Black men in her life. Smith issued a memo to his firm's staff, stating: "Let's each of us hold the people we love a little tighter this weekend, and do our part to make of this old world a new world. We have work to do." Frazier conducted an interview on CNBC where he said: "I think business has to go beyond what is required here. It has to go beyond just statements." And for these and several other Black faces in high places that's exactly what they did: go beyond statements and *take action.*

On June 26, 2020, Vista Equity Partners was among the first to join the Modern Leadership initiative, comprising companies that were each committed to placing minorities with no prior board expertise in five new board seats. Smith had previously pledged to cover the college debt of Morehouse College's 2019 graduating class.

On September 23, 2020, Citigroup launched Action for Equity, a $1 billion investment in strategic initiatives "to help address racial equity and justice in the US." As a part of the official press release, Mason said, "The commitments we are announcing today are just the starting point."

On October 8, 2020, JPMorgan Chase pledged $30 billion to "address key drivers of the racial wealth divide, reduce systemic racism against Black and Latinx people, and support employees." Duckett would later be named CEO of the Teachers Insurance and Annuity Association of America (TIAA) and the second Black woman to currently lead a Fortune 500 company (her predecessor, Roger Ferguson, was a Black man).

On October 14, 2020, the Starbucks Foundation awarded $1.5 million in neighborhood grants to support racial equity. This was on the heels of a public apology in 2018 for the arrest of two Black men, Rashon Nelson and Donte Robinson, at a Philadelphia Starbucks. The earlier incident also invoked Brewer's leadership and prompted the company to close eight thousand US stores for implicit bias training. Brewer would later be named CEO of Walgreens, becoming the first Black woman to currently lead a Fortune 500 company.

On December 12, 2020, Merck announced that it was joining OneTen, "a coalition of leading executives who are coming together to upskill, hire and advance one million Black individuals in America over the next 10 years into family-sustaining jobs with opportunities for advancement." OneTen was cofounded by Frazier along with Ken Chenault, former chairman and CEO of American Express; Charles Phillips, chairman of the Black Economic Alliance; Ginni Rometty, executive chairman and former CEO of IBM; and Kevin Sharer, former chairman and CEO of Amgen; it's led by OneTen CEO Maurice Jones. Frazier and Rometty served as cochairs.

* * *

On April 20, 2021, Derek Chauvin was found guilty of two counts of murder and one count of manslaughter in the killing of George Floyd. On June 25, 2021, he was sentenced to twenty-two and a half years in prison. Once again, several elected officials, corporate CEOs, civil rights activists, university presidents, and civic leaders released statements and expressed a mix of sentiments. Their words ranged from sympathies for the Floyd family, to solidarity with the Black community, to hailing the verdict as a sign of progress, to the need for redoubling efforts toward greater social justice and racial equity.

Apple CEO Tim Cook tweeted a quote from Rev. Dr. Martin Luther King Jr.'s book *Where Do We Go From Here: Chaos or Community?*: "Justice for Black people will not flow into society merely from court decisions nor from fountains of political oratory. . . . Justice for Black people cannot be achieved without radical changes in the structure of our society." We found these words to be quite apropos and still resonant fifty-four years after they were written during the penultimate year of the civil rights movement. While the events of 2020–2021 symbolized a different crossroads than the events of 1967–1968, they sounded the same clarion call for action.

The Crossroads for
Black Faces in High Places

Duckett, Brewer, Mason, Smith, and Frazier all arrived at a crossroads stemming from the murder of George Floyd, and they all responded with strategic action. And while these Black faces in high places experienced several challenges that were particular to being at the top, they were not unlike challenges they had faced in getting to the top. In fact, Black faces in high places often find themselves at multiple crossroads representing moments of significant challenge or crisis. It is not the crossroads but, rather, how they respond to the crossroads that ultimately defines them.

THE CROSSROADS OF A FAILED MERGER

In 1999, Cathy Hughes, founder of Radio One and Robert L. "Bob" Johnson, founder of Black Entertainment Television (BET), had already reached the top when they found themselves at a mutual crossroads in attempting to merge their well-known companies. According to Hughes, "It was Syndicated Communications [an investor in BET and Radio One] who sat us down and said, 'Listen, both of you are doing great, but look how powerful you would be if, in fact, you (Cathy) had a cable network and . . . Bob, if you had a radio network.'" After a series of discussions and analyses and negotiations to try to consummate the landmark deal, the merger failed. It was a missed opportunity of historical proportions to create the largest Black-owned media enterprise in the world spanning radio and television. Despite this pivotal setback, however, Hughes and Johnson were able to remain at the top.

Hughes, the first African American woman to chair a publicly held corporation, would go on to establish TV One and Urban One—the largest African American–owned broadcast company spanning radio, television, and digital media—and merge with Reach Media, the media company owned by Tom Joyner. Johnson would go on to sell BET to Viacom for $3 billion, establish the RLJ Companies, which owns or holds interest in a diverse portfolio of companies, and become the first African American to own a majority stake in a major American sports franchise, the Charlotte Bobcats. When asked if she had any regrets, Hughes said, "No, not at all. If I have any regrets about not merging with BET, it's that it would still be Black owned. It wouldn't be owned by Viacom." Johnson added, "And to this day, I do not know of a major company that came about as a result of a merger of Black business owners."

THE CROSSROADS OF BEING BYPASSED

By 1998, Angela Glover Blackwell had risen to the top of the legal advocacy, nonprofit, and philanthropic sectors, and she was poised to rise even higher. Glover Blackwell had submitted her candidacy and was confident that she would become the first African American and the first female president of the internationally renowned Rockefeller Foundation, where ten white men had served as presidents.

Glover Blackwell's resume reflected an accomplished career with impressive qualifications. From 1977 to 1987, she served as a law partner at Public Advocates, a nationally renowned public interest law firm giving voice to the voiceless. In 1987, she expanded her national reputation as the founder of Urban Strategies Council in Oakland, California, which received national recognition for pioneering an innovative, community-building approach to social change. From 1995 to 1998, she assumed the role of senior vice president of domestic programs at the Rockefeller Foundation and was responsible for directing the foundation's domestic and cultural divisions.

There were 265 applicants. The selection process spanned eight months. Glover Blackwell was selected as a finalist. She was one of two strong internal minority candidates, including Lincoln Chen, an Asian American expert in international health. In the end, Glover Blackwell was bypassed for Gordon Conway—not only another white man but also the first non-American to head the then eighty-four-year-old foundation. The decision was disconcerting as much as it was disappointing.

According to the *New York Times*, "Some foundation officials expressed surprise that the board had passed [Glover Blackwell and Chen]." Alice Stone Ilchman, chairwoman of Rockefeller's board, said the foundation leadership hoped both Glover Blackwell and Chen would remain at Rockefeller to continue their "cutting edge work." Glover Blackwell respectfully chose to take her talents elsewhere.

In 1999, Glover Blackwell left the Rockefeller Foundation to launch PolicyLink after successfully petitioning the foundation to provide the financial capital to establish the organization. PolicyLink not only represented the totality of her life's work but also her propensity to reach the top and stay there.

"I recognized we needed a new kind of policy organization, and so from Rockefeller, Ford [Foundation], and others I got resources to start PolicyLink. It includes advocacy, which I learned at the public interest law firm. It includes community building, which I learned at Urban Strategies, and it is infused with the respect for community, which I learned as a community organizer, and it understands how to do that in negotiation with and partnership with philanthropy, which I learned at the Rockefeller Foundation. It has been a remarkably successful endeavor." Today, PolicyLink is indeed a successful and nationally renowned research and action institute advancing economic and social equity. Glover Blackwell has stepped down from her role as founder and CEO but remains involved as founder in residence.

THE CROSSROADS OF BANKRUPTCY

David Steward was three years into his latest venture, World Wide Technology, when he found himself at the most challenging crossroads of his career.

A railroad industry veteran and former top salesperson for Federal Express, in 1984 Steward set out to buy a business and convinced the owner of Transportation Administrative Services (TAS) to sell the auditing company to him for no money down. Three years later, when Union Pacific Railroad needed to audit three years' worth of freight bills, they hired TAS to do the job. Recognizing the power of technology to automate such tasks, he parlayed this opportunity into World Wide Technology (WWT) in 1990.

Steward borrowed money to get the WWT venture going. He then borrowed more money to keep WWT going. And eventually he found himself in $3.5 million of debt with bill collectors hawking him down on a regular basis. "It was one of the most difficult times in my life," Steward said. "I didn't know if the company was going to make it." In fact, on one occasion he looked out his window and saw his car being repossessed. While Steward had reached an extremely difficult crossroads along his path to the top, he did not give up and did not give in. "I had no money, all the trappings of two kids and a wife and a mortgage and all the other things that go along with it, and I didn't have any resources to be able to do it, but I was determined to buy and grow a company," he said.[1]

By focusing aggressively on sales, delivering exceptional solutions, and developing a key strategic partnership with Cisco, today, World Wide Technology has become the largest Black-owned business in America, generating more than $13 billion in annual revenue with fifty-six hundred employees across the globe. WWT ranks number twenty-six on the Forbes Largest Private Companies list of 2020. Steward was able to reach the top and stay at the top, notably as one of five Black billionaires in America.

THE CROSSROADS OF A CRISIS

It's hard to imagine facing a more difficult set of circumstances within the first few months of reaching the top than the crossroads that faced Ken Chenault in 2001. Chenault was named CEO of American Express, a multinational financial services company, on January 1, 2001. He was named chairman of American Express on April 23, 2001. Less than five months later, on September 11, 2001, tragedy struck the epicenter of the financial services industry when terrorists flew airplanes into the Twin Towers of Lower Manhattan, also the location of the global headquarters for American Express. Nearly three thousand people lost their lives. "That was an incredible challenge at any point in someone's career but particularly in my first year as CEO," said Chenault in reflecting on this moment.

Chenault subsequently faced an untold number of challenges such as coping with the death of eleven American Express employees; dealing with the grief of surviving coworkers and the rest of the country; relocating five thousand employees; rebounding from the ensuing economic downturn (which led to a downturn in American Express transactions); and a painful layoff of fifteen thousand employees. "This was a time where, frankly, a number of people were writing off the company [and] did not think we were going to be able to come back. That was a very, very challenging time."

Chenault was able to lead American Express not only through these difficult times but also through the economic recession of 2008. "One of the things I said to [my team] was that this was an incredible crisis and what was most important was to take care not only of our customers but people who were not customers in the affected area— that American Express had to use its service capabilities to really take care of anyone who was impacted," said Chenault. "We emerged stronger as a company; but certainly, the leadership of this company and my leadership was tested at the highest level."

Chenault conveyed a wise, inspiring, and compassionate style of leadership, while achieving strong profit growth and stock value increases. Quite impressively, from the end of 2001, revenues grew from approximately $21 billion to about $34 billion in 2014. It took Chenault twenty years to reach the top at American Express, and he was able to stay there for an additional seventeen years. He retired in 2018 as one of the most respected and admired CEOs.

The Rise and Fall of Black Faces in High Places

Unfortunately, not every story of Black faces in high places has a positive outcome. There are also Black faces in high places who reach the top but do not stay there.

THE RISE AND FALL OF AN ICON

Lauryn Hill reached the pinnacle of entertainment success. In 1998, on the heels of widespread acclaim with the hip-hop group the Fugees, Hill's first solo album, *The Miseducation of Lauryn Hill*, debuted at number one on the *Billboard* music chart. For the 1999 Grammy Awards, Hill became the first woman to be nominated ten times in one year. She set a record in the industry, becoming the first woman to win five Grammys and the first and only hip-hop artist to win the coveted "Album of the Year." She subsequently graced the covers of *Time*, *Esquire*, and *Teen People* and was propelled to the status of an international superstar.

Shortly after her 1999 achievements, Hill dropped completely out of the public eye for several years. She described this period of her life to *Essence*, saying: "For two or three years I was away from all social interaction. It was a very introspective time because I had to confront my fears and master every demonic thought about inferiority, about insecurity or the fear of being Black, young and gifted in this western culture."

Hill resurfaced in 2001 with an erratic performance on *MTV Unplugged* and developed a reputation for being regularly late to concert appearances. In 2013, she was incarcerated for three months after failing to pay $1.8 million in federal taxes. After her release, Hill continued to perform and record music, and her songs became a pop culture fixture, but she has yet to reestablish her former status. She made it to the top but, unfortunately, was unable to stay there.

THE RISE AND FALL OF A TRAILBLAZER

Rodney Hunt went from mowing lawns as a youth to running one of the most successful Black-owned businesses in the country. After leaving his position as a senior associate at the recognized consulting firm Booz Allen Hamilton, Hunt launched in 1992 RS Information Systems (RSIS), an information technology, systems engineering, and telecommunications firm. Hunt remained committed to the venture even after his wife, Leila, was killed in a car crash leaving him to raise their son, Bradley, as a single father. After securing its first government contract for $5,000 in 1992, RSIS grew to its peak in 2015 at $363 million in revenue and seventeen hundred employees. "I'd like to be the Robert Johnson of government IT," Hunt told *Minority Business Entrepreneur*. "I'd love to be the first African American–owned firm to do a billion dollars' worth of services with the federal government."[2] Along the way, he bought a $5.3 million parcel of land upon which he built a twenty-thousand-square-foot mansion that was featured on *MTV Cribs*. Hunt sold RSIS in 2007 at a time when his estimated net worth was more than a quarter of a billion dollars.

At the age of fifty-one, Hunt unsuccessfully tried to translate his technology success into other arenas. Astonishingly, this included a failed record label, RPH Entertainment, which signed several local acts including Bradley (aka "A Kid Named Breezy") and released a compilation of music called *Money, Cars, Clothes and Hoes*. This also included a failed hip-hop fashion label, a failed sports complex, a failed real estate development, arrests, lawsuits, and the 2012 foreclosure of his $23.1 million mansion home. This all culminated in a 2015 bankruptcy filing citing debts between $10 and $50 million. "It frustrates me more that Mr. Hunt was a prime example [of] an entrepreneur who built a successful business outside of those stereotypical domains and after his success he chose to go backwards and blow it all away in those very same stereotypical industries. He chose to be flashy and chase fame over finding comfort in protecting and growing his substantial wealth," wrote *The Paper Chaser*. Hunt had made it to the top but, unfortunately, was unable to stay there.

It's hard to get to the top.

It's harder to stay at the top.

Why We Wrote
Black Faces in High Places

The lessons from Hill and Hunt lead to the simple yet powerful premise of this book: we want you to reach the top *and stay there.*

More than ten years ago, we wrote our first book together, *Black Faces in White Places: 10 Game Changing Strategies to Achieve Success and Find Greatness.* It was a book about rising to the top and navigating professional environments to make a positive impact on community and society. We encouraged our Black readers to see their ethnicity as an asset and not a liability; take charge of their careers; establish their circle of influence; and be strategic in developing their career path, entrepreneurial journey, or agenda for change. Arguably, we spent most of our time in that book on establishing career trajectories, building new ventures, and traversing organizations and companies. We always envisioned a follow-up book on how to reach the top and stay there.

This book charts the path for those who are in the middle of their career or in the growth phase of their business or organization. It is the culmination of many hours of research, and it draws on the life lessons and professional experiences of Black women and men who have successfully made the climb to become a Black face in a high place.

We first heard the phrase "Black faces in high places" attributed to Rev. Dr. Martin Luther King Jr. and thought it was a clever way to describe the crossroads faced by Black professionals at or near the top of their organization, company, field, or industry. When we looked further into the phrase, the originator was none other than Mary McLeod Bethune, the founder of the National Association of Colored Women and the National Council of Negro Women. In 1930 she said, "My people will not be satisfied until they see some Black faces in high places."[3] Known as the "first lady of the struggle" and an adviser to President Franklin D. Roosevelt, Bethune recognized that the advancement of Black people would not be realized until there were more African Americans at the top making systemic changes. In 1971, Helen G. Edmonds, a history professor at North Carolina Central University, used the phrase as the title for her book on Blacks in government.

More recently, Dr. Cornel West and others have used the phrase as a rebuke of getting to the top and forgetting the communities and people left behind. Dr. West expounded on this dilemma by calling out on CNN that "we lost sight of attacking issues of poverty, class—with the death of Martin—and moved into an obsession with having Black faces in high places. As long as we had those Black faces in high places, the poor could live symbolically through them, vicariously through them. Or those Black faces themselves, middle class and upper middle class, could claim that somehow they were the index of progress."

We firmly believe that being a Black face in a high place means achieving a certain level of power and influence while giving back to the community, whether you are a local community leader or a global corporate executive. You must be a part of a larger agenda. If not, the Black community will remain stagnant with one or two examples of success stories and a slow stream of "Black firsts" to crack the ceiling, while never developing a sea of "Black faces" to sit at the tables of power and influence and make sure everyone is included, valued, and treated fairly. We wrote this book to share the journey of Black leaders who fit this mold and, based on their lessons learned, outline a road map for others who endeavor to do the same.

That is why, throughout this book, we highlight the experiences of Black faces in high places who were able to navigate various crossroads in reaching the top and staying there. We offer additional insights from Cathy Hughes, Bob Johnson, Dave Steward, Angela Glover Blackwell, Ken Chenault, and our own experiences in corporate America, entrepreneurship, and academia. We provide a lens into the careers of other prominent figures, across several industries and sectors, such as Barack Obama and Michelle Obama (public service); media mogul and billionaire Oprah Winfrey (entrepreneurship); Ursula Burns, former CEO of Xerox who became the first Black woman to lead a Fortune 500 company (corporate America); Geoffrey Canada, president and CEO of the Harlem Children's Zone, which is breaking the cycle of intergenerational poverty for children, families, and communities throughout the country (nonprofit); Darren Walker, the first Black president of the Ford Foundation (philanthropy); and many more.

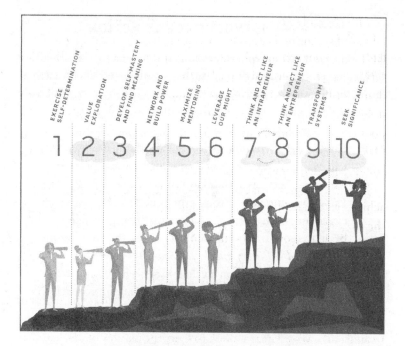

1 EXERCISE SELF-DETERMINATION
2 VALUE EXPLORATION
3 DEVELOP SELF-MASTERY AND FIND MEANING
4 NETWORK AND BUILD POWER
5 MAXIMIZE MENTORING
6 LEVERAGE OUR MIGHT
7 THINK AND ACT LIKE AN INTRAPRENEUR
8 THINK AND ACT LIKE AN ENTREPRENEUR
9 TRANSFORM SYSTEMS
10 SEEK SIGNIFICANCE

The 10 Strategic Actions to Reach the Top and Stay There

Our approach to understanding the challenges and opportunities of being a Black face in a high place is captured in the "10 Strategic Actions" graphic. This is the journey that the Black leaders and executives we have interviewed and studied have taken to reach the top and stay there. In doing so, we have identified 10 strategic actions that are common to all that make this climb. For each of these strategic actions, we present models and action steps that will empower you to make the climb too.

In the chapters that follow, we delve deeper than just showing examples and telling stories of successful African Americans in high positions. This book provides concise, detailed, strategic actions to reach higher heights and to benefit others along the way. The 10 strategic actions represent an outline and a road map for this book across four levels of action.

LEVEL I: INDEPENDENT ACTION

At Level I, your actions will only require *independent action.* These are actions taken by an individual, for her or his own benefit, such as self-determination, exploring, meaning, and self-mastery, which are concepts developed further in Strategic Actions 1, 2, and 3.

1. *Exercise Self-Determination*—In this strategic action, you will evaluate and strengthen your identity and purpose, which will serve as a foundation as you ascend to the top.
2. *Value Exploration*—Through the process of exploring new experiences and cultures, you will broaden your mind and begin to move from your comfort zone to the growth zone.
3. *Develop Self-Mastery and Find Meaning*—Here, we elaborate extensively on a valuable concept, *ikigai,* and how you can achieve a level of maturity and introspection to develop self-mastery and find meaning.

LEVEL II: INTERDEPENDENT ACTION

At Level II, we outline strategic actions taken by two or more individuals for their mutual benefit, such as networking and mentoring. This action level requires *interdependent action,* and the key to this type of action is relationships—networks, mentors, and partnerships. Each of these keys is described in Strategic Actions 4, 5, and 6.

4. *Network and Build Power*—There are many studies that demonstrate how increasing the value of your relationships can lead to important career and professional outcomes. You will learn how to network strategically and, of even greater importance, how to translate those relationships into influence and power.
5. *Maximize Mentoring*—If you are seeking to affect the world, you must embrace this strategic action— mentoring—as a part of your personal strategy for growth, achievement, and advancement.

6. *Leverage Our Might*—Through this strategic action you develop the skills to build teams, strengthen organizations, and form coalitions that will effect impactful change.

LEVEL III: COLLABORATIVE ACTION

At Level III, we highlight actions that require *collaborative action*. These are actions taken by groups of people that benefit the group, such as creating a nonprofit organization or launching a business. These concepts are discussed in Strategic Actions 7 and 8.

7. *Think and Act Like an Intrapreneur*—You will not only discover how to effectively navigate your company or organization but also how to build bridges between your company or organization and outside stakeholders, with significant benefits accruing to you and others.
8. *Think and Act Like an Entrepreneur*—This means creating new Black-owned businesses and growing existing businesses into multimillion-dollar and multibillion-dollar enterprises. We break down the principles of entrepreneurship and offer concrete steps for you to create a successful business enterprise.

LEVEL IV: AMPLIFIED ACTION

At Level IV, we outline the necessary actions for people and organizations to make a lasting impact. These actions require *amplified action*, which creates social and economic value by transforming systems, a concept we describe more fully in Strategic Action 9.

9. *Transform Systems*—You will identify and understand the various forms of strategic partnerships—competition, co-opetition, cooperation, coalitions, consortium, joint ventures, mergers, and acquisitions. We explain the "what," "why," and "how" to create these structures for synergy, scale, and impact.

At the top of the climb, we find examples of Black leaders and executives who have moved beyond success to significance. Thus, we conclude this book with examples of amplified action in the spirit of "paying it forward."

10. *Seek Significance*—Through innovative examples of strategic giving and philanthropy, we go into detail as to how you can use your position to positively contribute to the Black community, societal change, and the greater good.

The Strategic Action Plan: Mindsets, Skill Sets, and Tool Sets

This book gives you the detailed blueprint to reach the top and stay there. Along the way, we introduce a strategic action plan comprised of *mindsets, skill sets,* and *tool sets* that will be essential for your journey.

As shown in the "Strategic Action Plan" graphic, the five mindsets correspond to each of the action levels:

Level I: *Growth Mindset*
Level II: *Global Citizen's Mindset*
Level III: *Entrepreneur's Mindset*
Level IV: *Game Changer's Mindset* and *Servant Leader's Mindset*

The 10 strategic actions we have already presented represent the skill sets presented in the graphic.

Lastly, every Black face in a high place must know how to use the tools that allow them to execute the plans and strategies they develop. This leads to greater influence and impact. Therefore, the tool sets are the different forms of "capital" required to make a difference at that action level.

When most people hear the term *capital,* they only think of financial capital, but capital is anything that can be acquired, exchanged, converted, or invested. Each of the five forms of capital has an important role to play with you, your organization, your company, or any endeavor:

The Strategic Action Plan
to Reach the Top and Stay There

Action Levels	Mindsets 5 Ways of Thinking	Skill Sets 10 Strategic Actions		Tool Sets 5 Forms of Capital
LEVEL I: Independent Action	Growth Mindset (Personal)	1	Exercise Self-Determination	Human Capital and Cultural Capital
		2	Value Exploration	
		3	Develop Self-Mastery and Find Meaning	
LEVEL II: Interdependent Action	Global Citizen's Mindset (Interpersonal)	4	Network and Build Power	Social Capital and Intellectual Capital
		5	Maximize Mentoring	
		6	Leverage Our Might	
LEVEL III: Collaborative Action	Entrepreneur's Mindset (Entrepreneurial)	7	Think and Act Like an Intrapreneur	All Forms of Capital including Financial Capital
		8	Think and Act Like an Entrepreneur	
LEVEL IV: Amplified Action	Game Changer's Mindset (Systemic)	9	Transform Systems	
	Servant Leader's Mindset (Cultural/Spiritual)	10	Seek Significance	Time, Talent, Treasure, and Touch

1. *Financial* capital is the money that you have, acquire, or borrow.
2. *Human* capital is the level of skill, training, education, and experience that you possess.
3. *Social* capital is the collection of meaningful relationships that you and your team have.
4. *Cultural* capital is the knowledge of cultural norms and values, and the social resources that come as a result.

5. *Intellectual* capital is the capital that resides in teams of people and is often the source of innovation and intellectual property.

We say much more about each of these forms of capital in the appropriate chapters.

This journey is ultimately about a personal commitment to expanding your mindset, embracing new skill sets, and applying new tool sets. It is about undertaking a paradigmatic shift that moves from simply being an independent success to being a servant leader. And it is about effectuating this shift on Monday, not "someday."

With that, your journey has begun. If you follow the strategic actions offered in this book, we believe you will reach the top, stay there, and at every step along the way, make a lasting difference for those who aspire to follow in your footsteps.

The Redefine the Game Institute (RTGI) is a yearlong career and leadership development program for Black business professionals and community leaders. Founded in 2018 by Willie Barney, Damita Byrd, and us, RTGI is organized by the Omaha Empowerment Network, RDB Resultants, and our company, BCT Partners. Each year, the program selects a new cohort of rising stars to learn and apply the various strategies outlined in both of our books, *Black Faces in White Places* and *Black Faces in High Places*. RTGI has successfully accelerated participants' career advancement and expanded the pipeline of Black senior leaders and executives. Learn more at www .redefinethegame.com.

LEVEL I

Independent Action

Action is the real measure of intelligence.
— NAPOLEON HILL

Perhaps the quintessential Black face in a high place is President Barack Obama. His story offers unique insight to the foundations of what it takes to reach the top and to provide value. We break up the journey to the top into four levels of action. Here, in Level I, we discuss strategic actions that only require Level I Independent Action. To this point, it is important to note the journey that Obama took independently, from the start that catapulted him to the top.

On October 15, 2007, Dr. Randal Pinkett had the opportunity to attend, along with other minority business owners, a fundraiser for then senator Obama in Chicago, while he was campaigning for the presidency. It was a moment that has left a lasting impression on him to this day.

This fundraiser took place approximately one year before the election, at a point during the campaign when Obama was still far behind in the polls. Not very many people gave him a chance of winning, including, quite honestly, Dr. Pinkett. Don't misunderstand: He attended the fundraiser because he thought Obama was the best candidate and he wanted to be supportive of him but, at that time, Dr. Pinkett didn't think Obama could beat Hillary Clinton.

After entering the venue with his cool stride, Obama began his remarks, and the very first thing he said was, "I know most of you don't believe I can do this. I know most of you don't believe I can win." He then paused and said, "You will believe I can win when you see me on January 20, 2009, standing next to Michelle, [and their daughters] Sasha, and Malia, and place my hand on the Bible and get sworn in as the forty-fourth president of the United States of America." Dr. Pinkett said to himself, "Wow!" He was floored . . . speechless! But not for reasons you might expect. Dr. Pinkett was floored and speechless because he thought Obama was crazy to think he could win! In fact, Dr. Pinkett turned to the person next to him and whispered, very skeptically, "This guy really thinks he can win!"

To our amazement and pride, nearly one year later, based on a campaign that engaged people from all walks of life—men and women, young and the elderly, urban and suburban, Black and white and Asian and Hispanic and more—on November 4, 2008, at approximately 11:01 p.m., at Grant Park in his home city of Chicago, Obama said, "Yes we can!" the world said, "Yes we did!" and we excitedly said, "Oh no he didn't!" win the election! And, just as Obama so firmly predicted, on January 20, 2009, he stood next to Michelle, Sasha, and Malia and was sworn in as the first African American and the forty-fourth president of the United States of America.

The Obama Identity

Before Obama becoming known as president of the United States or as a United States senator, he had mastered the strategic actions that Level I of this book outlines as necessary to becoming a Black face in a high place. Obama exercised self-determination (Strategic Action 1), valued exploration (Strategic Action 2), and found meaning (Strategic Action 3) before ever reaching any of those high places.

Born in Honolulu, Hawaii, to a Kenyan father who left him at an early age to be raised by his mother and her parents, Obama sought his identity throughout his academic career. He graduated from Columbia University and became a community organizer on the South Side of Chicago. As told in his book *Dreams of My Father,* there he encountered a Black Muslim he calls Rafiq al-Shabazz who caused him to question whether politics rooted in Black nationalism was "a politics inadequate to the task" because "it contradicted the morality [his] mother had taught [him]." He concluded that such an orientation was more talk than action, which then prompted him to be introspective on matters relating to identity, purpose, race, and culture. Obama writes:

> The continuing struggle to align word and action, our heartfelt desires with a workable plan—didn't self-esteem finally depend on just this? It was that belief which had led me into organizing, and it was that belief which would lead me to conclude, perhaps for the final time, that notions of purity—of race or of culture—could no more serve as the basis for the typical black American's self-esteem than it could for mine.

Clearly, Obama was not only in search of a political ideology that combined talk with action, but he was also exploring the relationship between his identity as a Black man with his self-esteem, his sense of wholeness, and his bloodline. He would confront these very themes during his first visit to Kenya in 1987 at the age of twenty-six, five years after his father's death in a car accident. He traveled to his father's homeland with the hope of filling "a great emptiness" he felt inside, reconciling his identity and determining where he fit in the world. A truly revelatory moment emerged at the edge of a cornfield as Obama stood between two graves near the foot of a mango tree— one with an unmarked tombstone, belonging to a person whose identity would remain forever lost, and one belonging to his great-great-grandfather.[1] Obama writes: "The pain I felt was my father's pain. My questions were my brothers' questions. Their struggle, my birthright."

In this moment, Obama came to terms with his Black life and his white life; his African ancestry and his American ancestry; and his unique juxtaposition within the African Diaspora. Or, as Obama states, "My identity might begin with the fact of my race, but it didn't, couldn't, end there. At least that's what I would choose to believe."

The Obama Presidency

The following year, Obama began attending Harvard Law School and met his future wife, Michelle Robinson, when she was assigned as his mentor at a law firm where she was employed and he was a summer associate. He became the first Black editor of the *Harvard Law Review* while also studying the community organizing methods of "the father of community organizing," Saul Alinsky. Soon after graduating from Harvard magna cum laude, he married Michelle and they moved to Hyde Park, Illinois, where he led voter registration efforts in Chicago. During this time, he not only became more connected to the Chicago political scene but also to elected officials, businesspeople, and wealthy, liberal elites such as Chicago mayor Richard Daley, John W. Rogers of Arial Capital Management, and David Axelrod, who would later become his campaign manager.

In 1996, Obama was elected to his first of three terms as an Illinois state senator. He then ran for Congress in 2000 against a longtime incumbent and former Black Panther, Bobby Rush. He lost in a landslide: 61 percent to 30 percent. But that did not deter him. Four years later, in 2004, after the incumbent Illinois senator Peter Fitzgerald announced he was not going to seek reelection, Obama successfully ran for his seat to become only the fifth African American senator in US history. And he did not stop there.

The Obama Mindset, Skill Set, and Tool Set

Obama's story illustrates an artful weaving of three distinct but interrelated assets that will be interwoven throughout this book (see figure 1). The first asset, your *mindset*, is how you see, perceive, and view the world around you—your beliefs and way of thinking that determine your behavior and outlook; how you'll interpret and respond to situations. Specifically, Obama's mindset evolved over the course of his career to the point where he genuinely believed he could become the next president of the United States despite those who doubted him (including Dr. Randal Pinkett, who eventually came to believe it too).

For our purposes in this book, we will show you how Obama and other Black faces in high places expand their mindsets from a Level I (personal) growth mindset to a Level IV servant-leader mindset, which Obama developed by the time he ascended to become president.

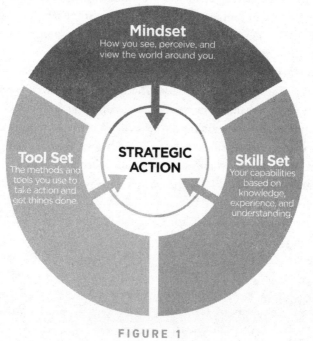

FIGURE 1

Adapted from Simon Dueckert, lernOS

The second asset is developed by exercising the strategic actions we outline in this book. We refer to these strategic actions as *skill sets* because once you master the action, this asset will become a part of your capabilities, knowledge, and understanding. Obama's skill set reflects self-determination, having established a strong identity after his moment of calmness and epiphany at the mango tree in Kenya; exploration to diverse places such as Hawaii, New York, Boston, Chicago, Kenya, and even Bali, Indonesia, where he traveled with Michelle to write *Dreams of My Father* for several months; and a sense of meaning and purpose that has permeated his community organizing, public service, and postpresidency careers, which is to be of service and to help others.

The third and final asset is your *tool set*, which represents the methods and tools you use to take action and get things done. We discuss how to leverage the specific tool sets that revolve around the various forms of capital ranging from social and cultural capital, as seen in Level I with Obama's search for identify and meaning, to financial capital and human capital in later levels of this book.

At the intersection of all three assets—mindset, skill set, and tool set—lies success, leadership, innovation, and more. This was certainly the case for Obama. But to reach the top and provide value, like Obama, not only do you need to effectively combine all three assets, but you need to continue this process at every stage of your development, from Level I where you begin your journey, to Level IV where you arrive.

Mindset: Broaden It

Skill Set: Deepen It

Tool Set: Sharpen It

Your Mindset, Skill Set, and Tool Set at Level I: Independent Action

The mindset to achieve at Level I: Independent Action is the *growth mindset*—a concept based on research by Stanford University professor Carol Dweck. In her book *Mindset: The New Psychology of Success*, Dweck writes, "For thirty years, my research has shown that *the view you adopt for yourself* profoundly affects the way you lead your life. It can determine whether you become the person you want to be and whether you accomplish the things you value. How does this happen?

How can a simple belief have the power to transform your psychology and, as a result, your life?" Dweck believes that the way you approach and view situations and challenges can be a defining factor in how successful you are. We agree. This explains why we begin all of the levels of action by focusing on your mindset—your beliefs—because a poor mindset can render the very best skill set and tool set useless (see figure 2).

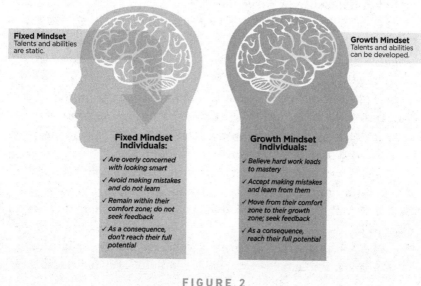

Fixed Mindset
Talents and abilities are static.

Growth Mindset
Talents and abilities can be developed.

Fixed Mindset Individuals:
✓ Are overly concerned with looking smart
✓ Avoid making mistakes and do not learn
✓ Remain within their comfort zone; do not seek feedback
✓ As a consequence, don't reach their full potential

Growth Mindset Individuals:
✓ Believe hard work leads to mastery
✓ Accept making mistakes and learn from them
✓ Move from their comfort zone to their growth zone; seek feedback
✓ As a consequence, reach their full potential

FIGURE 2

Adapted from Carol S. Dweck, PhD

People with a *fixed mindset* believe that their talents and abilities are fixed traits that you are born with and that they are carved in stone. People with a fixed mindset avoid risks or challenges that may reveal their deficiencies. They often strive to be perfect and succeed all the time.

Conversely, a growth mindset is the belief that you can cultivate your talents and abilities through effort, application, and experience. People with a growth mindset do not necessarily believe that everyone's the same or that anyone can accomplish anything, but they do believe that everyone can grow their abilities and skill set. They are less interested in proving how smart they are than in improving themselves with every new challenge and experience.

Janice Bryant Howroyd, founder and CEO of ActOne Group, a multibillion-dollar global organization that leads the human resources industry in talent aggregation and technology platforms, learned about the value of a growth mindset from her sister, Sandy, and her brother-in-law, Tom, early in her career. She writes: "The many lessons I learned from Sandy and Tom taught me I had a lot more to learn. They helped me realize the importance of always learning, always being curious, not judging, and soaking up as much knowledge as possible from as many experiences as I could." Powered by Howroyd's willingness to take risks and learn from mistakes, ActOne Group is the largest privately held, woman- and minority-owned workforce management company in the world, operating in over thirty-two countries across the world with more than seventeen thousand clients and twenty-six hundred employees worldwide.

The growth mindset and the skill sets in Strategic Actions 1, 2, and 3 translate directly to two tool sets or forms of capital, namely, *human capital* and *cultural capital*. Capital represents something that has value to you and others and can be acquired, exchanged, and converted. Within the context of Level I: Independent Action, both human capital and cultural capital reside within you as an individual.

Human capital is your education, experience, training, and abilities. People in a growth mindset believe that their human capital can be developed over time through learning, hard work, and focus. With the world constantly evolving, what is learned can very quickly become obsolete, so once you make it to the top you should never stop growing. The growth mindset naturally translates into behaviors that enable you to remain current, stay sharp, and be competitive in the marketplace through continuous learning, microlearning (that is, short-term learning activities and e-learning), and lifelong learning.

Robert D. Blackwell Sr., founder of Blackwell Consulting, which was one of the largest Black-owned management consulting firms when he sold the company in 2008, describes a similar mindset as "sweat curve." He writes: "What separates the middle into those who end up closer to the top or closer to the bottom are words that we hear very often but don't value as much as we should—words like commitment, perseverance, hard work, determination, and steadfastness. Those are the qualities that sort people out. The key to being successful is not native ability; it's the willingness to do whatever is necessary to be the very best we can be. That's why I say it's a sweat curve that separates people."

Cultural capital is your knowledge, comfort, and familiarity with different cultures and cultural nuances. People in a growth mindset challenge themselves to try new things that increase their cultural capital. They take risks and they view mistakes or even failures as great opportunities to learn. This leads to behaviors such as continuous effort to move beyond your comfort zone into your growth zone.

The three strategic actions that make up Level I and enhance the growth mindset are:

Strategic Action 1: Exercise Self-Determination—This is the foundation of a growth mindset because knowing who you are and where you are going establishes the basis for a positive belief system.

Strategic Action 2: Value Exploration—The growth mindset is cultivated through experience and exploration that provides the basis for high achievement.

Strategic Action 3: Develop Self-Mastery and Find Meaning— Whereas meaning and a positive belief system are foundational to a growth mindset, self-mastery of one's own skills and abilities is an outgrowth and the result of a growth mindset.

A growth mindset is key to seizing the opportunities in front of you and helping to ensure your continued growth and development. When undergirded by a growth mindset, Strategic Actions 1, 2, and 3 are the essential skills you need, and human capital and cultural capital are the essential tools you need, to achieve Level I: Independent Action. This action level benefits you by improving your personal abilities, deepening your insights, and enhancing your sense of purpose.

1

Exercise
Self-Determination

Be yourself. Everyone else is taken.
—UNKNOWN

The paramount importance of self-determination in reaching the top and staying there cannot be overstated.

The Secret to Life: Self-Determination

From among all of the strategic actions highlighted in this book, Strategic Action 1: Exercise Self-Determination is the foremost and most foundational one. We have also found it to be an action that is frequently mentioned by successful and great African Americans, albeit in different words and in different ways. This includes everyone from billionaire media mogul, businesswoman, and talk show host Oprah Winfrey, who said, "You become extraordinary when you know who you really are," to billionaire entrepreneur, music executive, and hip-hop artist Jay-Z, who said, during a masterclass with Oprah, "Belief in oneself and knowing who you are, I mean, that's the foundation of everything great," to Grammy-nominated performing artist Ledisi, who once shared, "If I can't be myself; my true authentic self, then why do it." This is all summed up in the words of the evangelical leader and former head of Youth for Christ and World Vision International Dr. Ted Engstrom, who said, "The secret of life is to know who you are and where you are going." Stated even more simply, self-determination is the secret to life, and it is defined as a combination of two underlying concepts: *identity* (who you are) and *purpose* (where you are going and why you exist; see figure 3).

SELF-DETERMINATION

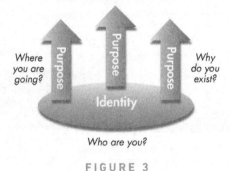

FIGURE 3

Identity: Who Are You?

Identity is the story you tell yourself about yourself. It represents the personal characteristics you hold dearest and absolutely would not want to give up such as race/ethnicity, gender, nationality, family origins and ancestry, physical appearance, personality traits, professional and career status (for example, community leader, entrepreneur, school principal), organizational affiliations (such as membership in a fraternity or sorority), and more. Identity is the narrative you have built up around yourself (personal identity) and that society has built up around you (social identity). It is the things you pride yourself on being, aspire to be, or believe you are destined to become.

Identity can be a *very* powerful construct as it can sustain you or derail you once you make it to the top. For example, imagine that your core identity is that of an athlete. That is, you define who you are as an athlete. When you reach retirement age or, even worse, possibly suffer a career-ending injury, it can be an extremely difficult situation to cope with, beyond the harsh reality of no longer being able to compete. If you realize that being an athlete is not the totality of your identity—that it is something you do but not who you are—then while retirement or injury may be disappointing, it is not devastating. Good illustrations can be found in the independent actions taken by three professional basketball players after they had reached the top.

When Michael Jordan retired *twice*, both times after winning three consecutive NBA championships with the Chicago Bulls, it was clear that his identity was not wholly defined by being an athlete. "I've reached the pinnacle of my career. I just feel that I don't have anything else to prove. When I lose the sense of motivation and the sense of 'to prove something' as a basketball player, it's time for me to move away from the game of basketball," said Jordan after his first retirement. After his second retirement he said, "This is a perfect time for me to walk away from the game. I'm at peace with that." Jordan would go on to become the first athlete to become a billionaire as co-owner of the NBA's Charlotte Bobcats; Major League Baseball's Miami Marlins;

Air Jordan, a subsidiary of Nike; and various other ventures including car dealerships, restaurants, and a golf course.

After a fifteen-year professional basketball career, three-time WNBA champion Swin Cash arrived at her own retirement crossroads. "You've done something your whole life, waking up for almost thirty years with something about basketball involved that day, whether it's practicing, eating right, or training," she said. "Then, all of a sudden, you wake up and you're not preparing for that thing you do so well. For me, it was like 'Okay, how do I keep a routine where I'm waking up to do something and still have that purpose?' That's where I think a lot of athletes get lost. They're just trying to figure out what purpose they're getting up for, what drives them every day. That's what I didn't want to have."

Cash's commentary is not confined to athletes and speaks not only to issues related to identity but also purpose. Throughout her career, she took Level I: Independent Action to position herself for a life—an identity and a purpose—beyond playing basketball, which has included her own foundation, television appearances, motherhood, product endorsements, a position as vice president of basketball operations and team development for the New Orleans Pelicans, and before that, the director of franchise development for her former team, the New York Liberty, a first-of-its-kind front office position.

Similarly, after retiring from the Los Angeles Lakers, the late five-time NBA champion Kobe Bryant reinvented himself. He went on to become an author; a coach to his late daughter Gianna, and her girls' basketball team; and an investor in technology, athletics, and entertainment ventures, including *Dear Basketball*, a film he produced that won the best animated short film Academy Award. In a clear retort to Fox News host Laura Ingraham's comments that athletes should "shut up and dribble" rather than comment on political matters, Bryant jokingly said in his acceptance speech, "As basketball players, we're really supposed to shut up and dribble, but I'm glad we did a little bit more than that."

There are two key lessons to be derived from the legendary careers of Michael Jordan, Swin Cash, and Kobe Bryant as Black faces in high places. The first lesson is that you should never confuse *what you do* with *who you are.* The second lesson is that your identity comprises many different facets and should never be reduced to just one. Jordan, Cash, and Bryant did not make these mistakes. "You're given very little chance in life to express yourself. Life more so is about masking. You have a lot of . . . labels put on you. And somewhere in there is who you really are," said Viola Davis. "And if someone does not give you permission to express that, if someone never gives you permission, then you implode." Jordan, Cash, and Bryant did not implode. By comparison, we have seen successful corporate executives forgo their obligations to family and friends because their identity was so inextricably linked to climbing the corporate ladder. They, in essence, became a public success and a private failure. We've also seen broke and failing entrepreneurs refuse to obtain full-time employment because to do so was incongruent with their identity as a business owner. It's a thin line between faith and foolishness. When evaluating who you are, never forget that your personal identity is defined by so much more than your professional trajectory.

Unlike the NBA and WNBA, when you are a Black face in a high place, you often see very few reflections of yourself. As a result, while your identity may indeed comprise many facets, we believe it is your cultural identity that is challenged most often (and it is your spiritual identity that can sustain you most often) as you become a Black face in a high place.

A strong cultural identity reflects a deep and abiding pride in being an African American. In America, where race and racism are such prominent issues, without a strong cultural identity, when stereotypes and prejudice and discrimination arise, you are "a leaf in the wind." A colleague characterizes your abilities in a negative light because of your skin color and you buy into it. Biased behavior is directed at you, and it derails your performance. You have earned your way to the top of your organization and you question whether you belong there. In each situation, a strong cultural identity is the solution.

Don't sacrifice yourself

because you won't like yourself.

We recommend viewing the movie *42*, which chronicles the life of Jackie Robinson, a pioneering Black face in a high place as the first African American to play Major League Baseball after an All-Star career in the Negro League. There is a particularly moving scene after a difficult game where Robinson experienced particularly harsh and overt racism. While engaged in dialogue with his wife, he asserts that *he knows who he is*, which demonstrates the quintessential importance of Robinson's strong cultural identity, and his wife's support, to his ability to overcome racism. Robinson once said, "The most luxurious possession, the richest treasure anybody has, is his personal dignity."

As a clever assertion of his strong cultural identity, retired four-star general, former chairman of the Joint Chiefs of Staff, and former US secretary of state Colin Powell once said, "Many interviewers when they come to talk to me, they think they're being progressive by not mentioning in their stories any longer that I'm Black. I tell them, 'Don't stop now. If I shot somebody, you'd mention it.'"

For us, the most powerful aspect of our identities is that we are children of God. We believe we can do all things through Christ who strengthens us (Phil. 4:13) and that belief sustains us during moments when we are being tested, undergoing trials, or experiencing tribulations, both personally and professionally. Above all, this spiritual identity is one that can never be taken away from us.

Purpose:
Where Are You Going? Why Do You Exist?

Purpose is your reason for being. It is your mission and your ministry. Purpose represents what you are meant to accomplish and what you are called to do with your life. It's been said that the two most important days of your life are the day you were born and the day you figured out why you were born. This speaks directly to your purpose. "Purpose is an essential element of you. It is the reason you are on the planet at this particular time in history. Your very existence is wrapped up in the things you are here to fulfill," said the late, great actor Chadwick Boseman. "Whatever you choose for a career path, remember, the struggles along the way are only meant to shape you for your purpose."

The first African American First Lady of the United States, Michelle Obama, offers a wonderful illustration of how finding a sense of purpose is something you can still grapple with even after you've reached the top. Following the inauguration ceremony in January 2009, she and Barack Obama conducted their first overseas visit to the United Kingdom in April 2009. During the visit, the First Lady visited the publicly funded, all-girls Elizabeth Garrett Anderson School in the Islington neighborhood of London to deliver her first speech abroad as First Lady. In her book *Becoming,* she shares her trepidation as she entered the school auditorium of approximately two hundred working-class girls of color. As the girls performed Shakespeare's *The Tempest,* modern dance, and Whitney Houston's "Believe," she contemplated how these girls reflected her own identity and upbringing. And, even as First Lady of the United States, she wrestled with her sense of identity and purpose in that moment:

> At this point, I'd been First Lady for just over two months. In different moments, I'd felt overwhelmed by the pace, unworthy of the glamour, anxious about our children, and uncertain of my purpose. There are pieces of public life, of giving up one's privacy to become a walking, talking symbol of a nation, that can seem specifically designed to strip away part of your identity. But here, finally, speaking to those girls, I felt something completely different and pure—an alignment of my old self with this new role. Are you good enough? Yes, you are, all of you. I told the students of Elizabeth Garrett Anderson that they'd touched my heart. I told them that they were precious, because they

truly were. And when my talk was over, I did what was instinctive. I hugged absolutely every single girl I could reach.

Obama's experience at the Elizabeth Garrett Anderson School highlights the evolving importance of purpose, even at the highest levels, and the close interrelationship between identity and purpose (that is, self-determination). She also reminds us that sometimes we have to let go of who we think we should be in order to embrace all of who we really are.

Independent Action Steps
for Exercising Self-Determination

Exercising self-determination—defining who you are and why you exist—is ultimately about finding yourself and fulfilling your destiny. It is the foundation of Black faces in high places who are secure in themselves and confident in what they are there to accomplish. The following are action steps for Black faces in high places to exercise self-determination.

DR. PINKETT'S JOURNEY TO
FINDING IDENTITY AND PURPOSE

There are experiences in life that are difficult to put into words. As it relates to my identity and purpose, I have had three such experiences, and they reflect the three things I believe every Black person absolutely must experience to solidify her or his identity and purpose.

The first experience I had that I could not put into words was when I got the results of my AfricanAncestry.com test and had conclusive, scientific evidence of my African origins. You must know that you have an identity beyond slavery and exactly what that identity is. Are you Akan? Ashanti? Mandika? Fulani? How can you know who you are if you do not know your ancestry?

The second experience was when I traveled to West Africa, and the first words uttered to me at the airport when I landed in Dakar, Senegal, were from a Senegalese man who said, "Welcome home." You have to know where you come from and you have to go there or, at minimum, research that country. How can you know where you're going if you don't know where you've been? Alex Haley taught this to us decades ago.

The third experience was when I was baptized at the age of twenty-six and gave my life to Christ. Now, just to be clear, I am not suggesting that everyone needs to get baptized and give their life to Christ. Religious practices are a very personal choice. I am suggesting, however, that every African American must experience what baptism allowed me to experience, which is to reconcile your understanding of who you are and whose you are (that is, who created you). How can you know yourself until you reconcile your understanding of who created you? For me, I have come to understand that Randal Pinkett was created by God and created in His image. That is a core component of my identity: I am a child of God.

CULTIVATE A SOLID SPIRITUAL FOUNDATION

When asked how he overcomes moments of self-doubt, Rey Ramsey, founder and former CEO of One Economy Corporation, said, "I'm a spiritual person. At the core of everything I do is my spirituality. And I don't wear it on my sleeve, but it comes from the Bible and a sense of submission. You submit. And that gives you that extra strength, and boy, if you were ever praying before, boy do you pray then."

We have found spiritual foundation and perspective to be a critical resource for many people, including ourselves, in our professional and personal activities. This spiritual foundation will help you deal with much of the adversity you will face on your path to high places. It could manifest as prayer, mindfulness, meditation, yoga, and quiet reflection time.

Our personal spirituality has empowered us to endure because we believed that greatness was something that God wanted for us and that "doing the right thing" was going to yield a better life than going off of the "straight and narrow path." We recognize that a large part of this identity and purpose for us has been influenced by the time we spent in church, in church youth groups, and in church-related activities. These activities provided a context for our identity and purpose. We encourage you to situate yourself in a spiritual context so you may begin to view your relationships and actions from a spiritual perspective.

In our estimation, reading, studying, and becoming one with your spirituality will lead to four important life lessons related to your identity and purpose:

1. A solid spiritual foundation grounds you in a set of principles for living well.
2. A solid spiritual foundation provides boundaries for your actions and is instrumental in developing a conscience that limits unhealthy actions and unproductive activities.
3. A solid spiritual foundation helps you prioritize what is important in life.
4. A solid spiritual foundation helps establish a belief system that puts life and living into perspective.

These four lessons are essential elements of identity and purpose because they provide a context that is beyond the activities of everyday life. The development of this aspect of your identity and purpose is of critical importance.

STUDY YOUR CULTURAL, NATIONAL, AND WORLD HISTORY

The great poet, memoirist, singer, and civil rights activist Maya Angelou once said, "I have great respect for the past. If you don't know where you've come from, you don't know where you're going." A grounded understanding of our history both in America and dating back to ancient Africa, including the African origins of civilization, has had an indelible impact on us. It has raised our awareness, fostered our self-esteem, and deepened our pride.

As the adage goes, to determine who you are or where you are going, you must learn where you have been. Look to the past for an understanding of who you are as a Black person today. Visit museums and cultural institutions to learn about the links that you have to other parts of the world. Not only is there a history of Africans in America before slavery, but there is a whole world of African history to tap into. This involves *education, exploration,* and *exhortation.*

- *Education*—Learn about African American culture and its influences. By this we mean study the basics of the history of Africans in America—from preslavery times, through slavery, and on to modern day. There are amazing stores of triumph and trials that we all can learn from. You can enroll in a formal course or read books that provide a history of our people.
- *Exploration*—Go beyond the basics and learn more about a time period, a region, a form of expression, or a topic. For example, Dr. Robinson has been interested in jazz for many years. Jazz is described as both the only uniquely American form of music and the music that originated in the Black community in New Orleans. Everywhere he travels, he looks for a jazz club or museum related to the history of jazz and jazz artists. Following this history of jazz has not only been enjoyable for Dr. Robinson, but it has also been rewarding for him to understand its relationship with African American culture.
- *Exhortation*—To exhort is to give advice. Particularly in the context of Black faces in high places, this simply means sharing what you've learned with others. It involves looking at what you've been exposed to and introducing that to

others. Dr. Robinson's father became fascinated by Black inventors. In the mid- to late-1990s he created a traveling exhibit that he would take to schools and youth groups to help them see the history of inventors, engineers, and scientists in African American history and culture.

READ HISTORY

The following are recommended books that had a significant impact on the coauthors:

- *The African Presence in Ancient America: They Came Before Columbus* by Ivan Van Sertima
- *Stolen Legacy: Green Philosophy Is Stolen from Egyptian Philosophy* by George G. M. James
- *Nile Valley Contributions to Civilization* by Anthony T. Browder
- *The African Origin of Civilization: Myth or Reality* by Cheikh Anta Diop
- *The Isis Papers: The Keys to the Colors* by Frances Cress Welsing
- *Afrocentricity: The Theory of Social Change* by Molefi Kete Asante
- *The Miseducation of the Negro* by Carter Godwin Woodson
- *The Autobiography of Malcolm X* by Malcolm X

DISCOVER YOUR ANCESTRAL ORIGINS AND CULTURAL HISTORY

Here are some good resources to help discover your ancestral origins and cultural history:

AfricanAncestry.com helps people of African descent recover their history, reconnect with their ancestors, and create a lasting legacy for future generations. Founded in 2003 by Dr. Gina Paige and Dr. Rick Kittles, African Ancestry is the world leader in tracing maternal and paternal lineages of African descent having helped more than 750,000 people reconnect with the roots of their family tree. Using the power of DNA and the most comprehensive database of indigenous African genetic sequences in existence, African Ancestry is the *only* company that can trace your ancestry back to a specific present-day African country and ethnic group of origin dating back more than five hundred years. They also offer a private digital community, weekly online trainings, and a guide, *The African Ancestry Guide to African History and Culture.* Learn more at: www .africanancestry.com.

The National Museum of African American History and Culture is the only national museum devoted exclusively to the documentation of African American life, history, and culture. It was established by an act of Congress in 2003, following decades of efforts to promote and highlight the contributions of African Americans. To date, the museum has collected more than thirty-six thousand artifacts, and nearly a hundred thousand individuals have become members. The museum opened to the public on September 24, 2016, as the nineteenth and newest museum of the Smithsonian Institution. If you are in Washington, DC, or able to get there, you should visit the museum. You can also explore, learn, and engage with the museum through their number of digital resources at: nmaahc.si.edu.

The 1619 Project is an ongoing initiative by Nikole Hannah-Jones from the *New York Times Magazine* that began in August 2019, the four hundredth anniversary of the beginning of American slavery. It aims to reframe the country's history by placing the consequences of slavery and the contributions of Black Americans at the very center of our national narrative. The 1619 Project won the Pulitzer Prize for Commentary (alongside investigative journalism trailblazer, educator, and civil rights icon Ida B. Wells, who was honored posthumously). The 1619 Project's official education partner, the Pulitzer Center, has helped connect this curricula to tens of thousands of students in all fifty states. You can explore this interactive project at: nyti.ms/37JLWkZ.

The DuSable Museum was developed to preserve and interpret experiences and achievements of people of African descent. The museum, a Smithsonian Affiliate, promotes understanding and inspires appreciation of the achievements, contributions, and experiences of African Americans through exhibits, programs, and activities that illustrate African and African American history, culture, and art. Founded in 1961 by teacher and art historian Dr. Margaret Burroughs and other leading Chicago citizens, the DuSable Museum is proud of its diverse holdings that number more than fifteen thousand pieces and include paintings, sculpture, print works, and historical memorabilia. Learn more at: www.dusablemuseum.org.

LEARN YOUR FAMILY HISTORY

Since your identity and purpose are often informed by the paths of your ancestors, we believe it is important to put their experiences into perspective. Learning your family history is one of the ways you accomplish this. Here are some concrete actions that you can take to learn more about your family and about yourself:

- Take a DNA test that traces your ancestry such as AfricanAncestry.com and Ancestry.com.
- Research and create a family tree using websites such as AfricanAncestry.com, Ancestry.com, and RootsWeb.com.
- Organize or help organize a family reunion.
- Conduct your own oral history project by interviewing the oldest members of your family. Not sure how? Explore books like *Doing Oral History: A Practical Guide* by Donald Ritchie (Oxford University Press, 2003) or *The Oral History Manual* by Barbara W. Sommer and Mary Kay Quinlan, (AltaMira Press, 2002).

- Create a scrapbook of your family's story. Look for pictures and stories about the patriarchs and matriarchs. For inspiration visit CreatingKeepsakes.com and CKScrapbookEvents.com.

Q&AS ABOUT APPROACHING FAMILY HISTORY

The following is a list of common questions the coauthors get when they advise people to learn more about their family history:

1. *What if your family history is complicated?* Many of us have complicated family histories because of blended families, divorces, parents who were never married, adoptions, foster care families, and a whole host of other reasons. Even if it's complex, learning about your family history might be the kind of spiritual adventure that leads you to new insights about yourself and others. We know from our own personal experiences that families come in all shapes and sizes. The complexity makes for very interesting stories that you may (or may not) want to pass on to the next generations.

2. *What if I am biracial?* Both parts of your heritage are important. We don't see why being biracial should stop you from exploring both sides of your heritage. If you explore only one side of your heritage, you are exploring only one-half of yourself. You may lose out on a family history and heritage that could bring value to your life and the lives of others.

3. *What will I gain by exploring my family history or my culture?* You gain a broader perspective of your life in the context of a family and a history that stretches back generations. We believe you learn about yourself while you are learning about your family and culture, and that gives you perspective on what is happening to you and your family today.

DEVELOP A PERSONAL MISSION, VISION, AND VALUES STATEMENT

A personal statement of your mission, vision, and values directly relates to your sense of self/purpose, direction, and conduct. These tenets, combined with the cultivation of a strong cultural, spiritual, and familial grounding, are the necessary ingredients to pursue Level I: Independent Action that will empower you to exercise self-determination.

The concepts of mission, vision, and values are commonly associated with organizations, but they can be similarly applied to individuals (Strategic Action 6: Leverage Our Might will discuss the importance of mission, vision, and values in the context of organizations in detail). For your personal mission, you will simply answer the question "Why?" That is, "Why do I exist?" In your words, it describes your purpose or reason for being. There's no one way to express your mission statement. You'll see that our own styles differ.

Dr. Pinkett's Mission Statement
My personal mission is to bring glory and honor to God in all of my personal and professional endeavors, including being the man that God intends for me to be for my family, friends, and loved ones; to make a positive difference in business and the community; and be a true blessing to others, because I acknowledge that countless others have been a blessing to me.

Dr. Robinson's Mission Statement
I will make a positive impact on people, businesses, and communities.
I will make an impact on the people with whom I interact and build positive relationships, mentor others, and be an effective leader.
I will make an impact on businesses and organizations through research, writing, and consulting.
I will make an impact on communities through volunteer work and have influence on policy and professional activities.

Your personal vision answers the question "What?" That is, "What future do I see for myself?" In your words, it describes the direction you are heading and the person you are striving to become. Again, we'll provide our own statements as examples.

Dr. Pinkett's Vision Statement

My personal vision is to be an obedient child of God; a loving and supportive husband, father, son, and friend; a socially responsible and accomplished entrepreneur, speaker, author, and scholar; a passionate person who appreciates and enjoys each day, lives life to the fullest, maintains a healthy lifestyle and a healthy outlook at all times; a community servant who demonstrates the importance of giving back; and a blessed individual who maximizes his God-given potential and fulfills his God-given destiny for greatness to be a blessing to others.

Dr. Robinson's Vision Statement

I am a child of God—service to God is the centerpiece of my life. I serve God through obedience to his words and service to my fellow man.

I am a husband, father, and son—my relationship with my wife is important to me but also makes a statement about the importance of marriage in our community. I work hard to provide for my family and to create a better community for my children to grow up in. As a son I am a bridge between generations—I carry the legacy of my father to my children and connect my mother's generation to the future.

I am a scholar, entrepreneur, and an advocate for community economic empowerment. I use my gifts and talents to positively impact the African American community, America, and the world.

Your personal values answer the question "How?" That is, "How should I conduct myself while fulfilling my mission along the path to achieving my vision?" In your words, describe the behaviors, deeds, manners, and actions you desire for yourself on a daily basis. Examples of personal values that we uphold include the following: *love, service, honesty, integrity, balance, excellence, greatness,* and *faith.*

WRITE YOUR PERSONAL MISSION, VISION, AND VALUES STATEMENT

Find some quiet time to sit down and write down your answers to the questions:

What is my mission?

What is my vision?

What are my values?

See what comes immediately to your mind. Reflect on what you have written, revisit it, and revise it until you are comfortable that what you have on paper accurately reflects your core being.

Most people do not take the time to develop personal mission, vision, and values statements. We highly encourage it, but only if it is a meaningful exercise. For some people that do take the time to do so, unfortunately, their statements end up being merely ink on paper. Do not allow the statements to be words with no meaning. The mission does not make the man or woman; the man or woman makes the mission.

2
___

Value Exploration

The wise man belongs to all countries,
for the home of a great soul is the whole world.
— DEMOCRITUS

Comfort Zone to Growth Zone

The growth zone is the place where new opportunities exist and new goals are set. It is where your purpose and your planning come together so that you can make an impact on the world around you. If you value exploration, then you will always be in the growth zone.

Once our life activities and work start to get into uncharted territory, we can enter into some other zones. In our first book, *Black Faces in White Places*, we wrote a lot about the comfort zone and the growth zone. We all have our comfort zone—the place where we feel the most at ease and where we can maintain our performance with little effort. A diagram we saw online (thanks to @successpictures) made us think about two other zones that we travel through before we arrive at the growth zone (see figure 4).

FIGURE 4

The fear zone is the first stop once we leave our comfortable and safe space. It is in this fear zone that we sometimes hear that small voice that gives us every reason why we should not explore new circumstances and situations. In the fear zone, we make all kinds of excuses for not doing the activities that will help us grow. We have met so many people over the years who have let fear stop them from moving forward in life. The fear zone is real, but don't let it be the end of your journey.

When we can push past the fear, we get into the learning zone. Some of the most successful people we know have made a habit out of learning new things so that they can expand their territory and grow. They make a habit out of exploring new things, getting new information, and developing new ways of doing things. Entering this learning zone means gaining new skills and knowledge that you can use as you cross into the growth zone.

So, how do we stay in the growth zone? We engage in exploration through our experiences and learn new skills and ideas through exposure.

Once you expand your growth zone,

it never returns to its original dimensions.

The Three Categories of Experience and Exposure

Experience is the best teacher. But not all experiences (and exposure) are created equal. To help you in identifying the kinds of experiences and exposure that can be most beneficial to you, we have attempted to organize these concepts into three types or categories, as shown in figure 5. The categories are not mutually exclusive, but rather, they are representative of the kinds of things you might actively pursue.

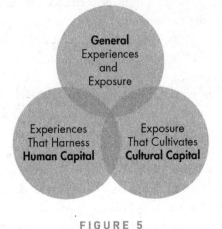

FIGURE 5

GENERAL EXPERIENCES AND EXPOSURE

The first grouping is made up of very general exposure and experience. The items described here are those that foster engagement with various *people*, *places*, and *possibilities*:

- *People:* Experiences meeting different kinds of people—this could be as close as neighbors you've never met to as far as meeting people from a foreign country.
- *Places:* Exposure to different kinds of spaces—visit a farm or explore a different country or even a virtual world.
- *Possibilities:* Exposure to different and new possibilities—learning that you can combine an ability in law and an interest in hip-hop to pursue a career as an entertainment lawyer.

While these activities may seem basic, they can have a very powerful impact. As we meet people, travel to and from places, and learn about new possibilities on a daily basis, we expand our perspective and add more tools to our tool belt. These tools empower us to think creatively, innovatively, and differently about how to overcome challenges and seize opportunities.

There is no comfort in growth

and no growth in comfort.

Some people make the mistake of thinking they have to be connected to someone famous, powerful, or with years of experience to benefit from the relationship—but sometimes the people who make the biggest impact are much closer. Dr. Pinkett's relationship with Wayne Abbott began as children growing up in New Jersey. The Abbott family was from St. Thomas and had moved to Twin Rivers—just a few miles from East Windsor—at around the same time as the Pinketts. Growing up, Dr. Pinkett and his brother, Dan, spent a lot of time with Wayne at each other's homes as part of the "Our Kids" group.

Years later, Wayne helped ease the transition into life at Rutgers for both Dr. Pinkett and Dr. Robinson. It was Wayne who made sure they knew about the first National Society of Black Engineers meeting where they met and connected with other Black students with similar interests. Wayne was that guy on campus who tried to connect students with opportunities and information. He showed Dr. Pinkett and Dr. Robinson how a college student could be an entrepreneur. And that set them on their own entrepreneurial path.

EXPERIENCES THAT BUILD HUMAN CAPITAL

The second grouping is that of experiences that build human capital—the knowledge, experience, training, and abilities you possess—specifically in terms of your *capabilities*, *curiosities*, and *capacities*:

- *Capabilities:* Experiences that develop your skills—taking part in sports, arts, and crafts.
- *Curiosities:* Experiences that cultivate your interests—visiting libraries, museums, concerts, or plays.
- *Capacities:* Experiences that test or challenge you in new ways—giving your first public speech; traveling to a foreign country and testing your language skills; or even, as Dr. Pinkett did once, going to a Native American "sweat ceremony."

The sweat ceremony was part of Dr. Pinkett's experience in the Next Generation Leadership fellowship program sponsored by the Rockefeller Foundation. He and twenty-two other NGL fellows were invited to participate in the sacred event by another fellow/friend, Gail Small, and her family in Montana on an Indian reservation. The experience is one Dr. Pinkett will never forget.

Inside the sweat lodge, the group sat around burning coals—the temperature was high but not so bad, kind of like a really intense dry sauna.

Dr. Pinkett recalls:

I'm thinking, "Okay, this isn't so bad." And then they did the unthinkable. They poured water over the coals, which did two things: one, the temperature went up dramatically, I mean it went from hot to ridiculous, and two, the hut filled with steam so you could not see an inch in front of your eyes. And at that point, the heat was so intense, imagine every pore on your body secreting liquid; it's that hot. I had water coming out of my toes, out of my eyes, water coming out of my ears, water coming out of my head, water coming out of my arm, everywhere water was coming out of my body and that went on for another twenty minutes. It was over-the-top intense, but when it was all said and done, I felt purged, I felt cleansed. I was glad I did it for two reasons: it was a bonding experience for all of us and it was another triumph over fear—because I had been scared to death.

Conquering something new and challenging may give you a greater appreciation for, and confidence in, your own abilities, as it did for Dr. Pinkett. Attending an event may spark a new area of interest. Practicing something makes you better at it. The significance of these kinds of experiences is that they all develop your human capital.

―――――

Variety is the spice of life

and exploration activates the flavor.

―――――

EXPOSURE THAT CULTIVATES CULTURAL CAPITAL

Cultural capital refers to the resources that shape how you think and act in a local and global context. The third grouping involves exposure to different *concepts*, *cultures*, and *circumstances*:

- *Concepts:* Exposure to different concepts, ideas, and ways of thinking—this can be achieved through reading, researching, and having conversation with others. The simple act of browsing in a bookstore can reveal something new.
- *Cultures:* Exposure to different cultures or ways of living. Chances are, in your own city or town there are areas that are very different than where you reside. Maybe it's a very wealthy area as opposed to a working-class or middle-class environment or an area with a high density of people from one part of the world. Beyond your own geographic area, there are always opportunities to travel to other countries and immerse yourself in another culture.
- *Circumstances:* Exposure to different events, situations, and circumstances. This is incredibly varied and could range from attending a lecture, film festivals, and museum events to taking workshops, attending seminars, or taking enrichment

classes—these being courses that are taken not for a degree program but simply to enhance your knowledge of something new, like architecture in your city or a new language.

The kinds of exposure described above involve some kind of inter-action: reading a newspaper, debating an issue, traveling to a foreign country, or participating in a conference, and so on. These interactions then help you to build cultural capital—increasing your ability to generate new ideas, understand different cultures, or gain insight into situations.

When Dr. Pinkett was at Oxford, it was the first time he had encountered people who weren't fans of everything about the United States. This was an eye-opener. Growing up so close to New York City, the center of business, finance, fashion, and media in this country, Dr. Pinkett kind of felt like the world revolved around him. He, like a lot of young Americans, didn't have an awareness or appreciation for some of the criticisms of American foreign policy that he heard from his fellow Rhodes scholars—why did we favor Israel, but not Haiti? Why did we support the UK but have an antagonistic relationship with Cuba?

Dr. Pinkett recalls:

I didn't feel culpable regarding the negative or controversial aspects of US foreign policy given our history of slavery and racism in this country. When debates about US policy erupted, I'd ask, "Why are you mad at me?" And, of course, the response was, "You're an American, so you need to sit and listen to what I have to say about what the US does because you have to take some responsibility for it whether you agree with it or not." That blew me away. To some extent, they were right. I am an American. Whether I agree with our president or not, the American people elected him, and I am an American.

Independent Action Steps to Value Exploration

To this point, we have explained what your comfort zone is, why you need to grow beyond it, and the reasons why it is important to you in becoming a Black face in a high place. As you implement Strategic Action 2, always keep these points in mind:

- Recognize that personal *development* is as important as living. Without growth you become stagnant.
- Much like lifelong learning, you should actively seek *daily* opportunities to move beyond your comfort zone.
- Foster a healthy level of tolerance for *different* views/opinions/ways; listen, hear, and understand the perspectives held by others.
- Be *deliberate* in seeking to obtain broad exposure, both for you personally and for your children or other young people in your life.
- Seek experiences that produce a healthy level of *discomfort*; those that challenge you to do things you normally would not.
- Seek exposure to individuals and ideas that offer a *divergent* perspective from your own; those that challenge your outlook.

These points are guiding principles for executing the following action steps that conclude this chapter.

Strategic Action 1 is about looking within.

Strategic Action 2 is about looking around.

TRAVEL DOMESTICALLY AND ABROAD

Travel domestically and abroad, especially to the African continent, the Caribbean, and other places of the African Diaspora. Exploring different places around the country and around the world may be the easiest way to obtain broad exposure to people, places, events, and cultures. When you travel, you see different surroundings and (hopefully) gain an appreciation for the different styles, values, and perspectives of the people you meet. You learn by interacting with the local people, attending events, and visiting places of cultural or other significance. Buying a guidebook or searching the internet before you go may alert you to the cultural events or places of interest.

- *Plan Ahead.* Plan your vacations and time off to deliberately take advantage of your destination. Perhaps you will want to select a destination that is of significance to your family history or to African history. This would build some bridges between your identity and the global context.
- *Study Abroad.* Universities offer junior year abroad, study abroad, semesters-at-sea, and study tours that visit countries specifically for broadening their students' horizons. Some of these programs are also offered for alumni of universities or any person who can pay the tour fee. By joining an organized tour, you will have knowledgeable tour guides to give you the background on what you are seeing.
- *Extend Trips.* Business trips may offer an additional way to explore different places. Staying an extra day on your own expense may allow you to gain a better understanding of another part of the country or the world. This is an easy way to create additional exposure.

STUDY AND LEARN THE HISTORY
OF DIFFERENT CULTURES

In Strategic Action 1, we talked about the importance of studying and learning your personal or family history. In similar fashion, here we encourage you to study and learn about the history of cultures other than your own. The argument and benefits are similar to that of the previous action step (travel domestically and abroad). The good news is that you don't have to necessarily travel to be exposed to other cultures. Through formal and informal learning opportunities (reading books, using social media, listening to podcasts, watching films and documentaries, and the like), you can learn almost as much about another culture as if you were actually there!

STAY ABREAST OF CURRENT EVENTS

Keeping current on local, national, and world events is both a challenge and a necessity for being a Black face in a high place. Current events are conversation starters and also the type of information that is useful for decision-making.

Strategically, you must be cognizant of the *source* and the *type* of news you are receiving to properly evaluate the *quality* and the *accuracy* of the information. The source of the information may be via social media, in newspapers, on television, or on the radio. The source will determine if it is live or delayed; filtered or not; or coming from interviews or first-person experiences. The type of news may be objective, or it may be advocacy or partisan journalism—work that advances a particular point of view.

Staying abreast of current events is an essential part of obtaining broad exposure. We regularly listen to National Public Radio, which goes more in depth on many issues, and the British-based BBC News for a wider variety of news and perspectives. Websites like CNN.com, NYTimes.com, and NJ.com allow us to stay abreast of up-to-the-minute news all day.

READ BOOKS AND LISTEN TO MEDIA

Read books, watch movies, listen to radio and podcasts, and browse the internet to expand your knowledge base—there is always something to learn. Most of us do not spend enough time developing our knowledge base through print and other media. Books and other media provide the opportunity to be exposed to places beyond your immediate surroundings.

One way to do this is to join or start a reading or book club. If you join the right group, you will have a group of people you can talk to about the book. Especially, if you form a group in which members share insights that have helped them in the past. This will give you some new ideas and introduce you to new possibilities.

An alternative is to use technology to enhance your knowledge base. Use podcasts or social media to explore topics of interest to you. Some people set up alerts via search engines on topics they are trying to learn and then regularly review them. If you are a commuter, how are you using your commute time to and from work? Whether you are driving or sitting on a bus or train, you may be able to use that time to listen to radio broadcasts or even documentaries about topics you are researching or need more information on. These kinds of activities expand your interests and build your skills and capacity. Before going to China, Dr. Robinson listened to podcasts and audio books on Chinese history and modern China.

PARTICIPATE IN FORMAL
PROGRAMS AND ORGANIZATIONS

There are several formal programs and organizations that provide life-changing exposure for their participants. Some examples include:

* Aspen Institute First Mover Fellows (https://www
  .aspeninstitute.org/programs/business-and-society-program
  /first-movers-fellowship-program/) is a "global network

and professional development program for corporate social intrapreneurs. First Movers are accomplished innovators inside companies who are creating new products, services, and management practices that increase business value and make the world a better place."

- Executive Leadership Council (ELC) (https://www .elcinfo.com/) has programs that are designed for Black professionals at the top of the corporation and for midlevel managers aspiring to get to the top of their organization. Both programs include leadership development and networking.
- Fulbright Specialist Program (https://fulbrightspecialist .worldlearning.org/) allows professionals to use their expertise outside of the United States. These are short-term programs that allow you to use your expertise in the service of others.
- Young Global Leaders (https://www.younggloballeaders .org/) is a five-year experience affiliated with the World Economic Forum and provides exposure to a network of global business and social sector leaders interested in cooperation and positive change.

These are just a few examples of the useful opportunities available for exposure through formal programs and organizations. See the RedefineTheGame.com website for more information on these and many other programs.

SEEK BROADENING ACTIVITIES

Be deliberate when choosing a set of activities for yourself and for any young people you are working with. This could include any range of personal experiences, educational experiences, professional experiences, spiritual experiences, and more. Certain activities can seemingly be the complete opposite of the way you live now. For example, if you are a city dweller, why not travel to the county fair or the balloon festival to see a completely different perspective on life? If you are from the suburbs, why not volunteer for an urban soup kitchen for a day and learn about the issues being faced by the populations they serve?

As a student at Rutgers, Dr. Robinson spent some of his free time volunteering at Elijah's Promise, a soup kitchen in New Brunswick.

Dr. Robinson recalls:

> I really didn't even understand how people got to that point where they had to come to a soup kitchen or why they were homeless, but I knew this was a way to help. It just made sense that I would go there and help out and see some things. And you know, it made some connection to parts of the world, parts of the city that you wouldn't normally walk into and know. That to me was important because it kept me grounded.

These kinds of activities will expose you to ideas and possibilities that you would not see if you remained in your comfort zone.

If you are a parent or a mentor of young people, make sure that you are exposing them to a diversity of activities that push them beyond their comfort zone. Take them to work with you or let them go to an exciting event with you. Have them meet interesting people or see local places that they have never been to. These experiences will do something invaluable for them that obtaining broad exposure does for everyone: expand their range of *options* and *choices*. Needless to say, you can never have too many of these experiences.

All of the aforementioned action steps represent viable ways to experiment with your likes and dislikes and explore your strengths and limitations.

Develop Self-Mastery and Find Meaning

You become extraordinary when you know who you really are.
—OPRAH WINFREY

From Excellence to *Ikigai*

When we wrote *Black Faces in White Places*, we thought long and hard about what should follow *establishing a strong identity* and *obtaining broad exposure*. When we agreed that *demonstrating excellence* was the next foundational strategy for achieving success, we were excited to write about something that we found to be very important in our lives.

We were also excited because it gave us a chance to show how excellence is developed. As we wrote then, "Excellence is achieved when you bring empowering beliefs and old-fashioned discipline to the intersection of your true passion and God-given gifts." To be excellent means to find congruence amongst these four faces. To be excellent means to understand yourself so well that you know where your skills, talents, abilities, and hard work really pay off and make an impact. According to Ursula Burns:

> It's really important that we work hard and are good at something. You can't actually skip over the steps between the day you were born and the presidency of the United States just because you're bright. You earn your way up the ladder, and there are things that you have to experience and do. So find something that you're really good at, perfect yourself in that, and work really, really hard.

This is self-mastery. We have encouraged our readers and our audiences to find this highest level of self-mastery because it would lead to personal success. Our Diamond of Excellence was our way to visually represent this idea of polishing the different facets of excellence to find a higher level of success (see figure 6).

You don't get what you wish for;

you get what you work for.

FIGURE 6

IKIGAI

A few years ago, one of Dr. Robinson's colleagues at Rutgers Business School introduced him to a different concept that would push his own ideas on life and meaning to the next level. The concept is called *ikigai,* and it comes from Japanese language and culture. Simply put, *ikigai* is your "reason for being." In *Ikigai for Business,* James Della says, "Discovering one's *ikigai* brings the kind of profound satisfaction of finding meaning in your own life. Neither financial nor career success are requisites for *ikigai.*" In *Ikigai: The Japanese Secret to a Long and Happy Life,* Héctor García and Francesc Miralles, write, "Having a clearly defined *ikigai* brings satisfaction, happiness, and meaning to our lives."

Ikigai has two additional facets that make it a more complete concept than our Diamond of Excellence. First, *ikigai* connects one's personal choices and actions to community- and society-level outcomes. It is said that if everyone pursues their *ikigai* it makes communities and society better for all. Second, *ikigai* places the search for meaning into the center of the self-mastery process. *Ikigai* is not given to you. It is something that must be discovered through your life experiences.

Ikigai is usually depicted with overlapping circles that form intersections of key aspects of self-mastery (see figure 7). The *ikigai* graphic says so much about how we think about life. Once our basic needs are met and we get out of "survival" mode then we are able to think about what we want to do with our life. The *ikigai* graphic shows us four aspects of living. They are captured in four questions:

1. What do you love?
2. What are you good at?
3. What does the world need?
4. What can you be paid for?

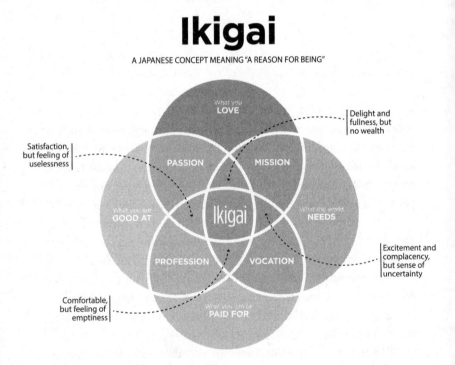

Ikigai

A JAPANESE CONCEPT MEANING "A REASON FOR BEING"

SOURCE: dreamstime

TORONTO STAR GRAPHIC

FIGURE 7

For many of us who seek success, these questions outline the contours of our lives. The answers to these questions help sort out where to spend time and energy. Finding the answers to these questions is a process that encompasses all three strategic actions of Level I: Independent Action to include self-determination (Strategic Action 1), exploration (Strategic Action 2), and of self-mastery and meaning (Strategic Action 3).

When the answers to these questions overlap with one another, there are some synergies released.

The intersections show us the areas of our passion, mission, vocation, and profession.

Passion = (What you love + what you are good at)
Mission = (What the world needs + what you love)
Vocation = (What the world needs + what you can be paid for)
Profession = (What you are good at + what you can be paid for)

When you think about it, passion, mission, vocation, and profession define much of how we live life. Our major activities in life, organizations we participate in, and where we spend our time and money are indicators of where our passion, mission, vocation, and profession truly lie. *Passion* and *mission* and *profession* are words we commonly use to describe these activities. *Vocation* is a word we don't use as often. Vocation and profession are similar to one another because they both require training and expertise. Both can be activities you are paid for. But vocation involves a sense of "calling"—an occupation that you take up because you are drawn to it because it is important to the well-being of others. There are certainly people who have professions that are also vocations. But every person's vocation is not necessarily their profession.

What if the activities that you love to do are also the things you can get paid for? What if the things you know that the world needs coincide with what you can get paid to do? And what would happen if you could simultaneously do what you love to do, what the world needs, and what you are good at? These are the times that energize us and make us want more! *Ikigai* represents the sweet spot in the middle of the *ikigai* graphic, where all of the circles overlap. Constructing a life that aligns your profession, passion, mission, and vocation can take many years. But pursuing and finding *ikigai* also allows you to perform at the highest levels.

Ikigai is a fascinating concept for us to think about and apply because it describes much of our own experience and the experience of high-performing leaders and innovators we have worked with, met with, interviewed, or profiled in this book. To us, *ikigai* is a unique combination of self-mastery and meaning.

> Ikigai *does not drive you to a life to live,*
>
> *but rather, a life to love.*

DR. ROBINSON'S JOURNEY TO FINDING PASSION AND PURPOSE

I have often told my students about how I leaped from a student of civil engineering to become an award-winning business school professor. It was not a straight route. After starting a very promising career at Merck as a project engineer, I became restless and began to search for more fulfilling opportunities. When I thought about it, there were a few things I knew about myself. First, I was a good speaker in front of an audience. I liked being in front of a room. I also knew that entrepreneurship and starting new businesses excited me. My emerging career in the pharmaceutical industry didn't offer opportunities for any of this.

Second, there were the community activities where I spent my time and thoughts. I would participate in mentor programs and activities to work with young people from urban areas. I wanted to make a difference in inner-city neighborhoods, and I knew that mentor programs were one way to participate. These activities built upon my undergraduate second major in urban studies. I believed in the transformation of cities and in uplifting urban neighborhoods.

Third, I wanted a career that allowed me the autonomy to do the things I wanted to do and not just because someone was telling me to do it. My dad saw an advertisement for something called The PhD Project, which introduced people to academic careers in business schools. I attended the conference in November 1997, and it changed the trajectory of my life. After nearly three years of working my "dream job," I decided to leave a "good paying job" and go back to school and study for a PhD at Columbia Business School. While there I pursued research in entrepreneurship and went deep into a study of urban entrepreneurship as my dissertation. Many of my colleagues didn't understand my decision to trade in a great career opportunity with financial security for a return to school and financial insecurity. What they didn't understand was that I wasn't passionate about engineering. I was passionate about transforming urban areas through entrepreneurship. I was on a mission.

Along the journey, there were signs that I was on the right path. My gifts and skills developed over the years and were rewarded by my new academic profession. This doesn't mean that every day was easy or that there weren't challenges on this path. As I worked I found more fulfillment and meaning in the work I was doing. Over time I was more confident that what I was doing was important work and key for communities, business, and society. I was no longer distracted by a lot of "side hustles" and other activities. I was able to find alignment of passion, mission, vocation, and profession to find *ikigai*. The ability to focus and become an expert in my area of choice led to award-winning performance.

By searching for more meaning in life, I landed in a place where I could follow passion and purpose. I was willing and able to take some risks to find some opportunities that changed my life.

IKIGAI IN ACTION

When we talk to accomplished entrepreneurs and business and social sector leaders, we hear the principles of *ikigai* in action.

Knowing Your Gifts and Talents

Cathy Hughes, founder of Urban One, the largest African American–owned broadcast network, knew at an early age she wanted to be in media, although she comes from a family of educators.

> I feel that of the many blessings that God bestowed upon me was the identification before I reached puberty of what it was that I wanted to do and needed to do with my life. And I knew that I would be in media. I was eight years old in the bathroom, pretending that my tooth-brush was a microphone. . . . I've had no detours on that route. . . . And that's a very special blessing. I happen to think that more of us received that blessing than not. But I think that the key is whether or not you are able to recognize it and not allow others to dissuade you from that road.

Commitment to Excellence and Love for the Work

Throughout this book, we will make repeated references to another book, *Breaking Through: The Making of Minority Executives,* by David A. Thomas and John J. Gabarro. *Breaking Through* compares the experiences of minorities who reach the C suite in corporate America ("minority executives") to three other groups: nonminorities who reach the C suite ("nonminority executives"), nonminorities who plateau in their careers ("nonminority managers"), and minorities who plateau in their careers ("minority managers") across three career stages: "Breaking In" (early career). "Breaking Away" (middle career), and "Breaking Through" (late career).

Figure 8 is a visual representative and summary diagram of the findings from the studies performed by Thomas and Gabarro at three different corporations. The figure depicts a few key observations pertaining to the career trajectories of minority executives: (1) they progressed at a very slow rate in the early stages of their career (slower than nonminority executives and nonminority managers) and (2) they progressed at an extremely fast rate during the middle stages of their career (faster than any other group and almost catching up to nonminority executives). This raises some interesting questions about the distinguishing characteristics of minority executives, including their ability to reach the C suite despite a relatively slow start. Thomas and Gabarro write the following, particularly related to Career Stage 1 (p. 102):

The most successful minority executives possessed two key traits . . . a passionate commitment to excellence and an inherent and unshakable love of the work itself. Their commitment to excellence led them to learn new skills. [They] consistently reported that their vocational interests and aptitudes matched their functional area of work in Career Stage 1; some of them even changed jobs once they perceived a mismatch. Minority executives described making early career choices in order to be at the leading edge of the work they liked. They were most enthusiastic about the work itself, and less so with how quickly—or slowly—they were promoted. In contrast, minority managers who

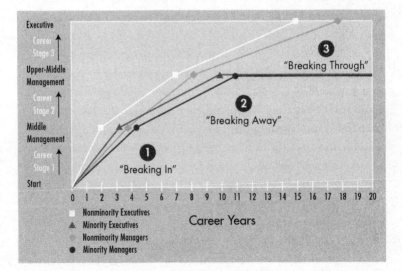

FIGURE 8

subsequently plateaued were more likely to describe choosing the company or organization for fast-track career opportunities to management rather than for the work itself.

Clearly, minority executives understood the underlying principles of *ikigai*—having strong alignment between passion, mission, vocation, and profession—very early in their careers. We will explore several other distinguishing characteristics of minority executives in subsequent chapters.

Linking Passion and Profession to High Performance

When passion and profession intersect, you can reach new heights of performance. Ken Chenault reached the top of the corporate world as the CEO of American Express. And yet, when people asked him what they should do to be successful he would say, "What you need to decide on, most importantly, what I would say is what are your passions? What is it that you want to do? Then get the training to make that happen." He understood that passion for what you are doing is just as important as technical skills.

Angela Glover Blackwell, the founder of PolicyLink, shows us that combining passion and profession can lead to higher performance.

> I would say that many people, many different walks of life, who know me and PolicyLink would consider me an expert in public policy, coalition building, advocacy, and organization building. And I would say that the way that I was able to achieve that level of confidence and mastery, the expertise, is that from the very beginning of my working career, I have sought to do the things about which I am passionate. I have never had a job about which I was not passionate, and if I did, I didn't linger there very long.

She goes on to say:

> Young people come to me constantly asking, "How can I be as satisfied in my work as you seem to be in yours?" And my response is, "Follow

your passion." It will take you where you want to be. It takes discipline. It takes commitment to hard work, and quality, but if you bring a commitment to hard work and quality, and you combine it with what you're passionate about, you will find that many opportunities will open up for you. I would never, and I hope no one would ever describe me as a careerist, which is not to put down careerists. I think that people achieve things often because they are focused on doing so, but I have always just been trying to fulfill my lifelong passion, and actually the way I say it to people is that over the course of the thirty years that I've been working, I have had many jobs but only one project—to do something to make a better world, to deal with issues of justice, and that's it for me.

Finding Meaning in Your Work and Life

Some of the people who work in large organizations see their work activities as an extension of higher goals and values. Ken Chenault said it this way in an interview:

> I think, at the end of the day, that it is a mistake simply to pursue a job. Instead, you should pursue a way of life. The opportunity for me is to make a fundamental difference in people's lives, both inside and outside the company. To lead a very successful enterprise that is not just focused on achieving business success. That's a consequence of doing the right things for our employees and our customers.

PRINCIPLES OF *IKIGAI*

- *Ikigai* is your reason for being, the meaning you find in your life, work, and other activities.
- Your unique gifts and talents will point you toward your *ikigai*. They are not only for you to find fulfillment but also for the community and the society around you.
- Finding the intersections between passion, mission, vocation, and profession can be a lifelong journey toward your *ikigai*.

- *Ikigai* is about aligning your passion, mission, vocation, and profession to achieve harmony in your life.
- Activities that are part of your *ikigai* will be energizing and exciting.

As you get closer to finding your *ikigai*, you will rise to higher levels of performance.

WHAT STOPS PEOPLE FROM FINDING THEIR *IKIGAI*?

Ikigai also gave us a lens into why some successful people are restless in their jobs or careers: they haven't found their *ikigai*.

When you find your *ikigai*, you lessen the conflicts and lower the stress levels in your life. Why? Because you aren't dividing your energy across too many divergent and often energy-draining activities. When you find your *ikigai*, the experiences, talents, gifts, and abilities that have shaped your life make sense because you can see how they help you make a difference, perform at a high level, and maintain productivity. Where others would perish, you thrive. What seems extremely difficult to others is easy to you.

For example, many people talk about how they feel unfulfilled at their job. The work isn't meaningful, the people are not supportive, and they are only there to make a living. When asked what brings them joy in their life, they reveal amazing stories about activities other than work that have so much more meaning and energizes them. When speaking about these other activities, their entire demeanor changes—they almost become a different person. Their eyes light up, they have a smile on their faces, and they talk about it with passion. For those of you that feel this way, ask yourself, is there a way to combine your profession/career with the things you are passionate about? For example, if accounting is your career but music is your passion, could you find a job in accounting in the music industry?

Some people have never thought about having a career that actually gives them fulfillment. They are just going along in a career path that they don't like and spend forty or more hours a week doing a job that they hate just to pay the bills. When they get out of work, they go and spend as much time as possible doing something else. Their job is draining the life right out of them. They could be happier if their work and their passion or mission were in alignment. But fear and finances keep them in jobs where they are not happy.

On the other hand, finding your *ikigai* changes everything in your life. It reduces stress and promotes harmony and gives you a life full of rewarding experiences and meaning.

We sometimes see people leave successful corporate careers to lead nonprofit organizations. On the surface, it seems like such a big shift. They often take pay cuts and lose all of the perks and status of corporate life. They are choosing to use their God-given gifts, talents, and abilities in a completely different area. People who have made this pivot often find that running an organization that has a mission they relate to and where they can harness their passion into productivity is life changing. They are so much happier and more fulfilled than they were in their corporate career.

If you look up *ikigai* online you'll often find references to the residents of Okinawa, Japan. Okinawa is one of seven "blue zones" where the residents have unusually high life expectancy. On Okinawa it is not uncommon for people to live into their eighties, nineties, or over a hundred years old. There are even some people who are over 110 years old. The secret to their longevity, they say, is diet and finding *ikigai*. When you have *ikigai* you have meaning and harmony in your life, and it pays off in good health.

(If you are still finding your *ikigai*, check out the callout box "What If You Haven't Found Your *Ikigai* Yet?")

By seeking *ikigai* you can find a use for the skills, abilities, talents, and gifts that you possess. *Ikigai* cannot be given to you, but you can be guided toward it. Many high-performing leaders and innovators have found out how to leverage their passion, profession, vocation, and mission to rise to new levels of performance while affecting their work places, communities, and society.

WHAT IF YOU HAVEN'T FOUND YOUR *IKIGAI* YET?

Finding *ikigai* is a process. Here are a few steps to help you find yours:

- **Complete a self-assessment.** What am I good at? Where are my gifts? There are some great assessments that will give you insights into your gifts, talents, competencies, and abilities. In our leadership institute, we have used StrengthFinders, Myers-Briggs Type Indicator® (MBTI®), Keirsey Temperament Sorter, Herrmann Brain Dominance Instrument® (HBDI®), and other assessments of personality, gifts, and intelligence to help people uncover their often-hidden talents and abilities. When these self-assessments are debriefed, we are always surprised by how much people don't think about themselves and where their strengths and talents may be. Taking these types of assessments and talking them over with a mentor, coach, or good friend will start you on your way toward finding your *ikigai*.

- **Assess your activities and organizations.** Write down all of the activities and organizations you are a part of. Ask yourself, what are the common themes in these activities? What do I gain from doing these activities outside of my job? Some of us spend a lot of energy with organizations and work on community projects that fulfill some aspect of our lives outside of our work. Examining what the themes and commonalities are in these activities will help you to think about what energizes you and what is exciting to you. Sometimes we put enormous energy into activities outside of our professional or work life because our work is not fulfilling or lacks the opportunities we are looking for. These energizing and exciting activities are definite hints for finding your *ikigai*.

- **Take a look at your work life.** Ask yourself the question "Is my work a job, a career, or a calling?" Organizational behavior professor Dr. Amy Wrzesniewski's research on work orientation is relevant here. Her work points to why people do their work. You might think of your work as a "job" if you are doing it only for the money and it isn't fulfilling in any other way. You might think of your work as a career if you are motivated by the thought of progressing through various jobs of increasing responsibility. Your approach to work might be career-like if you get excited by advancement and achievement. You might think of your work as a "calling" if you believe your work is part of a larger mission or if it has meaning that goes beyond money or achievement. People who think about their work as a calling often are motivated by ideals and the needs of society.
- **Do some self-reflection.** Think about the times in your life when you were excited about getting up to go do an activity or to complete some task. Reflect on the times in your childhood that were energizing. Think about times when people have been impressed by what you have done and you think it was easy to do. All of these moments are indicators of where your passion, mission, and vocation may be.

After you do these activities, ask yourself three big questions: (1) What does all of this tell me about myself? (2) Am I combining self-mastery and meaning in my current choice of profession and vocation? (3) How can I move my life and use my energy in ways that draw me closer to my *ikigai*? Write the answers to these questions down in a journal or in another way that you reflect on your life. By writing these things down, you will begin to focus on establishing new goals for yourself. The answers to these questions will help you to find new opportunities to pursue self-mastery, meaning, purpose, and *ikigai*.

Independent Action Steps
to Develop Self-Mastery

LEARN YOUR CRAFT

According to Thomas and Gabarro, Career Stage 1 for minority executives is characterized as a period of fewer departmental changes,
functional changes, lateral assignments, line to staff moves, location
changes, and even fewer promotions when compared to minority
managers who eventually plateaued, as shown in table 1. This may
seem counterintuitive that minority managers who plateaued had
more promotions than minorities who became executives. How can
these seemingly contradictory insights be understood?

RELATIVE FREQUENCY OF ASSIGNMENTS IN CAREER STAGE 1
FOR MINORITY EXECUTIVES AND MINORITY MANAGERS

Note: Average frequency of assignment per participant per period

TYPE OF ASSIGNMENT	MINORITY EXECUTIVES	MINORITY MANAGERS
Departmental Change	0.4	1.1
Function Change	0.5	1.1
Lateral Assignment	0.7	2.0
Line to Staff Move	0.1	0.5
Location Change	1.2	1.5
Promotions (within level)	0.7	1.9

TABLE 1

Source: The Breaking Through: The Making of Minority Executives
in Corporate America by David A. Thomas and John J. Gabarro

The data suggest that minority executives were relatively stationary,
thus allowing them to better hone their abilities and learn their craft. By
minimizing the frequency of their assignments, they were able to deepen
their technical/functional expertise (and deepen the relationships

within their team and/or department, which we will revisit in Strategic Action 4: Network and Build Power) as a means to establishing a solid experiential foundation when compared to minority managers. For Black faces that aspire to high places, this speaks to the importance of developing technical/functional excellence in the early stages of your career as an associate pastor or staff attorney or entry-level teacher, because it sets the tone for excellence in the subsequent stages of your career to becoming a law firm partner, senior pastor, or school principal.

"From the beginning of my career I found something I could be passionate about—that was the business of health care. I have always been inspired by the work that I do as a leader in a profession that makes a difference in people's lives," said Dennis Pullin, president and CEO of Virtua Health. "From this foundation I invested the time and energy to prepare myself, learning as much as I could and developing those areas in which I wasn't as strong as I wanted to be. Along the way I have been lucky to work with many great people. And so for me as a leader, the stars aligned."

PURSUE "DEVELOPMENTAL HEAT"

Pursuing "developmental heat" means taking deliberate steps to place yourself in situations where you have to perform under "extreme conditions" (but not dangerous), such as limited resources, limited time, limited support, heavy reliance on others, or other "high stakes" environments. Some examples of "developmental heat" include the following:

- Academic and Extracurricular
    intense academic programs
    performing arts auditions and oratorical contests
    athletic competitions
    semesters abroad
    outdoor challenges
    pledging a fraternity or sorority

- Professional
    rotational programs
    special assignments
    turnaround efforts
    high-consequence and high-visibility projects

Why is "developmental heat" so important to demonstrating excellence? The answer is found in a comment that was made by Brenda Wright, former senior vice president at Wells Fargo, one of the sponsors of a program where Dr. Pinkett first heard the term *developmental heat*. She said, "You play at the level you practice." Developmental heat challenges you to practice at a high level, so you can perform at a high level. Zaila Avant-garde personified this life principle at the age of fourteen when she became the first African American to win the Scripps National Spelling Bee in 2021 after almost one hundred years of contests. Her success came as a result of the tens of thousands of words she pored over with her father in just two years of preparation!

Moreover, the research by Thomas and Gabarro found that the examples of professional developmental heat listed above were also instrumental in minority executives breaking through in Career Stage 3, as these experiences gave them the ability to demonstrate their executive potential. We will revisit this in Strategic Action 7: Think and Act Like an Intrapreneur.

PURSUE PROGRAMS AND ORGANIZATIONS THAT PROMOTE EXCELLENCE

There are several formal programs and organizations that promote personal and professional excellence among their participants. Some examples include:

- Academic and Early Career
    Academic enrichment and college preparation
        (such as Arthur Ashe Institute for Urban Health,

Postbaccalaureate Achievement Program, Minority
Summer Research Program at MIT, Detroit Area
Pre-College Engineering Program)
Academic placement (such as A Better Chance)
Graduate education (such as National GEM Fellowship
Consortium, The PhD Project, The Consortium)
Career development (such as INROADS)
Public speaking (such as Toastmasters International, New
Jersey Orators)
* Mid- to Late-Career
Executive Leadership Council
Information Technology Senior Management Forum
NMSDC Advanced Management Education Program at
Northwestern University's Kellogg School of
Management
Tuck Diversity Business Programs at Dartmouth College

These are just a few examples of the plethora of opportunities available to promote excellence. See the Redefine the Game Institute website for more information on these and many other organizations.

LEARN FROM FAILURE

If you look closely at people who have achieved any measure of success, there are undoubtedly two things they have in common. First, they have been persistent. They never allowed failures or setbacks to discourage them. As we discussed earlier in this chapter, persistence stems from an empowering belief in your ability to overcome obstacles. And throughout our lives we've seen talented individuals outperformed by others who were unwilling to accept failure. *Failure is unavoidable if you desire to be successful.* Successful people understand that failure does not suggest that something is wrong with them. Rather, failure is an opportunity for learning and growth.

Take Senator Cory Booker, for instance. Booker lost one mayoral race in 2002 against longtime incumbent Sharpe James before becoming mayor of New Jersey's largest city in 2006. "I learned more lessons in my loss than in my victory," he says.

Just as important, because some of our most valuable learning comes from failure, successful people have taken the time to learn from their failures. "I say to my staff all the time, you can't lose the lesson when something goes wrong," Booker says. "It's one of the professors you can find in life—mistakes and what some people call failures. I don't put myself in a lens of having mastered anything as long as we are a nation that has not fulfilled itself. I'm a part of a larger, we all are part of a larger, unfolding story of a nation that's put forth profound ideals into the universe; yet the story of America is the constant story of individuals trying to make real the promise to this country. And so there is no time to rest on laurels or to claim how we have achieved ourselves or as an individual. As we get better and learn more, the world demands that we rise to the challenge. And I am in the process of trying to rise."

Taking the time to learn from failure is not difficult. It simply requires a moment of reflection. If something hasn't worked out well, instead of beating yourself up about it, learn from the answers to these questions:

- What could I have done better?
- How would others have attacked the problem?
- How will I approach it differently in the future? Were there things I overlooked that could have led to a better outcome?

You may even take the time to document your lessons learned in a journal. No matter how you perform this action step, you should use what you learn from any failure as feedback. Failure as feedback is an important part of the never-ending process of growth and development.

LEARN FOR LIFE

We live in a world where the only thing constant is change. Anything you learn can become obsolete very quickly. New information, new knowledge, new approaches, and new best practices are always being introduced within any given field. *Maintaining excellence* requires that you constantly learn and apply new things. Dr. Robinson makes a point of learning a new technology each year. This is a growth mind-set as discussed in the Level I introduction.

Lifelong learning can take any number of forms. Certainly, formal education is an excellent way to establish a solid educational foundation (for example, high school diploma or GED) including the study of core areas (for example, associate's or bachelor's degree), more advanced areas (for example, master's degree), and various professional subjects (for example, degrees in business, law, medicine, divinity, and so on).

Generally speaking, we are strong proponents for obtaining a graduate degree. We believe a bachelor's degree has become today what a high school diploma was thirty years ago: a prerequisite for entering the competitive job market. The other benefit of formal education is that you're not just learning, you're also learning how to learn. This makes it easier to acquire new knowledge more quickly and easily because you've developed an ability to get up to speed in any number of areas.

But there are several other avenues to lifelong learning, many of which do not necessarily include formal education:

- Attend lectures or seminars being offered in your community or webinars offered online.
- Attend a conference including the workshops, panel discussions, plenary sessions, and keynote speeches.
- Enroll in a class at a local community college or online.
- Read books, which, in our opinion, represent some of the best value you can get for your money.
- Peruse materials at your local library.

- Subscribe to magazines and publications, including publications that are specifically geared toward your field or industry.
- Participate in a continuing education program, which is an accredited and sponsored course delivered by a qualified instructor for which you earn continuing education units (CEUs). (Completing a certain number of CEUs is often required by certain licensed professionals.)
- Research and study material on the internet including articles, reports, blogs, audio and video podcasts, and so on. (A cautionary note: just because something is posted on the internet does not mean the information comes from a reliable source.)

Independent Action Steps to Find Meaning

PURSUE YOUR PASSION
INSTEAD OF WHAT'S "PRACTICAL"

We've come across far too many people who are passionate about one thing but whose job is in a completely different area. The reason being that they are convinced, or even told, that their passion is not "practical." The argument is made that what they are passionate about is not lucrative or is not important or is not worth pursuing.

Dr. Cheryl L. Dorsey knows what that's like. Before discovering her passion, she spent many years preparing for a career in, and practicing, medicine.

"In my heart of hearts I wasn't that passionate about being a physician," Dr. Dorsey said. "But I was the first person in my family to go to an Ivy League school; I was the first person in my family to consider being a doctor, so there were a lot of expectations and hopes wrapped up into me becoming a physician even though in my heart of hearts it was not really my calling or my passion."

During the time Dr. Dorsey was in medical school, there was an effort to train more doctors about the business of medicine because the managed care system was emerging. Scholarships to the John F. Kennedy School of Government at Harvard to study policy were being offered with the hope that if doctors understood the business and policy side, they would operate better under managed care. "I didn't have a grand plan, but when the opportunity presented itself, I knew enough to take advantage of it," she said.

The program was designed to allow the medical students to take a year off for the policy studies and then finish the two degrees concurrently the next year. So when Dr. Dorsey emerged from school with the medical and policy degree, what did she do? "At the time, Black babies were dying at three times the rate of white babies in inner-city Boston, and I worked with another African American physician to start this mobile health unit to create a bridge between the community and the medical and health services in the Boston area," she explained. The unit, called the Family Van and founded under a fellowship program, still operates today.

After two years of working to get the Family Van established, Dr. Dorsey resumed her traditional medical career doing a residency in pediatric medicine. She still wasn't happy. Next, she decided to pursue a PhD in history to meld her interest in history and science, and that didn't feel right. Then she took a job at a for-profit company. That wasn't a good fit either. Some family members were less than impressed with her indecision.

"My aunt said you are the village idiot—she said those precise words," Dorsey said with a big laugh. "What are you doing? Your parents spent all this money and time sending you to medical school and you got this great education and you're not a doctor?"

But Dr. Dorsey pushed past the expectations and stayed true to her passions to lead her to the career she's in today. "I was interested in helping at a more policy and systems level than at the family or individual level," she said. "Most of us are pursuing careers, not jobs. Careers are an important part of our identity, and you do need career satisfaction to feel whole. If you think you deserve to be happy and you think your work should provide you with some measure of satisfaction, the notion of getting up every day and doing something that doesn't make you happy, to me, is just misery."

Today, Dr. Dorsey is the president of Echoing Green, a New York–based organization that provides funding and technical support to social entrepreneurs. And it is no coincidence that Echoing Green was the organization that awarded Dr. Dorsey the fellowship to start Family Van.

Professional excellence is not just about finding the intersection between your passion and your gifts; it is also about staying true to your passion when you realize what you're doing is not the right fit. This is where some risk is involved. You will have some very practical considerations such as income, quality of life, student loans and other debt, family support and obligations, and so on when making these decisions. You may need to take some time to prepare before taking on the next opportunity. Our point is that even when you must sacrifice practicality over your passion, try to seek opportunities that provide enough flexibility so that you do not have to completely give up on your passion, or seek ways to still explore your passion simultaneously and in other creative ways. In doing so, you will be able seek opportunities to bring your passion and profession together in one path, which we know leads to greater fulfillment, harmony, productivity, and performance.

EMBODY THE "POWER OF 'AND'"

You don't necessarily have to choose one area to go deep or to pursue excellence. We believe in something we refer to as the "power of 'and,'" which is the empowering belief that you can achieve excellence in multiple arenas. This is the notion that you can do this *and* this *and* that, as opposed to having to choose between this *or* this *or* that.

The latter is what we refer to as the "tyranny of 'or,'" or the disempowering belief that you must necessarily choose between one area or the other. For example, you could become a world-renowned scientist *and* a public official *and* a noted professor *and* the president of a university. In fact, this is the case for Dr. Shirley Jackson who was one of the few African Americans studying physics at MIT in the 1960s and '70s. She later became a professor and president of Rensselaer Polytechnic Institute. Like Queen Latifah, you could become a rapper, singer, model, actress, and producer. We are both entrepreneurs, scholars, speakers, and authors. The possibilities are endless if you possess the empowering belief that they are indeed possible. Therefore, we encourage you, if not challenge you, to seek out the connections between your seemingly disparate gifts and passions—between your passion in foreign countries *and* your gifts in business; or your passion for hip-hop *and* your gifts in entrepreneurship; or your passion in art or poetry *and* your gifts of finance or accounting. You may find that these talents can find harmony together.

We should be clear that what we do *not* propose is that you spread your time and effort too thin by seeking excellence simultaneously in several areas. More often than not, excellence is achieved in a specific area, before branching out into other areas. Dr. Jackson began as an excellent physicist. Queen Latifah started out as an excellent rapper. We began as excellent scholars. Once you've seen what is required to achieve excellence by focusing in on a specific area, it is easier to transfer many of the same principles to other areas.

MAKING A PIVOT TOWARD PASSION TO FIND YOUR MEANING

Darryl Cobb wouldn't describe his career before he found his passion as misery, but like Dorsey, he knew something was missing. He was traveling and making a good living as a consultant. He had earned an MBA at Northwestern University's Kellogg School of Management, one of the top business schools in the nation. All in all, he liked his work.

"But, while I was happy doing it, it wasn't my life's passion," he explained. But when he came home to the South Side of Chicago, he questioned the value of his work. "My heart would just die every Thursday, when I came home as a consultant. I'd ask myself, 'I did great work this week. How does it change the set of opportunities for kids of families in my neighborhood who don't have the same opportunities that I have? Because I'm no smarter than those kids are. In fact, many of them, given what they're dealing with, are probably a lot smarter and more savvy and intelligent than I am. They're just not provided with the opportunities to show that. So for me, through conversations with my wife, I realized that I had a passion for trying to create a different set of opportunities for children."

"The pivot" is a term used to describe a sharp change of direction. When people pivot in their careers, they are changing from one career path to another. They often use the same skills in a different context. And in making the pivot toward their passion, they find a higher meaning in their work.

Fatimah Williams, CEO of Beyond the Tenure Track, is an expert in helping people navigate through pivots. In her executive coaching business, she gives clients space to make adjustments in their life. When we talked to her about coaching people through pivots, here is what she said: From the outside, successful people's pivots appear to be sharp, unlikely turns from one industry or role to the next that culminate in magical, prestigious careers. But pivots are not sharp turns; they are a series of steps rooted in trust in self, calculated risk-taking, and persistence to take the next step, even when family, colleagues, or society don't fully understand it.

The first steps toward a meaningful career is to have the courage to identify what's not working. Even if it's within the context of a high-paying or prestigious position, ask yourself what you want next, and embrace your desired future without self-judgment. Until you attend to those self-reflective inquiries, you can bet on remaining frustrated and stuck.

Cobb's pivot came after talking with a career counselor at his alma mater, Kellogg. After hearing about the things he was passionate about, the career counselor connected him with the Knowledge Is Power Program (KIPP), a charter school organization being run by some Kellogg graduates. "I called them to set up an informational interview just to find out what does someone with an MBA do with education? And it so happened at that time they were actually looking for somebody to be in the Midwest, who had the flexibility to travel, who had a finance and operations background, and who could work to help the new school leaders with setting up the finance and operational aspects of their schools." After working for KIPP for six years in many roles including as chief learning officer, he moved on to become CEO of ACT Charter School in Chicago.

Cobb eventually has moved into an area of funding and investing in the growth of charter schools. Which brings his journey full circle by combining his in-school leadership experience with his financial and school development acumen. If he didn't make the pivot at a critical moment in his life, he would still be in "misery."

We have met many people over the years who describe similar life-changing moments when they could continue down a path where they were not happy and did not find meaning in their work or they could pivot toward work they had a passion for and find meaning along the way. And by finding meaning in your life, the quality of your life goes up. You might find your *ikigai* too.

LEVEL II

Interdependent Action

*We are not here on earth to see through each other;
we are here to see each other through.*
— UNKNOWN

The most important asset you will gain in Level II is your *mindset*. You will embody a global citizen's mindset by creating meaningful, productive, and mutually supportive relationships that are global, diverse, and that build bridges across lines of difference. When you're a global citizen:

- You are establishing real relationships with real people who are like you and, perhaps more important, people who are *not* like you: people who don't look like you; don't talk like you; didn't grow up in the same neighborhoods as you; don't eat similar foods as you, and so on.
- You are leveraging online tools to help establish, maintain, and manage connections to the global society we live in and translating those connections into relationships.
- You are building bridges between otherwise disconnected people, teams, departments, divisions, organizations, and communities.

• • •

The global citizen's mindset is about stepping outside of your comfort zone into your growth zone to develop relationships reflecting greater personal diversity.

The Benefits of Personal Diversity

We believe the arguments for leveraging diversity have been made very clear from an *organizational* perspective. For example, it attracts the best talent, generates the best ideas, and develops understanding and engagement of different cultures. For example, studies have found corporations that embrace diversity outperform their competition financially by as much as 35 percent. This is in addition to other measurable benefits such as increased employee satisfaction, enhanced decision-making and innovation, improved productivity, and more.

The *personal* benefits of embracing diversity have to do with cultivating *your* best talent, and generating *your* best ideas, and understanding the different cultures *you* engage. Studies have shown that people with strong social networks receive: (1) better performance evaluations, (2) earlier promotions, and (3) higher compensation.[1] Similarly, people who have more diverse, equitable, and inclusive relationships should also enjoy: (1) a richer human experience, (2) a more balanced worldview, and (3) more edifying interactions.

So, being a global citizen does not mean having the most *diverse* relationships. It means having *diversity* within your relationships; and not just your acquaintanceships, but also your friendships, if you want to be competitive in the twenty-first century.

DR. PINKETT'S RHODES TO ENGLAND

When I won the Rhodes Scholarship, I was the first African American from Rutgers University to receive this honor in the school's history. I subsequently traveled overseas to study at Oxford University, as one of five Black Rhodes scholars out of thirty-two American Rhodes scholars. There, in England, I experienced several culture shocks.

Oxford's student population was less than 1 percent Black at the time I arrived there. I would go days without seeing another Black face other than mine in the mirror, and I experienced what it was like to be part of a minority group within a minority group. Unlike US colleges and universities where African Americans are typically the largest contingent among the Black students, African Americans were one of the smallest contingents among the already underrepresented Black students at Oxford. The majority of the Black students at Oxford were from Africa, the Caribbean, and the United Kingdom. I was so myopic that I once asked some of my African classmates if they wanted to play spades and bid whist only for them to look at me sideways because they had never heard of these American card games.

I also came to realize the subtle but distinctive differences between the United Kingdom and the United States. This ranged from anticipated differences, such as driving on opposite sides of the road and dissimilar power outlets, to unanticipated differences, such as light bulbs that screw in (US) versus those that snap in (UK) and referring to deep-fried, thin slices of potato as "chips" (US) versus "crisps" (UK). But the biggest culture shock I experienced was the stark differences between African American and British cuisine. Suffice it to say that Oxford's dining hall food did not offer the same satisfaction as southern-style soul food!

Sadly, not only did my appetite diminish, but I lost so much weight that my mom became concerned when I returned home for break. I vividly remember to this day the profound advice she gave me. Rather than teaching me how to cook my favorite meals, she encouraged me to ask some of my Oxford classmates if they could teach me how to cook their native dishes.

I started preparing food from classmates who hailed directly from Africa, China, France, the Caribbean, and more. Perhaps most importantly, I learned not only about cuisine, but I learned about culture. This experience did more than just expand my culinary repertoire, it expanded my *mindset as a global citizen*.

Global Citizen Trends

Three trends have set the stage for the global citizen's mindset and those three trends are:

TREND ONE: DIVERSITY

The first trend is that *we live in an increasingly diverse society*. According to the latest US Census Bureau figures from 2017, 42 percent of the US population consists of Hispanics/Latinos, African Americans, Asian Americans, Native Hawaiian or other Pacific Islanders, American Indians, Alaska Natives, and two or more races.[2]

According to census projections:

These so-called minorities will make up a majority of the US population by the year 2045.[3]

These groups already make up a majority of the population of Hawaii, California, and Texas (85.2 percent, 67.5 percent, and 61 percent) and are projected to become the majority in New York and Florida within the next decades.[4]

The majority of babies born today (50.2 percent) are racial or ethnic minorities.[5]

According to a *Washington Post* analysis of US Department of Labor data, most new hires of prime working age (twenty-five to fifty-four) in the US are people of color.[6]

The implications of increasing societal diversity are that now, more than ever before, we are being called upon to work with, interact with, and lead people of different backgrounds. You can see this trend as a challenge, or you can see this trend as an opportunity; how you see it depends on your mindset.

TREND TWO: DIGITAL TECHNOLOGY

The second trend is that *we live in an increasingly digital and technological society*. From CDs to DVDs to MP3s to PSPs to HDTVs;

and, of course, from iPods to iTunes to iPhones to iPads, our world today is radically different in the twenty-first century even when compared to the twentieth century. According to Cisco,[7] as of 2009, the number of connected devices exceeded the number of humans on the planet (see figure 9). According to Statistica,[8] while the number of humans is estimated to be eight billion in 2025, the number of connected devices is estimated to be seventy-five billion, which is more than nine connected devices per person.

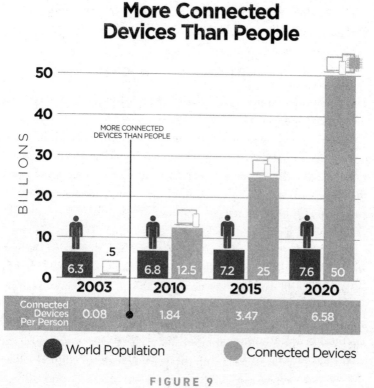

FIGURE 9

Source: Cisco IBSG, April 2011

These devices enable access to a growing cadre of social media platforms, with growing user bases, such as Facebook (2.45 billion users), Instagram (1 billion users), TikTok (800 million users), Reddit (430 million users), Snapchat (360 million users), Twitter (330 million users), Pinterest (322 million users), and LinkedIn (310 million users),[9] to name a few. These platforms allow us to connect with almost anyone, anywhere, anytime across the globe.

The implication of widespread digital technology throughout our society and growing use of social media platforms is that now, more than ever before, when you restate the old adage "It's a small world after all," remember what you are really saying is, "It's a small *global* world after all," and digital technology has been a key driver in creating it. You can see this trend as a challenge, or you can see this trend as an opportunity; how you see it depends on your mindset.

TREND THREE: DEMOCRACY

The third and final trend is we live in an increasingly divided country that threatens our democracy.

We believe the single greatest threat to our democracy is the growing divides within our society. We are talking about the growing divides between the "haves" and the "have nots"; the wealthy and poor; the "rich" and "the rest"; the young and old; Black and white; straight and LGBTQ; Democrats and Republicans; agnostics and believers; CNN and MSNBC and Fox News.

In her TED talk "The Politics of Fiction," Turkish novelist, activist, and academic Elif Shafak reminds us that we all live in some kind of a social and cultural circle and that we are all born into a certain family, race, ethnicity, class, and nation. She argues that if we do move beyond the worlds we take for granted and interact with people who are not like us—those who do not look like us, speak our language, eat the same foods, espouse the same political views, share our cultural values, and so on—then we can suffer the equivalent of a social and cultural death. If we only remain within our "cultural cocoons" of what is familiar and convenient—family, friends, loved ones, and colleagues— then our humanness becomes progressively and sadly diminished.[10]

Our society increasingly comprises what Shafak refers to as "communities of the like-minded." And the danger of these communities of the like-minded that surround so many of us is that we tend to associate with people who are like us and, as a result, we can become more prone to produce stereotypes and assumptions about those who are not like us—cast projections onto those outside of the communities to which we belong. The irony is that as our country continues to diversify, we *all* seem to be diving deeper into our communities of the like-minded. This not only undermines the benefits of America's greatest asset—cultural diversity—but also further exacerbates America's greatest liability—cultural ignorance. In the absence of real dialogue and real interactions and real understanding that breaks down the walls that can separate all of us, societal inequities will continue to exist because societal ignorance will continue to persist.

The solution does not lie in Blacks learning more about whites, or Hispanics learning more about Blacks, or even whites learning more about Hispanics, but in all of us learning more about one another, and that means embracing the global citizen's mindset. A mindset that sees diversity as something to be *valued*; a digital technology-enabled, small global world as something to be *explored*; and communities of the like-minded as something to be *bridged*. It is ultimately a mindset that sees an increasingly divided country as something that threatens our democracy and believes that if you are not a part of the solution, then you *are* the problem.

Your Mindset, Skill Set, and Tool Set at Level II: Interdependent Action

The recurring theme throughout Level II: Interdependent Action is relationships. We define interdependent action as action taken by two or more individuals for their mutual benefit (1+1=2), such as networking, mentoring, and teamwork, which all stem from relationship building. The *skill sets* you will learn to employ at this level are:

- **Strategic Action 4: Network and Build Power—**
  Networking leads to relationships, relationships translate into power, and power equates to influence. Becoming a

Black face in a high place builds power; being a Black face in a high place wields power.

- **Strategic Action 5: Maximize Mentoring**—Black faces in high places have often benefited tremendously from developmental relationships, such as mentorship (and sponsorship), and therefore have a necessary responsibility to mentor (and sponsor) others.
- **Strategic Action 6: Leverage Our Might**—As a Black face in a high place, you must connect with other like-minded and like-hearted individuals to pursue collective goals while being intentional about opening doors for those who aspire to exceed your accomplishments.

The global citizen's mindset and the skill sets making up Strategic Actions 4, 5, and 6 translate directly into two tool sets, or forms of capital: namely, *social capital* and *intellectual capital*. Social capital resides in individuals. It is your relationships, the people you know and the contacts you have. Intellectual capital resides in relationships between people such as teams and mastermind groups. It is the knowledge, experience, and skills resulting from a team's collective effort. It is both the art and the science of using these tool sets that forms the basis for putting the next three strategies into action.

Network and Build Power

Networking works when you understand that there is very little that
you can do or have in life without working with other people.

—DR. GEORGE FRASER

in *Success Runs in Our Race*

Understanding the Social Capital of Networks and Power

The social capital tool set can be the basis of your power within your company, organization, industry, or community. In an amazing TED Women talk in 2018, Carla Harris, the legendary vice-chair of Morgan Stanley, explained that we all carry around "relationship currency"—those investments we make in the people around us.[1] She stresses the importance of building these social relationships before you need them. When the time is right, you want these people to be willing to spend their own relationship currency on your behalf to get a job, a promotion, or an important connection. In other words, it's not about who you know but who knows you. That sums up social capital pretty well!

Four sociologists shaped the study of social relationships and networks: James Coleman, Mark Granovetter, Stanley Milgram, and Ronald Burt. Each contributed research that transformed the way we think about our interactions with others. Coleman called this study of the value and usefulness of these relationships a study of social capital. His area of focus was the set of "strong-tie" (that is, high familiarity and/or frequency) relationships that provide support around us. He used the term *network* to describe the set of interconnected relations each person has. The lesson here is that the value of a person's social capital increases as they build strong relationships with other people.

Granovetter's research advanced the idea that the strength of the relationships matter. Granovetter's work emphasized that it isn't just the strong ties that are valuable in a person's network; so-called weak ties (that is, familiarity and/or frequency) are very important. Weak ties bring unique information and connect you to resources. The value of your social capital increases as you develop good contacts from a diverse set of people.

Milgram introduced the term "six degrees of separation" to the world. His work on networks was trying to answer the question "How is everyone connected to everyone else?" Social scientists have continued to research the connections between us and have concluded that there are no more than three or four "degrees" of separation between every person on the earth. What seems to make a difference in how successful you will be in connecting with a specific person is the quality of your network and your connection to key "connectors" in the global network.

Burt introduced the concept of the network structure of social capital. This structural approach looks at the shape of our networks and how the people in our networks are spread across departments, levels in the organization, and different social groups. If there is a missing connection within a network, known as a *network gap,* it presents opportunities to not only connect disconnected people and groups but also for the person who brokers these connections to benefit.

THE NETWORKS OF WANDA AND JAMES

When we talk to rising executives about their networks, we often use the networks of Wanda and James to visually illustrate the structure of social capital (see figure 10). Imagine that letters A, B, and C in the figure represent different departments or divisions within an organization (for example, accounting, marketing, and operations). The solid lines represent strong ties and the dashed lines represent weak ties for both Wanda and James, respectively. Both Wanda and James

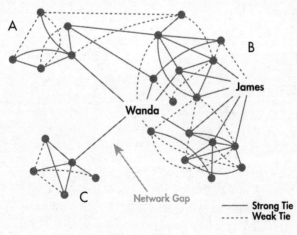

FIGURE 10

have the same number of strong ties and weak ties. Who do you think has a stronger network? The answer depends on their career stage.

DENSE NETWORKS

James's network is excellent for establishing credibility during the early stages of one's career. Why? Because James's network is very *dense,* that is, several people in his network are connected to one another. While there are limits to the kinds of social capital that James can build, those overlapping relationships of redundant ties within group B represent people who can deepen his technical and functional expertise and vouch for him and his abilities. For example, imagine group B is the marketing department. James has the right network to become an excellent marketer and to have relationships to people who can affirm that he is an excellent marketer, which can benefit him well into the future. We saw in figure 8 the career stages and career trajectories of minority and nonminority managers who plateau in their careers and minority and nonminority executives who reach the C suite. The networks of minority executives during Career Stage 1 look like James's network.

Thomas and Gabarro explain further:

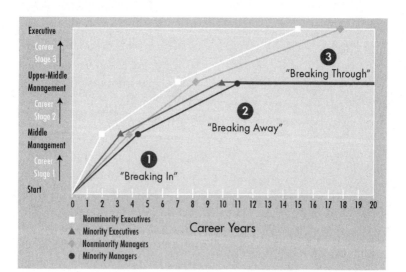

Minority executives' constellations of relationships expanded quickly beyond their internal mentors to include peers and people below them in the hierarchy. These networks tended to be full of redundant ties [known people] . . . and often mirrored the initial mentor's own relationships. Maintaining these networks over the relatively long time spent in Stage 1 served to create a strong social consensus within their immediate group or organization about their abilities, performance, and potential to succeed, lending them credibility and developing their professional reputations.

SPARSE NETWORKS

By comparison, *Wanda's network is excellent for exercising control during the middle stages of one's career.* Why? Because Wanda's network is very *sparse*; that is, several people and even groups in her network are not connected to one another. Her network spans network gaps. She can take advantage of the unique information given to her from groups A, B, and C, and she is the broker (the bridge) between these groups for the flow of information and projects. By having a network that spans network gaps and organizational boundaries, she is more likely to build long-term social capital than her colleague James. She is in a more powerful position than James and, according to the research in this area, she will have more opportunities and move faster through an organization. Referring back to figure 8 again, minority executives' networks transitioned from looking like James's network in Career Stage 1 to looking like Wanda's network in Career Stage 2. Thomas and Gabarro explain further:

Stage 2 is a period of building the network of relationships beyond the boundaries of the original functional area(s) in which the person began their career during Stage 1. This process is facilitated by the opportunity to work in key roles that require spanning organizational boundaries and interacting with managers and superiors in other parts of the company.

You may now be wondering: What is an effective way to transition from a dense network like James's to a sparse network like Wanda's? The answer for Black faces that aspire to high places is to borrow the network of a more powerful ally.

BORROWED NETWORKS

Ronald Burt conducted a study that compared the promotions of high-ranking men to women and entry-rank men based on their type of network. As shown in figure 11, Burt found that high-ranking men were best served by a sparse network as evidenced by being 0.9 years ahead in promotions when compared to their counterparts with dense or borrowed networks. By comparison, women and entry-rank men were best served by a borrowed network as evidenced by being 1.4 years ahead in promotions when compared to their counterparts with sparse or dense networks. Burt describes women and entry-rank men as "outsiders," that is, "a category of people for whom success depends on borrowing social capital" and "a category of people who have a legitimacy problem." We would argue that African Americans and other emerging majorities can also often experience legitimacy problems, that is, unfounded challenges to our competence and credibility. We are therefore also likely to be best served by a *borrowed* network from Career Stage 1 to Career Stage 2.

Wayland Hicks, a senior executive at Xerox, saw tremendous potential in Ursula Burns and tapped her to become his executive assistant. In this role, Burns began to borrow Hicks's network. Burns was later assigned to work directly with then CEO Paul Allaire and subsequent CEO Anne Mulcahy, both of whom took Burns under their wing and gave her the ability to borrow their networks. These relationships were instrumental in Burns becoming the only Black woman to ever helm a Fortune 500 corporation. A similar progression transpired in Ken Chenault becoming the first Black CEO at American Express when he borrowed the network of his predecessor, Harvey Golub. Their success also touches on themes related to mentoring, which we will explore further in Strategic Action 5: Maximize

Mentoring. The implication is that it is often better to borrow someone else's network than to build a network yourself.

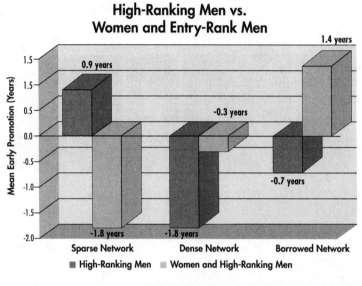

FIGURE 11

Source: Ronald S. Burt, "The Network Structure of Social Capital,"
Research in Organizational Behavior, *Volume 22, 2000*

EVALUATING YOUR NETWORK

Here is a rudimentary way to figure out what kind of network type
you have. Take out a sheet of paper to do the following exercise.

1. Think about the fifteen people you talk to for career advice, to
   solve business problems, and for personal counsel. Write their
   names down on a piece of paper. If you were to write down
   all of your contacts, how many more people would you write
   down?

2. Ask yourself the question, "How many of these people know
   each other?"

3. Fill in the chart about each person on your list. For every person who has the same characteristics as you, write "same" in the box. For every person who is different, write "different" in the box.

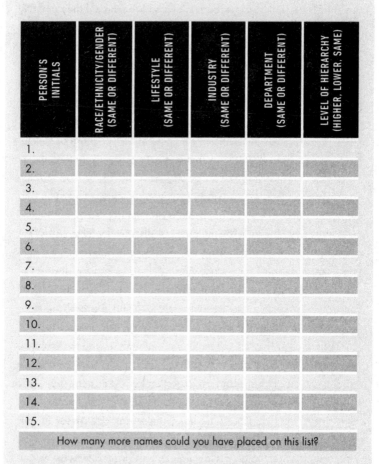

PERSON'S INITIALS	RACE/ETHNICITY/GENDER (SAME OR DIFFERENT)	LIFESTYLE (SAME OR DIFFERENT)	INDUSTRY (SAME OR DIFFERENT)	DEPARTMENT (SAME OR DIFFERENT)	LEVEL OF HIERARCHY (HIGHER, LOWER, SAME)
1.					
2.					
3.					
4.					
5.					
6.					
7.					
8.					
9.					
10.					
11.					
12.					
13.					
14.					
15.					

How many more names could you have placed on this list?

Now let's evaluate your network for size, density, diversity, and hierarchy.

Size. Was it easy to come up with the fifteen people for this exercise? How many more people do you turn to for career advice, business problems, and personal counsel? The real question here is how many people can you really count on to listen to you, assist you, or provide valuable advice? There are people who claim to have hundreds of contacts, but a true assessment of their network would be an assessment of the resources available to them if they actually asked people to help them out. To assess your network, consider how many people you regularly keep in contact with. Remember, the size of your network alone does not equal effectiveness.

Density. How many of the people on this list know each other? In the densest networks, everyone in the network knows everyone else. In the sparsest networks, no one knows anyone else. Look at what you have written down and determine if your network is dense or sparse. Many studies show that dense networks are good for getting things done and for building cohesive groups that trust and are loyal to each other. Sparse networks are good for getting diverse information and for getting ahead within organizations and companies.

Diversity. The table on the previous page is a way to assess the diversity in your network along five dimensions: race/ethnicity, gender, industry, organization, and hierarchy. To assess the diversity in your network, evaluate how many of the boxes are filled with the word *same*. The more times you see the word *different* in a box, the more diverse your network is. Even for Black professionals, diversity matters.

Hierarchy. The last column of the table allows you to determine the level of hierarchy that is in your network. How many people do you talk to that are lower in the organizational hierarchy than you? These people may be sources of different kinds of information than you receive from your peers. Do you have at least one person in your network that is at a higher level in the organizational hierarchy than you are? This person may allow you to *borrow* their network in certain circumstances or may serve as a mentor to you. The potential borrowed social capital may help you in your career aspirations.

Now, think about how you can improve your social network and therefore build your social capital. Answer the following questions:

- What have you learned about your network from this evaluation?
- What are the strengths and weaknesses of your network?
- What is one action you can take in the next seven days to build the weak aspects of your network?
- What are two actions you can take in the next month?

The answers to these questions become your action plan for future relationship building.

Independent Action Steps for Networking and Relationship Building

LEVERAGE YOUR VIRTUAL NETWORK

Today, technology allows us to keep in touch with and maintain relationships with thousands of people simultaneously. It is important that you extend your online presence and leverage social networking tools.

The world of social networking websites can be broken down into three categories:

1. *Business Contacts and Networking Sites*—Social networks like LinkedIn have a business or professional purpose.
2. *Online Community Sites*—Community sites like Facebook, Twitter, and Instagram can be used to generate customers or for purely social purposes.
3. *Alumni Sites*—Alumni associations' websites help graduates from a college or university connect with one another.

Here's how the four compelling findings on social capital that we discussed earlier in the chapter play out online.

1. *Strong Ties Form the Basis of Your Network*—Any technology that helps you stay connected to your strong-tie network is vitally important. Using group text messaging or social network apps such as Facebook is ideal for this kind of connecting.

2. *The Strength of Weak Ties*—LinkedIn, Facebook, Twitter, and Instagram are good for organizing your weak ties. Through these websites, for example, you can be updated when people change jobs or make other shifts. You can also inform everyone in your network about changes in your life or send out questions you need answered. Your weak ties will be able to funnel information back to you via the website or directly to you via email.

3. *Six Degrees of Separation*—Websites that make it clear who you are connected to and who is connected to those people are excellent ways to make connections. LinkedIn has a function on its site called "Introductions" that allows trusted contacts to make connections to others in their network. The recipient is more likely to respond to the inquiry just by virtue of the fact that the new contact was introduced by an existing contact.

4. *Network Gaps*—The best social networking sites to help you bridge relationships are those that help you evaluate if the different groups and communities you are talking to are talking to each other. For example, on LinkedIn, there are many groups that are related to industries, technologies, geography, or other common interests. By monitoring the conversations taking place in your various groups, you may see an opportunity for you to bring information from one group to another group that may value that information. This would be a sign that you are bridging network gaps.

MAKE YOURSELF "PORTABLE"

Dr. Pinkett's auto mechanic once told him that he could not fix his car because he did not have the necessary tools. Other mechanics in the garage had the tools, but he was unable to use them. The mechanic explained that each mechanic was responsible for maintaining his own set of tools independently and would, in fact, take his tools with him as he moved from employer to employer. Tools do not belong to the repair garages but to the mechanics, and the more tools a mechanic is able to bring to a garage, the more value the mechanic brings.

This same concept is true in the twenty-first-century workplace. Of course, the more knowledge, skills, and relationships you bring to the workplace, the more value you bring to an organization. But what you take from an organization is just as important as what you bring. Just as Dr. Pinkett's mechanic was "portable"—able to personally retain value independent of his employer—you must make yourself portable too. There are several ways to do this:

- *Maintain your own personal contacts in an organized way.* You can do this by using a database, customer relationship management software, or spreadsheet of scanned business cards that captures information about when, where, and how you met each contact. This will have long-lasting benefits.
- *Take resources with you (when allowed).* To the extent that your employers allow you to take material resources with you upon departure—papers, books, checklists, templates, methodologies, and so on—you should always do so. Most employers have justifiable legal safeguards that prevent employees from taking certain information. We are not suggesting that you violate such agreements; instead, you should understand the limitations of them thoroughly so you don't bypass the opportunity to legitimately take some resources with you.
- *Safeguard intellectual capital that you bring to the table.* There may be instances when you are bringing intellectual

capital or proprietary knowledge to an employer. In this case you would want to try to put in place your own safeguards to ensure that you retain ownership of your intellectual property. You and your employer could draw up a nondisclosure agreement, intellectual property rights agreement, or other legal agreement. It would spell out how you will retain ownership or engage in profit sharing for intellectual property that belongs to you.

- *Maintain a professional journal.* As you move through your career, chronicle the lessons learned from each job assignment in a journal. This is something that you can do either at the end of each day, when you complete a project, or monthly—whatever is appropriate given your workflow. This enables you to generate your own independent knowledge base to be used in the future.

Interdependent Action Steps for Networking and Relationship Building

BRIDGE THE NETWORK GAPS BETWEEN PEOPLE AND BETWEEN ORGANIZATIONS

Synergy is the result of creating mutually beneficial connections between people and between organizations to fulfill their collective purpose. Scale is achieved by amplifying efforts of everyone for the broadest possible impact. As you will see, it is through the combination of synergy and scale that incredible things can happen. In Strategic Action 9: Transform Systems, we will discuss synergy and scale in more detail. As we make our way there, there are a couple of key behaviors we must discuss here to help you unlock this potential:

- *Seek mutually beneficial opportunities to bridge network gaps.* You can be an agent of synergy by identifying and connecting networks, whether they are disconnected people, disconnected organizations, or even disparate groups within, or across, organizations. This requires developing relationships with a diversity of people and with people in different organizational units so you can identify the gaps. Sometimes these people or groups may be unaware of one another or may not realize the natural synergy that can be unleashed by working together.

- *Bring disconnected people and organizations together for mutual gain.* Once you identify network gaps, the next step is to find ways to bring the right people or organizations together to explore possibilities together, pursue an initiative together, or launch a collaboration together between departments, businesses, nonprofits, churches, and so on.

Later, in Strategic Action 9, we elaborate on exactly how bridging network gaps for a common agenda brings together organizations and people who are otherwise disconnected.

THE SEVEN LAWS OF NETWORKING

1. Law Number One: Networking is a social-first, business-second activity.
2. Law Number Two: You are your word, your work, then your network.
3. Law Number Three: It's not who you know, it's who knows you.
4. Law Number Four: Weak ties can be your most valuable ties.
5. Law Number Five: All networks are not created equal. (They can be dense, borrowed, and sparse.)
6. Law Number Six: All networks do not lead to the same outcomes. (Dense, borrowed, and sparse networks lead to different outcomes.)
7. Law Number Seven: You get out what you put into your network.

KNOW THE DIFFERENCE BETWEEN A BROADCAST SEARCH AND A DIRECTED SEARCH

Although we live in a world where we can seemingly reach out and touch anybody through social media, email, or some other technology, the basis of our close relationships is still the same. Referrals from "trusted others," or people who share some commonality with you, remain the best way to make a new connection or contact.

- Use a *directed search* to obtain confidential information or a personal introduction. If you want information of a confidential nature, or you want a meeting with a specific individual, your best bet is to identify someone with whom you have a personal relationship. The relationship could be based on some similarity or common experience—perhaps a college friend, a neighbor, or a sorority sister.
- Use a *broadcast search* to harness your entire network. If you need to find the answer to a general question, or if you are a hiring manager looking for a certain kind of job candidate, you will likely find it more efficient and effective to send an email or a query to your entire network on social networking websites. You may recall earlier in this chapter we discussed Granovetter's findings that the most common way people find out about job opportunities is through weak ties. The larger your network, the greater the possibility that someone in your immediate network, or someone in their network, knows of an opportunity.

BE VISIBLE AND ESTABLISH YOURSELF AS A PLAYER IN THE GAME

Visibility is an important aspect of building your network. Being visible provides a platform for displaying your excellence.

While it is important to be "there"—whether there is an industry conference, seminar, cocktail reception, or other event—it's also important to be excellent, as mentioned previously in Strategic Action 3. When you demonstrate excellence, people will often take notice, which only increases your visibility. Maintaining both a positive reputation and a highly visible profile is important to becoming a person of influence. You want to be visible for the right reasons, and you want to be known for excellence and not for mediocrity, incompetence, or for exhibiting poor behavior.

Roland Martin credits much of his ability to move up in the ranks of journalism to attending National Association of Black Journalists (NABJ) conventions. He attended his first convention in 1989. There he met the person who made the connection that helped him get a job at the *Austin American Statesman*, the editor who hired him to become the city hall reporter at the *Fort Worth Star-Telegram*, the person who hired him to be editor of Tom Joyner's blackamericaweb .com, and the person who was editor-in-chief when he was hired to work at *Savoy* magazine.

Martin traces his role on CNN back to NABJ's 1989 and 1991 conventions. "I [was] on CNN because I first met Henry Mauldin, who was the head of talent for CNN, and he remembered me from a convention in 1991. And he said, 'We were in a room with all of these bigwigs, I was the only student in the room, but everybody in the room knew [you].' Had I not gone to that convention [in 1989], I would not have been in a position to be on the board to be in that room." (Essentially, Martin established a borrowed network through connections brokered by Mauldin.) In discussing Strategic Action 5: Maximize Mentoring, we will further explain the role of mentors in providing this kind of sponsorship as well as their role in helping you to determine the most effective ways to increase your visibility given the nuances of your organization.

In addition to demonstrating excellence, the following are additional ways you can increase your visibility, some of which we introduced while discussing Strategic Action 3: Develop Self-Mastery and Find Meaning:

- Join task forces.
- Engage in special projects.
- Pursue high-consequence assignments.
- Participate in rotational programs.
- Accept opportunities to give presentations.

When it comes to increasing visibility, the general rule of thumb is to not take for granted that others are aware of your accomplishments. Share your accomplishments with others during one-on-one meetings, meals, receptions, and other informal opportunities. Just be sure to do so in a way that is prideful without being boastful; confident without being cocky; and humble without being haughty. Similarly, let your voice and opinions be heard during meetings among colleagues. Of course, never talk just for the sake of talking. It's been said, "Better to remain silent and be thought a fool than to speak out and remove all doubt!" Instead, when you have something substantive to offer to the conversation, do not be afraid to stand up and speak out.

When you reach a certain level within an organization or make significant achievements, there will be people who will come to you with jobs or other opportunities. When given several choices or options, you might consider the visibility of the position, because greater visibility may expose you to those powerful others who can assist you or provide resources to your projects or help you in your career. Thomas and Gabarro advise aspiring executives to pursue visible assignments because these positions are seen by upper management, and people in them have a better chance at promotion.

The Social Capital Basis of Power

Power is exerted through relationships, organizations, and institutions, and without it you cannot achieve your goals.

We introduce this topic at this point because networks can be a source of power and influence. Before you get too excited about the word *power*, let us define what we mean by it. *Power* is, as defined by Jeffrey Pfeffer in *Managing with Power*, "the ability to influence others to do what you would like them to do." It is the ability to change the course of events and circumstances whether for yourself or for others.

Some people prefer not to use the word *power* and talk about it in terms of *influence*, but they are essentially the same. Some prefer the word *influence* because it is not a word that carries as much baggage as *power*.

On a larger scale, the word *power* is associated with those who are "in power." When the most powerful people in the country are mostly white, that means that all others do not have a say in what will happen in the future. In America, this kind of power has been concentrated in the hands of a few and passed on from generation to generation. This is not only a story of family wealth but also a story of "white privilege," or a sense of entitlement. And, white privilege is reinforced by networks of organizations, corporations, and institutions that have historically left Black people and other people of color out of the game.

When people make reference to institutional racism, they are speaking of the power structures of the nation not being sensitive to the concerns or issues of Black, Indigenous, and People of Color (BIPOC). If the most important institutions of society—government, education, business, finance, and banking—do not have diversity at the highest levels, then, with few exceptions, they are not responsive to the needs of all the people. Therefore, people of color do not have full access to what these institutions can do to protect their rights, property, and success.

It may be comforting for some to believe that these networks are open to all and that as long as we have achieved a certain educational, financial, or celebrity status then Black faces in high places will always have entrée in the circles of the most powerful people in the nation. Unfortunately, this is not the case. Hollywood producer Mara Brock Akil (*Black Lightning*, *Love Is*, *Being Mary Jane*) would seem to have it all—and enough connections to have it made. But as she wrote in a guest column on RushmoreDrive.com in March 2009, as her show *The Game* faced possible cancellation,[2] her future wasn't as feather-lined as many of her white counterparts even after she had created and executive produced the hit show *Girlfriends* and:

> After a 13-year-career in this business—from a Writer's Trainee on "South Central," a Staff Writer, on up to Producer on "Moesha," a stint as a Supervising Producer on "The Jamie Foxx Show" and after eight successful seasons of "Girlfriends" and now three successful seasons of "The Game"—I have to hustle for another job, another show. I had my first job interview in nine years the other day. Just in case The CW does really cancel "The Game," I need to staff on someone else's show. Sure on the one hand I am truly thankful for the blessing of opportunity, but on the other, I'm mad, frustrated and disappointed that my veteran experience, which includes running "Girlfriends" and "The Game" for two years at the same time, doesn't equal a cushy overall development deal somewhere, like my white male and sometimes female counterparts seem to land even in this time of economic crisis. Somehow, because my characters were of color, my shows don't count as much. Doesn't matter that at one point "Girlfriends" was the longest running comedy on television. Successfully producing 236 episodes (172 episodes of "Girlfriends" plus 64 episodes of "The Game") of television doesn't have as much value. But that is the plight of being black in this business. That is the plight of being a woman in this business.[3]

As Brock so eloquently infers, inside organizations and outside of them, power and influence determine which ideas are given credence and which ideas are tossed away; it determines who will receive resources to get the job done and who will have to be "resourceful" in getting things done.

SOURCES OF POWER AND INFLUENCE

Black faces in high places must understand the nature of power in organizations, the dynamics of power, and determine what power tactics to use to redefine the game. Therefore, it is important to understand where power comes from and how it is used.

Position Power

Power is often associated with the job or title that someone has. This is *position power*. Position power is interesting because it is often assumed that all positions at the same hierarchical level in an organization are equally powerful. This is not the case. The six dimensions that determine the true level of position power are:

1. *Authority*—Some positions have more authority than others. Roles that have high levels of authority have an array of responsibilities and are able to intervene in the activities of other parts of the organization.

2. *Resource Controllability*—These roles provide discretion over resources including human, financial, and productivity.

3. *Criticality*—There are always positions within an organization that are critical because they are important to the operations in the organization. These roles are more powerful than positions that have no direct impact on the operations.

4. *Nonsubstitutability*—These roles have less ease of replacement by people inside or outside of the organization. The functions usually cannot be substituted or outsourced.

5. *Centrality (or Relevance)*—Some positions have great importance to the core mission or business of the organization. Other positions are clearly in support of these functions.

6. *Visibility*—Some positions are more visible than others. These positions provide a large degree of work that is seen by influential people in the organization.

The more dimensions a specific position has, the more powerful it is. Power and influence are not necessarily tied to hierarchical level. Instead, it can be a function of who you know and how that allows you to control or broker information. But there is another type of power that is equally important: *personal* power.

Personal Power

Think about it. . . . Before Barack Obama ever ran for public office, his power was concentrated in the ability to organize communities to work for positive change on the South Side of Chicago. At seven feet one and 325 pounds, Shaquille O'Neal not only wields power on the basketball court because of his skills but also because of his size. Cathy Hughes wields tremendous power as she oversees a multimedia empire that spans television, radio, and digital media that also represents the largest African American–owned and –operated broadcast company in the nation. These are examples of personal power.

Personal power is related to the person. It is a source of power and influence that springs from the person's experience, personality, and personal network connections. Examples of personal power include:

- *Expertise*—Or how much a person knows. Others may be influenced by you or defer to you based on your knowledge and education.
- *Reputation*—Being known for getting results over time gives you credibility, which can translate into influence.
- *Characteristics*—Height, size, or personality can be used to exert influence on others.
- *Network Connections*—Bring together information, people, and trust to influence people at the right time. This is based upon your network and all of the things we have talked about in the first part of this chapter.

USE OF POWER

It's important to understand how to identify power and how to use it. There is a distinction between power being used at the individual level and at the societal level. The scale is different, but the implications are the same.

Using Power to Get Things Done Through Other People

At the individual level, getting things done through other people is using power. The other people can be *subordinates*, *peers*, or *superiors* in the organization. Consider the two sources of power that we discussed before—position power and personal power. These sources of power may work differently depending on your audience. Therefore, it is important to know the source of your power—is it your network? Is it your expertise? Or is it your position?

Your relationship with your *subordinates* is important because they are usually people you are counting on to get work done. Leading them well is going to pay off for you in the long run. But it should be clear that power is an indispensable part of these relationships. You are the supervisor, manager, or director or executive for a reason. You have more responsibility than your subordinates. Your performance is dependent upon their work. Some people do not want to use power in these situations because they are afraid of how people will regard their use of power on them.

If you are in charge of a group of employees and there are some employees who are always challenging your authority, you must be able to demonstrate your leadership by dealing with these people and not alienating the ones who are following your lead.

This becomes more complicated when we are talking about Black faces who are managing in white places. The race dynamic calls for an extra level of savvy when it comes to influencing other people. Because of the history of race relations in this country, personal experiences, and even what they view on the evening news, your white subordinates may have preconceived notions about Black people that can potentially undermine your authority and ability to lead effectively. They may scrutinize your actions differently than those of your white peers. This is a particular consideration for Black faces in white places.

When Black faces lead in high places effectively, the benefits reach beyond a company's bottom line or your performance review. A study conducted by Dr. Robinson and University of Virginia associate professor Greg Fairchild found that white respondents who were supervised by Black managers often had better views of Black people than those who were not supervised by Black people. When power is used appropriately, it can be transformative!

For these same reasons, your relationship with your *peers* is critical. In the organizational context, people who enter the organization at the same time or at the same level are your peers. They work on similar types of projects or have similar types of responsibilities. Often these relationships take on two forms. Peers and groups of peers will compete with one another for the attention of those above them in the hierarchy. Or they will band together and collaborate with each other to achieve mutual goals. Many of your long-lasting friendships are with those who have been your peers in school or in organizations.

Position power is not used under these circumstances because you are all at the same level. Personal power, in all its forms, is used extensively, and leaders emerge because of their expertise or network of relationships. Writer and community activist Kevin Powell began exerting his personal power with his peers in his early twenties.

"Many of us came of age together as Gen Xers, and many of us are now in very serious leadership positions in this country," Powell said. "A lot of these people I met when we were student leaders, some were at Columbia, some were at UCLA. You're talking about network. Twenty years ago, before there was the kind of use of the internet that exists today, I remember constantly being in touch with student leaders around the country, just on the phone, using our calling cards. You did what you had to do. You didn't wait for permission from someone to say you should connect with people."

Your relationship with people above you in the hierarchy—your *superiors*—is also about power. Those above you have authority over your area of responsibility as a function of their position. How do you influence this level of the organization? One study indicated that those with higher positions in the hierarchy wanted to be approached and reasoned with as a first approach to influencing decisions. In this situation, it is important for you to have all your information and be fully prepared to present it.

When this does not work, three other tactics may be necessary: coalitions, bargaining, and appealing to a higher authority. It may make sense to find other people who have similar interests to present a joint plan for influencing your boss. This coalition might be more convincing than if you were the only person making the case to your manager or director. You may opt to do some kind of bargaining or negotiating with your manager to get what you want. And you might appeal to a higher authority (that is, your manger's boss) for the decision that you desire and make the case that your solution is the best for the organization and should be reconsidered.

Keep in mind that each of these ways to influence others has implications and sometimes repercussions for which you must be prepared. For example, if you are going to use a higher authority, you should be prepared for a hard time in the short term. No one likes it when someone goes over their head to get something done. It can make your manager look incompetent, and you may pay for that later. Remember, power in the hands of insecure people can be dangerous because they may attempt to use it to crush those who make them feel threatened.

Using Power When Shaping Projects

In the previous section on networks, we wrote that one of the advantages of having a good network is the ability to shape projects. This may be more important than you first realized.

Every job or function has project work that must be completed in addition to the regular operations. Projects within an organization require some combination of information and resources to accomplish. Your network within and outside of the organization can be a vital source of both. When you have a network made up of the right people, it is like having the pieces of a giant puzzle. If you have the right pieces, you can put them together to make a beautiful picture. Your network comprises the pieces.

But when you have the discretion to create and shape your own projects within an organization, you have the power to make significant changes. This makes sense only when you have a network that is substantial enough to give you the information and the resources necessary to make the project work. Shaping a project requires you using your network. Getting the project approved requires you exerting influence on those inside and outside of your network. And when you do this, you are using your network to exert some power on the organization.

Using Power to Do Good Works and Make Positive Change

At the societal level, we are advocates of using power to do good works and to make positive change. Changing an organization or society requires building social capital and expending it. When you use social capital, you are using power toward a positive outcome. Of course, this means that you have investigated what a positive outcome will be. And that is no small step.

When you have the power and influence to do good work and make a positive difference in the lives of others, we believe you should do it. Some powerful people choose to wait for the "right" situation to use their power.

Oprah uses her power and considerable influence to do good things. She established a school in South Africa to educate young women to be whatever they want to be. In the US, she has used her power and influence to get media projects that she thought were important in bookstores and on television and the big screen. Her power is recognized by others, and she uses it to influence millions.

Strategic Action 4 has been primarily focused on influencing the people immediately around you and within groups, teams, organizations, and companies. Oprah's work is an example of how power and influence are exercised on a broader scale.

● ● ●

Interdependent Action Steps
for Using Power and Influence

UNDERSTAND THE RELATIONSHIP
BETWEEN POWER AND RACE

You cannot be afraid to use power and influence to complete projects and achieve noble goals. Here are four points to remember in this context:

1. Power is the ability to influence others to do what they would not normally want to do.
2. Power is not inherently evil. It is a tool to get things done.
3. Power does not concede power without a challenge.
4. Power in the hands of a few will attempt to maintain the status quo.

We've explained how power can be used on you and how you can use power. The challenge for Black faces in high places is to also develop a keen sense of how power can also be related to race. Because of white privilege and deep-seated psychological biases toward Black people, some of your white counterparts may: (1) have power and use it against you, (2) use power more severely against you, and (3) react more negatively to your use of power on them.

Some of you may not believe any of these three statements about race and race relations in modern corporations and organizations. But corporations and organizations are often a reflection of society. The same social stratification that exists in society is present in corporations and organizations of all sizes.

So there may be times when you will need to use power to address a situation with your white counterparts. Because power does not concede power without a struggle, do not fear using power to set the record straight. Just remember to use power wisely and to use it in proportion to how power is being exerted on you.

In early 2009, the *New York Post* ran a cartoon that depicted a chimpanzee, shot dead by two police officers. In the drawing one of the officers says, "They'll have to find someone else to write the next stimulus bill." The cartoon created a furor. Historically, bigots have attempted to dehumanize Black people by comparing them to primates. At the time the cartoon was published, Barack Obama, the first African American president of the United States, had just signed a stimulus bill designed to help the US economy recover from the worst economic crisis since the Great Depression. Initially, the *Post* held its ground, refusing to apologize. Then, after the uproar swelled, the paper issued this statement:

> It was meant to mock an ineptly written federal stimulus bill. Period. But it has been taken as something else—as a depiction of President Obama, as a thinly veiled expression of racism. This most certainly was not its intent; to those who were offended by the image, we apologize. However, there are some in the media and in public life who have had differences with The Post in the past—and they see the incident as an opportunity for payback. To them, no apology is due. Sometimes a cartoon is just a cartoon—even as the opportunists seek to make it something else.[4]

Instead of acknowledging that its cartoon crossed a line that has been used to create pain and division—whether it was intentional or not (also at the time a chimpanzee had been killed by police after mauling a Connecticut woman)—the *Post*'s editorial team focused approximately one-third of its statement—56 out of 151 words—swiping at its detractors—namely activist Rev. Al Sharpton who spoke out against the cartoon and had previously been critical of the newspaper's opinion pieces and news coverage.

The only way to challenge ignorance at this large scale is to use the power of a significant coalition to act as one voice and to get others to do what they do not want to do. (This will be explored more closely when we discuss Strategic Action 6: Leverage Our Might.) Protestors converged, politicians expressed outrage, celebrities like film director

Spike Lee suggested boycotting the *Post*, and Sharpton even suggested challenging *Post* owner News Corp's waiver from the Federal Communications Commission that allows it to operate multiple media properties in the area.

Finally, five days later, News Corp's iconic chairman, Rupert Murdoch, stepped up offering what many viewed as a more sincere apology:

> Last week, we made a mistake. We ran a cartoon that offended many people. Today I want to personally apologize to any reader who felt offended, and even insulted. Over the past couple of days, I have spoken to a number of people, and I now better understand the hurt this cartoon has caused. At the same time, I have had conversations with Post editors about the situation and I can assure you—without a doubt—that the only intent of that cartoon was to mock a badly written piece of legislation. It was not meant to be racist, but unfortunately, it was interpreted by many as such.[5]

We're not sure who or what exactly made Murdoch understand the situation, but it is clear that power challenged power and changed the game along the way.

DEVELOP AND NURTURE A NETWORK OF POWERFUL ALLIES

The relationships you build will be a basis for your power so you must continuously nurture your networks. Try not to let your connections become dormant because it could shift a strong tie to a weak tie or to a nonexistent tie.

We realize it may be a challenge to make deposits with a network that includes hundreds of people. But remember, all of your connections have power, so try to nurture them all. With information technologies, you are able to send emails and newsletters and stay connected virtually. But we cannot forget the "old-fashioned" ways of maintaining relationships: going to dinner, sending a personal handwritten note, having coffee, and talking on the telephone.

"Networking is really, really basic," Powell says. "It could be something as simple as not only getting people's cards but making sure you send them a follow-up note or email or call or finding out when their birthdays are and just saying, 'Hey, I just wanted to acknowledge you.' People appreciate that."

The emotional bank account is a great analogy for maintaining relationships. You must make deposits before you can make withdrawals.

Also note, there is an additional level of care in maintaining relationships with powerful allies. When dealing with powerful allies, remember two things: (1) they are busy people and do not have a lot of time, and (2) they must get something out of the relationship, even if it is just knowing that they have contributed to your success. So this means you can't expect your powerful ally to talk with you for hours on end as you ramble about your life and dreams. They want to know what you are thinking or doing, but they certainly want to do it in a timely manner. You should think about how you will use your short time with your powerful ally. You should also think about how your objectives can align with the goals of this person. There may be something they want in return for helping you. You should have an idea of what this is before you ask for help and make sure it is something you are capable and willing to do. This reciprocity—also called *quid pro quo*—is inherent in most relationships. When dealing with a powerful ally, you should take great care in understanding it.

Lastly, you should think about what you can learn from the experiences of the powerful allies you know. We are going to say a lot more about mentors and sponsors and others whom you can learn from in the next chapter, Strategic Action 5: Maximize Mentoring, but for now understand that you should organize your conversations and be able to show that by assisting you they will be meeting one of their own goals. As a result, you will be using your network as a source of power to get something done. We not only encourage this, we try to practice it every day.

Maximize Mentoring

Blaze a trail that will help others begin their journey
and it will never be lonely at the top.
—CARLOS WALLACE
in *Life Isn't Complicated, You Are*

Mentors and Protégés

Mentoring.

It is a simple action that means so many things to different people. Because of its ambiguity, it is supremely important to understand the nuances of mentoring as you rise to the top.

Cathy Hughes, the legendary media entrepreneur who created Radio One and TV One, explained to us in an interview that

> most successful entrepreneurs, most successful CEOs, even if they're not working for themselves, had someone in their lives who was a role model and a counselor to them. You know, now they call it mentoring. Back then it wasn't mentoring. It was an older person who was accomplished sharing with a younger person, if that younger person was receptive.

THE NINE ROLES OF A MENTOR

Mentors can provide a wide range of support spanning from career support, such as strategies for advancement, to psychological and social support, such as words of encouragement. The following are the nine roles of a mentor.

Career Support

1. *Coach or Adviser*—These relationships focus on task- and performance-related skills and work competencies.
2. *Sponsor*—These relationships provide career-focused support for advancement in the organization or within the profession.
3. *Advocate*—This is the often "invisible" mentoring function; it provide protection from negative career outcomes or consequences within your organization.
4. *Investor*—These types of mentors make investments in your career by helping protégés gain access to "stretch"

opportunities that allow people to see your skills and knowledge.

5. *Networker*—These mentors connect you to opportunities that expand your networks and support your access to important people who can support your goals.

Psycho-Social Support

6. *Role Model*—These mentors provide an example of valued norms or competencies.

7. *Supporter*—These mentors validate your skills, experience, and overall value to the organization.

8. *Sounding Board*—These mentors listen to you and sometimes provide advice on professional and personal issues.

9. *Ally*—The allyship of these mentors supports you and your career.

(Adapted from Kram and Isabella, 1985)[1]

GOALS OF MENTORING

A mentor can be invaluable to anyone who is trying to understand a new environment (that is, a department, division, or entire organization). In 1979, Daniel Levinson,[2] a professor at Yale University, identified the following six items that a new hire should learn about an organization. In the organizational context, mentors should be able to assist you with these:

- The politics of the organization
- The norms, standards, values, ideology, history, heroes/heroines in the organization—the "psychological contract," the implicit expectations that organizations and their members have of each other

- The skills and competencies that are necessary in the organization for succession to the next immediate step
- The paths to advancement and the blind alleys
- The acceptable methods for gaining visibility in the organization—the questions of who needs to know about what and what these people need to know
- The characteristic stumbling blocks in the organization and the personal failure patterns

When Dr. Robinson came to NYU Stern School of Business, he had to learn all of the aspects of being a new faculty member at a prestigious institution. It was a difficult journey that led him to seek a mentor there early on to help him learn how NYU worked. He also had mentors from other institutions who helped him by providing a perspective on what he was seeing at NYU. Both of these were valuable for key decisions he had to make and for navigating the waters of a very large organization that was completely new to him.

By contrast, when Dr. Robinson moved to his alma mater, Rutgers University, to be part of the founding team of The Center for Urban Entrepreneurship & Economic Development, he had so many network connections within the university that it made the transition very easy.

GETTING STARTED WITH MENTORING

Strong mentor-protégé relationships do not happen overnight. They are established, cultivated, and should become stronger over time. In the next few sections, we offer some hints on how to make the mentoring relationship effective for both parties.

Consider these basic questions and have an explicit conversation about each.

- Who will take the lead in the relationship?
- What does each party expect from the other?

- When will you meet and how often?
- Why is each party involved in the relationship?
- How should advice and criticism be given and received?

BENEFITS OF MENTORING

Potential mentors and protégés should remember that both parties benefit from the relationship.

Benefits to the Mentor

When mentors are engaged and energetic about their responsibilities as a mentor, they can gain as much from the relationship as the protégé. Mentors learn from the new ideas and perspectives that the protégés share. Mentors expand their networks and often increase their visibility by participating in formal programs. Some mentors take pride in watching their protégé navigate his or her career journey. Because of the nature of the mentor-protégé relationship, mentors' interpersonal skills are improved because they have developmental or difficult conversations with their protégé. In the best mentor-protégé relationships, a strong friendship develops, and this can be valuable for both parties.

Dr. Robinson remembers Earl Thorne, one of his mentors at Merck, as being naturally skilled at mentoring. Thorne knew just what to say and just how to say it. He had learned the lessons of corporate life and was able to impart them to younger workers with ease. It was clear that Thorne was excited to see the new faces and that it motivated him to keep climbing higher in the company. The success of the young people he worked with was evidence that his hard work to recruit and retain talented Black and Hispanic engineers was paying off.

Some might say that being a mentor is a divine use of your time on earth. Roland Martin believes in the biblical model of mentoring. "If you go back and study, you will realize that Moses *chose* Joshua. Elijah *chose* Elisha," Roland says. "That means the mentor saw something in the potential mentee and said, 'I want to be your mentor to transfer my knowledge, my experience, to you,' because the mentor is making an investment in the mentee."

BENEFITS TO THE PROTÉGÉ.

It should be obvious what protégés gain from having a mentor. But just to be clear, here are some specific benefits. Protégés gain the following:

- learn practical skills;
- receive career guidance and advice;
- gain insight into the corporate culture;
- learn the "ins and outs" of how to succeed;
- learn the spoken and unspoken rules of the game;
- expand their networks;
- identify and connect with key players in the game; and
- gain a valuable friend and confidant.

When Treena Arinzeh, professor of Biomedical Engineering at the New Jersey Institute of Technology (NJIT), had to make a decision about whether to become interim chair of her department at NJIT, she took her concerns to her mentors, who were mostly people outside of her department and at other institutions. "I called upon a few people that have gone that route to weigh the pros and cons," she recalls.

Mentors can also influence how you think and how you express yourself. One of Dr. Robinson's mentors would never use the word *problem* when talking about the projects he was working on. He always referred to them as "challenges." To this day, Dr. Robinson rarely uses the word *problem* because he was heavily influenced by how his mentor framed work issues.

The benefits of mentoring can extend deeper than aiding a protégé in a traditional career environment, as Dr. Pinkett's relationship with Rey Ramsey, a social entrepreneur and former CEO of the One Economy Corporation, shows. With Ramsey's help, Dr. Pinkett's firm, BCT Partners, was able to prosper early. Dr. Pinkett recalls:

Rey was instrumental in mentoring me from a number of perspectives. He subcontracted work from One Economy Corporation to BCT. He introduced me to key leaders in the nonprofit, foundation, and government space. He served as an enthusiastic reference for other projects we pursued. We even later formed a joint venture between our two organizations. Were it not for Rey, BCT Partners may not have survived our first years in business, which are critical to the success of a start-up company. This is particularly true because there were several others whom I reached out to for assistance, but they were unwilling to lend a helping hand or appeared to be threatened by me. Rey genuinely wanted me to succeed.

BENEFITS TO THE COMPANY OR ORGANIZATION

Formal mentor programs and informal mentor-protégé relationships help emerging talent transition into the environment and ultimately perform effectively on the job. Mentors can help convey information about corporate culture to the protégé. Good mentors can help identify and cultivate future leaders of the organization. Mentor-protégé relationships, especially when they cut across racial, ethnic, or gender lines, facilitate diversity awareness and provide a means to break down barriers. Studies have shown that employees who have mentors are happier, perform better, are more motivated, and stay longer.

FINDING A MENTOR

We often get the question, "Where can I find a mentor?" from ambitious professionals. If it were easy to find an effective mentor, then everyone would have one, right? How do you find one? Here we give you some ways to be proactive in seeking a mentor for your personal and career development. Keep in mind that we believe that you should have more than one mentor at a time because there are many roles that a mentor can play in your career and life.

Here are five potential approaches to finding mentors:

- *Participate in formal mentor programs.* These mentor programs are organized by your company, organization, or a community group. Make sure that your personal objectives align with the stated purpose of the mentor program. Make sure you can live with the program requirements and go for it.
- *Ask a former manager to be your mentor.* The people who have seen you work and complete projects have an advantage in mentoring you—especially if you have developed a trusting developmental relationship. We say former manager because it is a very rare individual who can be both a manager and a mentor at the same time. But former managers you respect can be valuable in your personal board of directors because they know your work ethic and professionalism.
- *Get someone you trust to recommend a person as a mentor.* Your peers or managers can be very good sources of potential mentors. Talk to your trusted peers or managers who are interested in your success and ask them if they have any contacts that would be a good mentor candidate for you. You should, of course, do your own vetting to see if this potential mentor could fit in your mentor network. Use the list of mentor roles we describe in this chapter to guide your selection and expectations.
- *Expand your network through activities and programs.* Pursue opportunities to participate in committees, working groups, and task forces. Volunteer in the corporate-sponsored community service program. Organize the Black History Month or other cultural celebration. All of these options provide opportunities to meet colleagues from different parts of the company and to expand your network. You may even get some higher than usual visibility by participating in one of these activities. In doing so, you can identify new potential mentors or connect with people who can assist you in finding a good match. In some cases, your increased visibility will have upper-level executives finding you.

- *Participate in community leadership programs.* Almost every metropolitan area has a city-based leadership development program. Sometimes they are named after the city or state you are in (such as Leadership Newark or Leadership New Jersey). Other programs are run by the chamber of commerce or other community organizations. These programs have superb networks of alumni who serve as formal or informal mentors to participants.

STRENGTHENING A MENTORING RELATIONSHIP

When entering a mentoring relationship, remember to dedicate regular time to develop the rapport necessary for mentoring to be effective. During the first meeting of a formal mentoring relationship, we recommend that you get acquainted and discuss the needs and expectations of both parties. During the second meeting, we recommend that you brainstorm ideas for developmental activities, prioritize them, and possibly document goals, objectives, and a timeline. Here are some guiding principles for strengthening the relationship.

- Establish realistic goals and expectations.
- Meet and communicate regularly.
- Plan a topic or activity for each meeting (be flexible to change).
- Respect each other's time.

In our experiences in corporate America, academia, and the business world, we have always had mentors. We believe it is important that mentors and protégés are engaged and energetic to make the pairing successful. Next, we offer some action steps for both protégés and mentors.

Nobody is born wise.
— AFRICAN PROVERB

Independent Action Steps for Protégés

BE YOURSELF/DO YOU

We have seen early-career Black professionals come into organizations and try to be someone they are not. It is challenging to enter a place where the office culture is strong. It may be tempting to completely abandon your own identity and assume the dominant culture. This is more challenging if you are still in the stage of your life where you are learning about yourself and establishing your identity. We encourage Black protégés to see your ethnicity as an asset and not a liability. When you remain true to who you are, you are not only able to bring your best self but also bring a different perspective. The psychological difference will benefit you in the end because you will not suffer from the "groupthink" that often takes place in large organizations. As a protégé, learn the game and then recognize how your diverse experiences can contribute to the big picture.

In *Rage of a Privileged Class: Why Are Middle-Class Blacks Angry? Why Should America Care?*, author Ellis Cose describes the frustration and even rage displayed by educated, competent, and prosperous Blacks who came of age in the twentieth century. This was partly due to the prejudices and injustices they had to endure in the workplace. But it was also partly due to the fact that—regrettably—they felt they had to give up a part of themselves and assimilate in order to "fit in." This was the sacrifice they felt they had to make in order to reach the upper echelon of their organizations. Upon later reflection, it was not clear to them whether the benefits outweighed the costs. While it is not without its own challenges, in the same spirit as Strategic Action 1: Exercise Self-Determination, we believe you are not only far better served by remaining true to who you are and your identity, but you are also empowered to see your uniqueness as an asset to the world around you.

BE RECEPTIVE TO ADVICE AND FEEDBACK

Since the late 1990s, we have led mentoring workshops for the managers of several Fortune 100 companies. One of the biggest challenges mentors shared with us was that some protégés were not receptive to advice and feedback. They were mystified about how a protégé could become involved in a formal mentor program and not be willing to receive constructive criticism.

Not taking in and acting upon constructive criticism undermines the benefit of the mentoring relationship. As a protégé you should

- be open to advice and constructive criticism;
- be willing to learn;
- listen and ask questions;
- set goals and work toward them; and
- act on what you hear and learn.

Don't make the mistake that we have seen several up-and-coming professionals make early in their career journey; develop the capacity to accept constructive feedback and act upon it.

Interdependent Action Steps for Protégés

BUILD MULTIPLE MENTORING RELATIONSHIPS

Sometimes mentoring is framed as a solitary relationship with an all-knowing sage. From a practical perspective, this is not the best approach. What if something happens to that person or if the two of you decide not to continue as mentor and protégé? The reality is you can (and probably should) have several mentors—a network of mentors. Thomas and Gabarro's work demonstrates the value of multiple "development relationships" like mentoring and sponsorship and how their value only increases as you progress from one career stage to the next.

Their research found that not only did minority executives form more developmental relationships on average than both minority

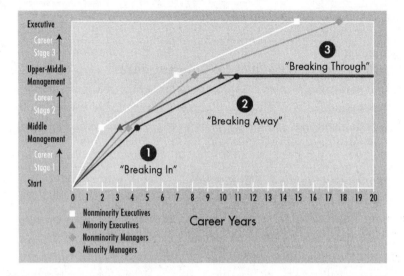

managers and white executives across all three career stages, but it was in Career Stage 3 that they formed the highest average number of developmental relationships (2.5) as shown in table 2. In the organizations the two studied, minority executives who made it to the top not only had multiple people fulfilling these mentor and mentor-like roles, but the number of people fulfilling these roles was larger for them than any other group.

RELATIVE AVERAGE FREQUENCY OF FORMING DEVELOPMENTAL RELATIONSHIPS

Number of Developmental Relationships Formed	CAREER STAGE 1: Start of Career to Middle Management			CAREER STAGE 2: Middle Management to Upper-Middle Management			CAREER STAGE 3: Upper-Middle Management to Executive Level		
Group	Min. Mgrs.	Min. Execs.	White. Execs.	Min. Mgrs.	Min. Execs.	White. Execs.	Min. Mgrs.	Min. Execs.	White. Execs.
Average Across Companies	1.4	1.8	0.8	1.2	2.3	1.5	0.5	2.5	2.0

Source: The Breaking Through: The Making of Minority Executives in Corporate America *by David A. Thomas and John J. Gabarro*

TABLE 2

Here are a few points that relate to creating a network of mentoring relationships.

Utilize Different Mentors for Different Needs

You may have a mentor that fills one or more of the roles of a mentor (see the callout box "The Nine Roles of a Mentor") but usually mentors don't fill all of these roles. It is not realistic to expect one person to be an all-encompassing mentor.

Identify a Diverse Set of Mentors

There is a universal preference for interaction with others that are like you. This is called homophily.[3] But in the case of mentors, we advise you to avoid this. Resist the temptation to find only Black mentors. We know that sometimes it takes a Black professional to understand the unique challenges facing Black professionals. But we firmly believe that diversity and differences in your mentors can be an asset, because you will gain useful insights from someone with a different perspective.

Marnie McKoy, former principal of Link Community School in Newark, New Jersey, which provides a rigorous college preparatory program to primarily African American students, says she has a diverse group of advisers with different skills and experiences as well as various ages and marital status. "I'm a mother, I'm a wife, I'm a school leader, I'm a student," she says. "To have one person would limit the scope of what I can learn. I am going to miss something inevitably. If I look to one person to speak to all of those areas, something is going to go lacking."

Similarly, Don Thompson, former CEO of McDonald's Corporation, seeks advice from diverse groups of people. "I try to leverage a lot of different people from a lot of different walks. And I've never limited myself to only one type of person. A lot of people can help you," he said. "I've got people from all walks of life, all races and backgrounds, that can give me some good counsel and advice."

Thomas and Gabarro's research also found that minority managers who plateaued tended to have homogenous networks (that is, predominantly Black or predominantly white), whereas minority executives tended to have more heterogeneous (diverse) networks of relationships, including their mentors.

Develop a "Personal Board of Directors"

A board of directors is a group of people who help a CEO think through strategic issues and make difficult decisions. Protégés should create their own personal "board of directors" or "board of advisers" as another way to seek the wisdom of others and leverage various developmental relationships in their lives.

Pinkett recalls:

When my name was placed on the official shortlist as a potential lieutenant governor running mate to New Jersey's governor Jon Corzine, it created a storm of public attention. As I contemplated whether this was an opportunity I wanted to pursue, I grew increasingly frustrated as certain segments of the media attempted to narrowly define me solely as a "reality TV star." I am extremely proud of my performance on *The Apprentice*, and while it should not necessarily qualify me for public office, it certainly should not disqualify me. To develop a strategy in response to my critics, I called upon a personal board of directors to counsel me.

The group included BCT cofounder and president Lawrence Hibbert, my public relations and business affairs manager April Peters, Dr. Robinson, and several prominent (past or present) clergy, government officials, corporate executives, and other professionals. They were people I've known and worked with in different capacities, people I trust and, above all, people who know me. We met weekly for almost two months as they guided me through various decisions. Our efforts culminated in a press conference that succeeded in bringing far more balance to the conversation concerning my qualifications.

Inasmuch as God orders our steps, while ultimately this was not the time for me to enter political life, it was a tremendous and humbling experience to be considered for the position. Moreover, I am eternally grateful to this group for their collective wisdom. I couldn't have navigated the waters of New Jersey politics without them.

If you are interested in opening a business, you should have a business coach or mentor. If you are considering entering the ministry, you should have someone who is already in ministry mentor you. If you are thinking about returning to graduate school, perhaps you should identify a current or former student who can help you think about what kind of graduate school you should attend.

You can certainly ask your board members about their area of expertise, but you may also ask your mentors about things outside of their expertise. This is a good approach because this is the set of people who know you well and are looking out for your best interest. By seeking developmental relationships with several individuals to meet various needs (for example, career support and psychosocial support), you gain valuable input when you are making important decisions and need advice in various aspects of your life. You'll be better informed and able to make more strategic choices as you move forward in your life—not just your career. This action step is a preview of concepts we will discuss in Strategic Action 6: Leverage Our Might.

In addition to these three principles, we would recommend that you also keep your supervisor or manager informed about how formal mentor relationships at work are going. Sometimes, supervisors are wary of mentor-protégé relationships when they are supervising the protégé. Supervisors may fear that the mentor will say things that will contradict them and make their job supervising the protégé more difficult. The way around this is to let the supervisor of the protégé know that mentors and managers have different roles. There is no need to feel or act threatened.

A final note here is to figure out a way to chart the progress you and your mentor are making. If you set goals and expectations at the beginning, this will be much easier. If there are certain things you want to achieve as a mentor or a protégé, write them down and periodically take inventory of how you are progressing.

SPONSORSHIP AND MENTORING

Carla Harris, the well-known vice chair of investments at Morgan Stanley, speaks about sponsors in her 2018 TEDWomen talk. When one of her colleagues said to her that she should have a sponsor, she asked herself:

"'Well, how do you get a sponsor? And frankly, why do you need one?' Well, you need a sponsor, frankly, because as you can see, there's not one evaluative process that I can think of, whether it's in academia, health care, financial services, not one that does not have a human element. So that means it has that measure of subjectivity. There is a measure of subjectivity in who is presenting your case. There is a measure of subjectivity in what they say and how they interpret any objective data that you might have. There is a measure of subjectivity in how they say what they're going to say to influence the outcome. So therefore, you need to make sure that that person who is speaking, that sponsor, has your best interests at heart and has the power to get it, whatever it is for you, to get it done behind closed doors."

The way we see it, sponsorship is among the most important facets of mentoring.

Independent Action Steps for Mentors

SAY WHAT YOU MEAN AND MEAN WHAT YOU SAY

Mentors must be dependable and must follow through with what they say they are going to do. Protégés should always believe that you are interested in being their mentor and that you are not too busy to keep your meetings or to do what you have promised to do.

Be sure to clearly state your commitment. Back up your words with actions, because your protégé will closely watch them. This means taking their phone calls or responding in a timely manner to emails or inquiries. It also means making time for them on your schedule.

Practice Active Listening

Mentoring should not only be about imparting wisdom to your protégés. It should also be about listening to what your protégés have to say and trying to understand their perspectives. Perhaps this is implied by all that we have written so far. But we know of many situations in which mentors saw mentoring as a chance to dominate the discussion and wax eloquently about their career success.

Active listening involves demonstrating your attentiveness through body language and empathy. Active listeners make eye contact with the speaker. Their gestures and posture show that they are ready to hear what the other person has to say. It may mean that a mentor leans toward the protégé and listens intently to what the protégé has to say.

Active listening will involve paraphrasing or summarizing what you've heard your protégés say in the conversation to make sure that you are clear and so that they know you are listening. Finally, active listening means being empathetic by acknowledging how they feel about a particular situation or circumstance. A mentor can help protégés separate the people from the problem so that there is room for a solution. A mentor can help protégés by listening and trying to understand their viewpoint. But don't confuse seeing things from another person's viewpoint with agreement with that perspective. You can respect a legitimate position and still disagree. Give protégés room to explain their perspectives by practicing active listening.

Keep It Real

In a competitive environment, there usually isn't a lot of time for "beating around the bush" or "candy coating" the realities of the organization or the environment. Doing so is a disservice to protégés because it does not prepare them properly for the future. It is important that mentors keep advice real and direct. Mentors should convey the *real* rules of the game (the good, the bad, and the ugly). Mentors are invaluable for explaining the explicit and implicit values and norms that shape an organization's culture. Mentors should not assume that these aspects of organizational life are already known or obvious to the protégé. If you are taking your mentoring relationship seriously, it is your responsibility to be honest and not take what you already know for granted.

Interdependent Action Steps for Mentors

BUILD MULTIPLE PROTÉGÉ RELATIONSHIPS

Building multiple relationships not only leverages your talents but gives you a lens into the worlds of several people. You will learn from a lot of different people with varied backgrounds and perspectives, and this will help you develop skills for sorting out complex issues. If your protégés are younger than you, they can provide insight to their generation and trends. Exposure to their perspectives will greatly benefit you in the long run. Protégés also expand your network—making it more of a sparse network as we described in Strategic Action 4. This creates a network of supporters for your efforts.

Of course, too much of a good thing can turn into a bad thing. We would not want you to spread yourself too thin. So, be mindful of how many active mentoring relationships you have at any one time.

MEETING IDEAS FOR MENTORS AND PROTÉGÉS

Once you have established a mentoring relationship, here are some ideas for specific activities for your meetings:

- Discuss any current issues of importance to you.
- Discuss career strategies within your organizations.
- Discuss events that have an impact on your field or the industry.
- Learn something about each other's area of expertise.
- Talk about the "rules of the game" and the "players in the game."

- Suggest visits to other parts of the organization to broaden your perspective.
- Meet other colleagues to discuss topics of interest and increase visibility.
- Discuss the projects you are working on.
- Discuss strategies for balancing work and family.
- Identify and discuss attributes of successful executives and discuss reasons for their success.
- Discuss books (like *Black Faces in High Places*!) or articles on topics of interest.
- Discuss recent courses or seminars that you've taken.
- Get together with other mentors/protégés to discuss topics of common interest.
- Learn as much as possible from each other's strengths.

The wise make mistakes but they

rarely make the same mistake twice.

Interdependent Action Steps for Mentors and Protégés

REVERSE MENTOR

You are never too young or too old to learn something new, and there is always something you can learn from someone else regardless of their age. Even a child can teach us very valuable lessons. *Reverse mentoring* refers to someone less experienced advising someone who is more experienced. This represents a valuable form of mentoring for Black faces in high places, which can also yield the benefit of remaining current on trends and perspectives related to more junior team members.

LEVERAGE BOTH ONLINE AND OFFLINE MENTORING RESOURCES

There are a growing number of opportunities to cultivate mentoring relationships both online (via the internet) and offline (face-to-face or in person). For example, iMentor (www.imentor.org) has been cultivating relationships between young people and volunteer adult mentors through an innovative combination of email correspondence and in-person meetings. MicroMentor (www.micromentor.org) connects via the internet microentrepreneurs, particularly in low-income communities, to volunteer mentors who have successfully navigated business ownership or management. The MentorNet E-Mentoring Program (www.mentornet.net) provides women and people of color in the white, male-dominated fields of engineering and science with information, encouragement, and support. This includes online mentoring of community college, undergraduate and graduate students, postdoctoral fellows, and untenured faculty. These are just a few of the examples of mentoring opportunities that are particularly or exclusively facilitated using technology.

To find opportunities to be a mentor or a protégé in your local community, visit www.caresmentoring.com for the National CARES Mentoring Movement (founded by Susan Taylor, editor-in-chief emerita of *Essence* magazine), or visit www.bbbs.org to identify the Big Brothers Big Sisters agency nearest you, or visit www.mentoring .org sponsored by MENTOR/National Mentoring Partnership to identify a program near you. Finally, inquire at your place of employment or a local organization appropriate to your needs (such as a faith-based organization, chamber of commerce, young professionals' organization, and so on) to learn more about academic, community, or professional mentoring programs they may sponsor.

You may also visit www.redefinethegame.com for additional information about mentoring programs.

The saying "Each one teach one" is an African proverb that originated during the period of African enslavement in America. Enslaved Africans were denied an education so when one learned to read or write they were responsible for teaching someone else.

BE A MENTOR AND A PROTÉGÉ

Much like networking and relationship building, mentoring is just as much about giving as it is about taking. It is therefore important to seek out opportunities not only to be a protégé of others but to also be a mentor to others. A college student can mentor a high school student. A young professional can mentor a college student. An executive can mentor a young professional. You can be a mentor at almost any stage of your career.

Formal and informal activities such as book clubs, Bible study, fellowship, discussion groups, and even one-on-one conversations are also a wonderful way of strengthening friendship ties while also exchanging useful information, sharing different perspectives, and learning about the experiences of others.

Mentoring is not just an opportunity; it is a responsibility. No one succeeds in life as a result of his or her abilities alone. Whatever successes we enjoy are due in large part to people who have helped us. We therefore have a responsibility to do the same for others. Always remember: "Each one reach one. Each one teach one."

6

Leverage Our Might

If you want to go fast, go alone.
If you want to go far, go together.
— AFRICAN PROVERB

It upsets us when Black people say that Black people can't work together, because it is simply not true. History has proven over and over again, not only that we can work together but also that when we choose to unite around an issue the results are nothing short of revolutionary. Two widely recognized and convincing examples can be found in the civil rights movement of the twentieth century and the Black Lives Matter movement of the twenty-first century. In fact, a deeper examination of the origins of both efforts reveals fascinating details about the prominent role that Black women played in transforming pivotal moments into widespread movements.

Two Moments, Two Movements

THE CIVIL RIGHTS MOVEMENT

DECEMBER 1, 1955

Rosa Parks refuses to give up her seat on a crowded bus to a white passenger and is arrested.

- Rosa Parks, civil rights activist: "I did not get on the bus to get arrested. I got on the bus to go home."

  "I knew someone had to take the first step, and I made up my mind not to move."

- Martin Luther King Jr., president, Montgomery Improvement Association: "That was the day when we started a bus protest, which literally electrified the nation. And that was the day when we decided that we were not going to take segregated buses any longer."

- Ula Taylor, professor, Department of African American Studies, UC Berkeley: "People know about Rosa Parks. People know about Martin Luther King Jr.—and they should. And they know that it was the Montgomery bus boycott that ignited a certain kind of southern civil rights movement. But what they might not know is that it was actually the behind-the-scenes organizing effort by

THE BLACK LIVES MATTER MOVEMENT

JULY 13, 2013

George Zimmerman is acquitted of the second-degree murder or Trayvon Martin.

- Alicia Garza, cofounder, #BLACKLIVESMATTER Network: "I personally got obsessed with watching the Zimmerman trial. I was at a bar, and I knew that the verdict was due because everything went silent. And that's when we started to check our phones. When I saw that George Zimmerman had been acquitted, I felt like I'd been punched in the gut.

  "Many people were trying to make sense of what happened, but I felt like the ways that people were trying to make sense of what happened and what we needed to be doing about it were actually destructive. How do we learn how to organize? How do we learn how to develop a set of demands that will actually transform conditions in our communities? I wrote a letter to Black people on Facebook saying that there was nothing wrong with us and we deserve dignity and respect." (Facebook post on July 13, 2013: "black people. I love you. I love us. Our lives matter.")

THE CIVIL RIGHTS MOVEMENT

the Women's Political Council, led by Jo Ann Robinson, that made the boycott successful.

"[The Women's Political Council] kept a critique of all of the horrific ways that Black people were forced to ride the bus. They wrote letters to the bus company. They wrote letters to the mayor, basically saying that there needed to be a more humane way of riding the bus.

"We're talking about at least two-hundred-plus Black women in the Women's Political Council in Montgomery, Alabama. And these were 'professional' Black women. Many of them worked at the historically Black colleges. Many of them were local teachers. Many of them had been formally educated at historically Black colleges.

"Yes, Martin Luther King Jr. was an amazing, charismatic leader for all of us, but it was because of the Women's Political Council that provided an anchor and grounding for him to even come into prominence."

- King: "Apparently indefatigable, [Jo Ann Robinson], perhaps more than any other person, was active on every level of the protest."

- Jo Ann Robinson, president, Women's Political Council: "Women's leadership was no less important to the development of the Montgomery bus boycott than was the male and minister-dominated leadership.

"That boycott was not supported by a few people; it was supported by fifty-two thousand people."

- Parks: "People always say that I didn't give up my seat because I was tired, but

THE BLACK LIVES MATTER MOVEMENT

- Patrisse Cullors, cofounder, #BLACKLIVESMATTER Network: "I came across Alicia's post hours later. I understood there is this thing called a hashtag, and you can make something go viral; and then I put a hashtag in front of it saying, 'Black Lives Matter'." (Facebook reply on July 13, 2013: "declaration: black bodies will no longer be sacrificed for the rest of the world's enlightenment. i am done. i am so done. trayvon, you are loved infinitely #blacklivesmatter").

- Jesse Williams, actor, activist: "The moment was electric. Black Lives Matter was a brilliantly framed set of marching orders/slogan/plea. I can't pretend that I saw a movement coming out of this particular moment. But young Black people, they are plugged in and they're moving this conversation. They're driving this conversation."

- Keeanga-Yamahtta Taylor, historian: "It was taking off like wildfire. But people were really beginning to ask the question, 'Is this just young people that are playing out on Twitter and in Facebook? Is this legitimate activism or just people using their phone? Is this a moment or a movement?'

"The Black Lives Matter movement is the most important development in Black life in the last forty years, and the most important aspect of it is that it's ordinary people fighting this fight. It is something that we have been responsible for getting out onto the streets, and I think the movement is here to stay."

- Deray McKesson, activist, cofounder Campaign Zero: "We're now talking about what does it mean to be a movement full of people who are

THE CIVIL RIGHTS MOVEMENT	THE BLACK LIVES MATTER MOVEMENT
that isn't true. I was not tired physically . . . . No, the only tired I was, was tired of giving in. "Each person must live their life as a model for others."	leading and doing their work in different ways and that there is no one way to organize, there's no one way to be in this work." • Michaela Angela Davis, image activist: "And that's what's different about this movement. We are seeing leaders come forward. And this is because they took social media and made it work for them. Black Twitter is *The Matrix*. Black Twitter popped it off and because of Twitter, we know who Patrisse is. We know who Alicia is. We know who [Johnetta "Netta" Elzie] is. This generation is not going to let them be nameless; and they're doing that. "I'm really proud of this generation. It's a revolution in a way. They have used this new tool, and I think Black Lives Matter will define this shift in America. I think we will look at Black Lives Matter like we looked at the civil rights movement."

When we leverage our might—like the civil rights movement, the Black Lives Matter movement, and even other lesser-known efforts—laws are enacted, racists lose their jobs, systems are reformed, communities are transformed, and companies are brought to their knees. But there are challenges not only for Black people working together but for any group of people seeking to do so. High among those challenges in the twenty-first century is a growing trend toward individualism, which is not representative of our historical reality but is most certainly representative of our modern society.

Individualism: "I Think; Therefore I Am"

The concept of individualism is perhaps best captured in a statement by the seventeenth-century French philosopher René Descartes: "I think; therefore I am," which translates to "*Cogito, ergo sum*" in Latin.

This was a philosophical attempt by Descartes to find a statement that was certain and irrefutable. The statement, however, is rooted in the idea that our individual existence is predicated on the existence of our thoughts and not in relationship to others. Arguably, it is the same underlying thinking that forms the basis for the concept of "rugged individualism," which was coined by President Herbert Hoover and is recognized as a cornerstone of American character. In the book *Rugged Individualism: Dead or Alive?*, authors David Davenport and Gordon Lloyd define the concept as a "combination of individual liberty in America's founding and the frontier spirit [which has] provided the rich soil in which it has grown and developed."[1] They acknowledge that even President Obama, no great fan of rugged individualism, has recognized it as being "in America's DNA" and that it "defines America." Sadly, we believe America has only grown to become more individualistic today than ever before. Particularly in our capitalist American society, there is increasingly more pressure to focus on an individual agenda and increasingly less pressure to focus on a collective agenda.

For example, as mini case studies, let's look at two industries that many people can relate to and that clearly illustrate these dynamics: (1) the entertainment industry or, more specifically, the recording music industry, and (2) professional sports or, more specifically, the National Basketball Association.

The modern recording music industry is saturated with solo performing artists. Solo artists used to be the exception, and then they became the norm, and now they are the rule. Music groups have practically disappeared. For example, we looked up the number of artists who reached number one on the Billboard Hot 100 in 1965, and then we looked up the artists who reached number one on the Billboard 100 fifty years later in 2015.[2] Take a guess how many music groups reached number one on the Billboard 100 in 2015?[3] Zero. None. Zilch. Believe it or not, this is generally true for the entire millennium. Most people are hard pressed to think of five music groups that reached number one in the new millennium, much less that are still together. By comparison, of the seventeen artists who reached number one on the Billboard 100 in 1965, take a guess how many of them were music groups? Fifteen!

There were only two solo artists on the list, and neither of their names is familiar to us: Petula Clark and Barry McGuire.[4] Almost 90 percent of the artists who reached number one in 1965 were music groups—a complete reversal when compared to 0 percent in 2015.

You are probably familiar with some of the music groups that reached number one in 1965, which included the Supremes, the Temptations, and the Four Tops. Moreover, we have fond memories of the music groups that were popular during the end of the millennium such as New Edition, SWV, TLC, En Vogue, Jodeci, and Guy! Sadly, music groups have been erased from the top of the music charts. Why? We're certain there are several factors involved, but among them our theory is that two trends make it less likely to establish and maintain music groups and more likely to produce solo performing artists: individualism and egotism. Nowadays, very few people want to dance in the background or sing backup while somebody else sings lead. Most people prefer having the spotlight to be on them or, at best, having someone collaborate on a song (that is, "featuring . . ."). Individual solo artists stand to make more money than members of groups. Egos get in the way of groups coming together and staying together.

A second example of this dynamic is the NBA.

The challenges associated with building and maintaining a winning NBA franchise are twofold. The first challenge is the increasing conflict between a player's individual agenda of making money and a team's collective agenda of winning a championship. It is difficult to preserve a roster of all-star-caliber talent that is collectively paid at a level below the salary cap (the maximum ceiling a team can spend on its players): if one player makes a lot, that is less for everybody else. To build and maintain a winning team, often one or more all-star players has to be willing to be paid below their market value in order for the team not to exceed the salary cap. For example, three NBA Hall of Famers bear this out: Kevin Garnett (amusingly rumored to be Dr. Pinkett's doppelgänger) took a $13 million pay cut to join the Minnesota Timberwolves and maintained that pay cut after being traded to the Boston Celtics.[5] Shaquille O'Neal took a $30 million pay cut after joining the Miami Heat.[6] Tim Duncan cut his salary by more than half, from $21 million per year to $10 million per year (from the third highest paid player in the league to the sixty-first), to keep the San Antonio Spurs team intact.[7] Why did Garnett, O'Neal, and Duncan do this?[8] Because they all wanted to win a championship, and they all did.

The second challenge to building and maintaining an NBA championship team is egos. Once an all-star-caliber roster is assembled, to win the title, the general manager, coaches, and players must ensure that everyone gets along and that their egos don't disrupt the team chemistry necessary. Shaquille O'Neal was traded to the Miami Heat one season *after* he and Kobe Bryant won three consecutive NBA championships because they couldn't get along. And it's irrelevant that Kobe and Shaq went on to win titles independently. The ends do not justify the means. The better question is: How many more titles could Kobe and Shaq have won if they had stayed together?

———

When you know who you are, you are not afraid to help people who look like you.

———

The undercurrents we have outlined in entertainment and sports are not particular to those industries. We could easily describe similar tensions among corporate professionals balancing their career objectives against their company's objectives; elected officials vacillating between their political aspirations, their constituents' needs, and those across the political aisle; entrepreneurs seeking to grow their companies while wrestling with decisions of whether to partner with competing companies in order to pursue opportunities together that they could not pursue alone; and more. These and other scenarios directly relate to the challenges and opportunities for Black faces in high places. We can easily get caught in a spiral of individualism and egotism that belies our ancestral African origins and undermines our attempts to make progress in twenty-first-century America. The good news is that there is an alternate philosophy that can guide and empower us to fully leverage our might.

Collectivism: "I Am Because We Are"

"I am because we are" is an ethic based on just one aspect of the humanist philosophy of *ubuntu*. *Ubuntu* is a Zulu proverb that says, "I am a person through other people. My humanity is tied to yours." The Archbishop Desmond Tutu says the following:

> One of the sayings in our country is *Ubuntu*—the essence of being human. *Ubuntu* speaks particularly about the fact that you can't exist as a human being in isolation. It speaks about our interconnectedness. We think of ourselves far too frequently as just individuals, separated from one another, whereas you are connected and what you do affects the whole world. When you do well, it spreads out; it is for the whole of humanity.[9]
>
> *Ubuntu* is very difficult to render into a Western language. . . . It is to say, "My humanity is caught up, is inextricably bound up, in what is yours."

Ubuntu has its origins in the Bantu people who currently and predominantly reside in southern Africa. They primarily speak Nguni languages, which are also spoken in Swaziland and Zimbabwe. *Ubuntu* carries several meanings, including behaving well toward others, acting in ways that benefit the community, selflessness, and a connection shared between people. According to Angela Thompsell, professor of British and African history at the State University of New York, *ubuntu* also refers to "the need for forgiveness and reconciliation rather than vengeance. It was an underlying concept in the Truth and Reconciliation Commission [that was formed after the end of apartheid in South Africa], and the writings of Nelson Mandela and Archbishop Desmond Tutu raised awareness of the term outside of Africa."[10]

By comparison to rugged individualism, we regard *ubuntu* as a foundation principle for compassionate collectivism and leveraging our might. Individualism is centered on the preservation and advancement of the individual, whereas collectivism is centered on the preservation and advancement of the group.[11] *Ubuntu* and collectivism are not only the antidotes to the aforementioned pitfalls of individualism and egotism, but they are also exactly what is needed for Black faces in high places to align with like-minded and like-hearted individuals, coalesce power, wield influence, and help others.

Leveraging our might requires a combination of Level I: Independent Action and Level II: Interdependent Action. In other words, to work with others toward a collective goal, you must first know who you are and where you are going. This refers to self-determination (Strategic Action 1), exploration (Strategic Action 2), and self-mastery and meaning (Strategic Action 3), which we discussed in Level I. Only then can you find strength in numbers through networking, building relationships, and power (Strategic Action 4), and mentorship and sponsorship (Strategic Action 5) at Level II. Strategic Action 6 ties all of this together and speaks directly to the responsibility of Black faces in high places to work together and to be intentional about opening doors for other Black faces who aspire to high places. The spirit of *ubuntu* and the principles of collectivism can guide us in coming together to pursue collective goals and, most important, staying together to achieve those goals.

A person is a person through other persons.

—Nguni Proverb

Examples of Leveraging Our Might

In his book, *How to Succeed in Business Without Being White: Straight Talk on Making It in America*, the late Earl Graves, founder and publisher of *Black Enterprise*, argues that the greatest challenge facing the Black community is "racism," and the second greatest challenge is "leveraging our might." Conversely, we believe the single greatest opportunity for Black faces in high places is leveraging our might. The following are some examples from the 1800s to the 2020s of exactly what this looks like.

MADAM C. J. WALKER (1867–1919) AND THE WALKER MANUFACTURING COMPANY

Madam C. J. Walker was "the first Black woman millionaire in America" and made her fortune thanks to her homemade line of hair care products for Black women. Born Sarah Breedlove to parents who had been slaves, she was inspired to create her hair products after an experience with hair loss, which led to the creation of the "Walker system" of hair care. A talented entrepreneur with a knack for self-promotion, Walker built a business empire, at first selling products directly to Black women, then employing Black women as "beauty culturalists" to hand-sell her wares. She single-handedly empowered scores of Black women as microentrepreneurs. The self-made millionaire leveraged our might and used her fortune to fund scholarships for women at the Tuskegee Institute and donated large parts of her wealth to the NAACP, the Black YMCA, and other charities.

BLACK WALL STREET (1921)[12]

Greenwood, Oklahoma, a suburb of Tulsa, was the type of community that African Americans are still today attempting to reclaim and rebuild. Black Wall Street was a community that was built entirely by Black people working together and doing so in the midst of reconstruction and the Jim Crow era. Josie Pickens describes Black Wall Street as a "modern, majestic, sophisticated, and unapologetically Black" community that boasted of "banks, hotels, cafés, clothiers, movie theaters, and contemporary homes." Not to mention luxuries, such as "indoor plumbing and a remarkable school system that superiorly educated

Black children." Undoubtedly, less fortunate white neighbors resented their upper-class lifestyle. As a result of a jealous desire "to put progressive, high-achieving African Americans in their place," a wave of domestic white terrorism caused Black dispossession. Tragically, Black Wall Street became the site of one of the bloodiest and most horrendous race riots (and acts of terrorism) that the United States has ever experienced.

THE BANKERS (1962–1964)[13]

Born in Willis, Texas, Bernard Garrett gravitated to entrepreneurship at a young age, running his own cleaning business while in high school. It should come as no surprise that when he moved to Los Angeles with his family, he started another cleaning business. He parlayed that into buying his first property, after convincing a white real estate developer, Patrick Barker, not only to sell him the building at below the asking price, but also to loan him the money to make the necessary renovations. After Barker died, Garrett approached Joe Morris, the owner of two successful nightclubs, to partner with him to further expand into the Los Angeles real estate market. At the height of their success, Garrett and Morris owned more than 170 buildings and achieved a net worth of $1.5 million and $2 million, respectively (equivalent to $14.3 million and $19.1 million in current times). A year later, when reflecting on their success, Garrett said, "The only time a man is really truly rich is when he controls money."

MAYNARD JACKSON AND
THE CITY OF ATLANTA (1973–1978)[14]

Maynard Jackson is an iconic example of leveraging elected office to foster Black economic empowerment. Jackson served two consecutive terms as Atlanta's first African American mayor and was responsible for significantly expanding the city's contracting with African American–owned businesses as a part of the expansion of Hartsfield Airport. According to the *Black Commentator*, "In 1973, fewer than 1 percent of [Atlanta's] contracts went to minorities. Five years later, it was 38.6 percent. At one point, more than 80 percent of all minority contracts at US airports were in Atlanta, prompting [Mayor Maynard] Jackson once to boast that he had helped create 25 new [minority] millionaires."

"Jackson was like Dr. Martin Luther King Jr. when it came to ensuring African Americans got a chance to participate in the nation's economic marketplace," says H. J. Russell, founder of H. J. Russell & Company, the nation's largest Black-owned construction company, which received several contracts as a result of Jackson's policies. Russell estimates that his company did approximately $100 million worth of work at Hartsfield Airport over a three-year period.

"Jackson unapologetically leveraged our might by working in partnership with Black legislators and the numerous Black entrepreneurs he helped make into millionaires. Those first 25 millionaires, with the assistance of the next three . . . Atlanta mayors, have helped to create scores of additional [minority] millionaires along with the thriving, empowered, well-connected and ambitious business and professional class which identifies with the people who run Atlanta to this day," writes the *Black Commentator*. Hartsfield Airport was appropriately and posthumously renamed Hartsfield-Jackson Airport after Jackson's death in 2003.

THE RUTGERS WOMEN'S BASKETBALL TEAM AND PASTOR DEFOREST SOARIES (2007)[15]

Syndicated radio host Don Imus was subject to intense scrutiny after making disrespectful and disparaging remarks about the Rutgers University women's basketball team by referring to them as "nappy-headed hos."

"The first thing that happened after Mr. Imus's remarks was that I called him," said Pastor DeForest "Buster" Soaries Jr., senior pastor at First Baptist Church of Lincoln Gardens and former New Jersey secretary of state in an interview with CBS2's Kristine Johnson. Several of the Rutgers women and their Hall of Fame head coach, C. Vivian Stringer, worshipped at First Baptist Church. "What I wanted him to understand was that these young women were living lives that would be impacted perhaps forever."

Eight days after the controversy began, Soaries had the team and Imus in a room at the New Jersey governor's mansion in Princeton, NJ. "And the ground rules were basically, 'Mr. Imus, first, listen,' and he listened for two hours," said Soaries. "Our goal going into that meeting was resolution. Our goal was not simply publicity or to inflame the matter; but the goal was resolution." While the Rutgers women's basketball team accepted Imus's apology after the private meeting facilitated by Soaries, his efforts ultimately contributed to Imus's firing alongside the related efforts of other powerful individuals and organizations such as Al Roker, Gwen Ifill, the National Association of Black Journalists, networks of Black employees at General Electric, Sprint, MSNBC, and the National Organization of Women (NOW).

Leveraging our might means turning to

each other and never turning on each other.

BLACK ECONOMIC ALLIANCE (2018–PRESENT)[16]

The Black Economic Alliance (BEA) is a coalition of business leaders and aligned advocates committed to economic progress and prosperity in the Black community with a specific focus on work, wages, and wealth. BEA is using Black collaborative action, power, and business acumen to advance policies that can and will create economic empowerment in our community. As mentioned previously, in the wake of George Floyd's murder, BEA chairman and Recognize managing partner Charles Phillips, along with a coalition of thirty-seven CEOs, including Merck chairman and CEO Kenneth C. Frazier, IBM executive chairman Ginni Rometty, and former American Express CEO and General Catalyst chairman and managing director Ken Cheanault founded OneTen. The aim of OneTen is to close the opportunity gap for Black talent in America by creating one million family-sustaining careers for Black Americans over the ensuing decade.

Independent Action Steps to Leverage Our Might

The following are independent action steps for transforming these ideas about collectivism and leveraging our might from broad concepts into concrete actions that can benefit you.

GET INVOLVED!

Our point here is plainly and simply summarized by the title of a song by James Brown, "Get Up, Get Into It, Get Involved!" Don't just get involved in charitable causes and social/racial issues, get *actively* involved. This could include any combination of the following:

- marching/protesting and then strategizing/organizing to seek reforms
- volunteering with a nonprofit organization and then joining the board of directors
- becoming a member of a church and then leading a church ministry

You should be deliberate in seeking opportunities to hone, develop, and/or leverage your skills. The more you know about the areas you would like to develop, or the areas where you can contribute, the more you will be able to shape your contributions in a way that is truly mutually beneficial. It is less likely to happen by accident.

Lastly, keep in mind that you get out what you put into any charitable cause or social or racial issue. Elbert Hubbard[17] once said, "Folks who never do any more than they get paid for, never get paid for any more than they do." The more you put in, the more you get out, and the more our communities and our society benefit. This is a win-win-win!

ENSURE ALIGNMENT

It is important to have alignment between your values and the values of the charitable causes and social/racial issues with which you are affiliated. Much like our earlier discussion in Strategic Action 1 about defining your personal mission, vision, and values, you should similarly take the time to understand the mission, vision, and values of any organization or entity with which you are considering membership and active involvement.

For those who seek to establish or have established their own organizations—executive directors of nonprofits, CEOs of start-up ventures, founding members of a charter school, and other new entities—you face an additional consideration. It is important that you maintain an organizational culture and values you can continue to embrace—values that are consistent with yours. But, inasmuch as your organization's culture is not completely under your control, you must be mindful of whether a disconnect evolves over time. If so, you must ask the hard questions about whether it represents a temporary shift away from the organization's core, the governing ideas that can be proactively addressed, or whether it is a more fundamental, permanent change that may be at odds with your core principles.

LEVERAGE INVOLVEMENT AS PREPARATION AND LEARNING OPPORTUNITIES

One of the benefits of organizational involvement is that it can be a wonderful training ground for future opportunities. If you would like to become a corporate executive, you can begin learning the basics of running meetings and managing people as an officer in an organization. If you want to establish your own nonprofit organization, what better way to prepare yourself than to learn the inner workings of an established 501(c)(3)? If you envision a future as an entrepreneur, you can gain experience in areas such as financial management, operations, marketing, and public relations, just to name a few, by volunteering to help with various programs or committees. Lastly, serving on a nonprofit and public board of directors could serve as a precursor to serving on a paid corporate board.

GO DEEP AND NOT WIDE

Once you reach a certain level in your career, you realize that "less is more." You will be able to gain more, and exert great influence, if you are active in a few charitable causes, social/racial issues, and organizations than if you spread yourself thin across several efforts. In other words, we advise you to go deep and not wide in order to have the greatest impact.

It also makes sense to vary your involvement in these organizations. In some groups, you will take the leadership role, which will require a heavier time commitment than if you are a committee member or general member. Are you ready, willing, and able to fulfill that commitment? Obviously, you can't do this with ten different organizations, so you have to choose when you will be in charge and when you will not. And, in some organizations, the leadership structure is a ladder of commitment. You start off as a lower officer and then over successive years you become the first vice president, the president (or chairperson), and then president emeritus. So when you run for office, realize that you are signing up for multiple years.

A meaningful role is not always a leadership role. In every organization, it is important to have stable and active members. That means paying your dues, going to meetings, and pitching in reliably when your service is needed.

Interdependent Action Steps to Leverage Our Might

The following are interdependent actions steps to leverage our might that can benefit you and others.

Strategic Action 1 is a "me" thing.

Strategic Action 6 is a "we" thing.

BE INTENTIONAL AND UNAPOLOGETIC

If you are a Black face in a high place, you have power: use it to help Black people and the Black community, and do so without apology. More specifically, be intentional about helping other Black people to reach their full potential (Strategic Action 3) by leveraging your relationships, power, and influence (Strategic Action 4), and providing mentorship and sponsorship (Strategic Action 5). Naturally, you will have to navigate some very important considerations such as the perceptions of your actions and the politics of your environment, but these factors should never impede your resolve to help others.

Actress, singer, and songwriter Cynthia Erivo, recipient of an Emmy Award, Tony Award, Grammy Award, and two Academy Award nominations, offers a simple example. Erivo used her power to demonstrate solidarity when, upon being rushed by her publicist to bypass the remaining media outlets on the red carpet at the 2020 Oscars, insisted that she stop to conduct an interview with Lola Ogunnaike, a fellow Black woman and reporter for PeopleTV, CNN, and MSNBC.

"Me being a Black man and being represented by [Rich Paul, who also represents LeBron James], who is also an African American man—it's huge," said NBA champion Tristan Thompson. "We want to find a way to put more people like us in positions of power."

Maynard Jackson's efforts, which we discussed earlier, offer a more elaborate example. Jackson would not have been able to accomplish what he did in Atlanta had he been concerned about perception or politics. He did what he did without apology.

CONVENE WITH LIKE-MINDED INDIVIDUALS

One of our favorite old adages is, "Show me your friends, show me your future." And this is not a principle we believe is confined to young people. Surrounding yourself with like-minded individuals is an action step for people of all ages and levels. It includes family, friends, neighbors, prayer partners, community members, parishioners and worshippers, coworkers and peer leaders. The importance of establishing and maintaining connections with fellow executives, entrepreneurs, and leaders is only heightened for Black faces in high places because you are often few and far between. Another old adage, "It's lonely at the top," can be very real.

It might seem obvious to some that this is an important action step. What might not be obvious is how important it is to be strategic in doing so. As you approach the top of your organization, membership in organizations that provide networking with other Black and non-Black professionals within your organization and outside your organization are vital. Which organizations are you spending your time in? What value are these organizations bringing you? How can your increased involvement benefit you, other Black professionals, and/or the Black community? While there are formal organizations and organizations comprising African American executives in corporate America (for example, Executive Leadership Council, Information Technology Senior Management Forum), entrepreneurship (National Minority Supplier Development Council's Advanced Management Education Program at Northwestern University, Dartmouth's Tuck Diversity Business Programs), health care (National Association of Health Service Executives), and more, there is an even greater number of formal organizations representing specific trades, professions, sectors, and industries. There is benefit to involvement in both kinds of formal organizations, and there is also a benefit to more informal gatherings, such as regular dinner meetings and self-organized retreats that take place behind closed doors. Not only is there the potential for networking in these various settings, but they also serve as excellent sources for mentors, sponsors, and professional development. The point is that involvement in local, regional, national, and international organizations should be strategic, focused, diverse, and appropriate to your career stage.

The research conducted by Thomas and Gabarro affirms this advice. They found that, across all three career stages, minority executives were engaged in "partnerships for change"—or "a set of relationships that involve stakeholders who collectively represent the interests of the corporation" and its emerging majorities and "who share a common goal of actively pursuing racial diversification"—as well as "minority activism" and other efforts to champion diversity, equity, and inclusion (DEI). This took the form of formal organizations such as affinity groups, employee resource groups, and business resource groups, informal networks among employees of color, and the unapologetic, conscious, overt, and intentional efforts of minority managers and executives to use their power to facilitate DEI. In fact, not only are these prime examples of leveraging our might, but they are also closely related to the next two strategic actions on intrapreneurship and entrepreneurship that constitute Level III: Collaborative Action.

CREATE HIGH-PERFORMING TEAMS

Whereas social capital was the foundational tool set for Strategic Actions 4 and 5, intellectual capital is the foundational tool set for Strategic Action 6. Social capital resides in individuals, and intellectual capital is the knowledge, experience, and skills resulting from the collective effort of interrelationships, or a team.

A high-performing team that will be able to leverage power should have these three features:

1. *Trust*—Highly effective teams trust each other. They know that each member of the team will honor their commitment, support one another, and have faith in one another.
2. *Communication*—High-performing teams communicate frequently, effectively, and efficiently with people outside the team about team activities. By leveraging tools such as

email, conference calls, text messaging, web conferencing, and good old-fashioned in-person meetings, regular communication allows these teams to make balanced decisions, handle conflict constructively, and provide one another with feedback.

3. *Roles*—Everyone on the team has a role or position that they play. Every team member will work with others to achieve the common goal. Each will contribute within and possibly beyond that role, if necessary, to meet the objectives.

TEAMWORK MAKES THE DREAM WORK: ARE YOU A LEVEL 4 OR A LEVEL 5 LEADER?

In the book *Good to Great: Why Some Companies Make the Leap . . . and Others Don't*, Jim Collins talks about the difference between a good leader, which he refers to as a "Level 4 leader," and a great leader, which he refers to as a "Level 5 leader." Using the metaphor of a bus, Collins explains:

- The "good" leader—the Level 4 leader—thinks "what then who": they set the vision for where to drive the bus and then enlist a crew of highly capable "helpers" to place in the right seats on the bus to make the vision a reality. The Level 4 Leadership Model is described as an organization led by "a genius with a thousand helpers."
- The "great" leader—the Level 5 Leader—thinks in the reverse. She or he thinks "who then what": they get the right people on the bus; build a superior team; and then once the right people are in the right seats on the bus, the team collectively figures out the best path to greatness.

The lesson being that you must pay careful attention to building and maintaining a core, solid team at all times.

ESTABLISH EFFECTIVE PARTNERSHIPS

A partnership consists of the formal members of a venture, initiative, or entity. You should be deliberate in assessing whether someone is well suited to enter into a partnership. Do not make the mistake that we once made to take the decision lightly. Our very first entrepreneurial venture was Mind, Body & Soul Enterprises (MBS), which comprised a retail sales division and an educational services division. Beyond the founding members of MBS and BCT Partners, which includes one of Dr. Pinkett's Oxford classmates, Munro Richardson, we have had several other partners who are no longer involved with our business ventures. Some of them left for understandable and legitimate reasons, but others had to be removed because they were not pulling their weight. Not surprisingly, we did not take the time to ask the hard questions as to whether these individuals were the right fit for the company and, more important, the right fit with the other partners. If you are considering entering into a partnership with someone, ask the questions: What is their track record? Do their personal values, motivations, mission, and vision align with yours? Do you have an understanding of their leadership style and the extent to which it is compatible with yours? The answers to these questions will reveal whether or not the partnership can work.

To the extent your partnership is one that will lead to a new entity—a new nonprofit organization, a new charter school, a new business, or a new church—there are a host of additional conversations that must take place. What does each partner bring to the table? Are there areas where the partnership is lacking? How can we make sure those areas are still being addressed? How can we strengthen our team in those areas in the future? What will be the organization's mission, vision, and values? Have we clarified roles and responsibilities? We will discuss some of these topics in greater detail in Strategic Action 8: Think and Act Like an Entrepreneur. Above all, in the spirit of *ubuntu*, establish partnerships that cast aside pettiness, posturing, personalities, and politics to pursue a greater purpose. This is something we have proudly been able to do among our various teams and partnerships from MBS to BCT, which span more than three decades dating back to college.

FOSTER AWARENESS OF TEAMMATES' AND PARTNERS' LEADERSHIP STYLES

For Black faces in high places, building effective teams is of paramount importance. Over our several decades as business partners we've seen, firsthand, the benefits of working on a team where we are all familiar with one another's personalities and leadership styles. Through regular and ongoing discussions with each other about how to approach work and our perspectives on leading and managing, we continue to deepen our understanding of one another. This allows us to assign responsibility, delegate tasks, and work together more effectively. The better you know your teammates, and the better your teammates know each other, the better you can work together to achieve your shared goals.

We recommend using a formal instrument to assess the personalities and leadership styles of your teammates and partners. This is common in leadership development programs. We have found the Myers-Briggs Type Indicator (MBTI)® and the Keirsey Temperament Sorter II® to be extremely useful. Both are related to the work of Katharine Cook Briggs and her daughter Isabel Briggs Myers—the pair is popularly known as Myers-Briggs—as well as the theories of Carl Jung. We have also found to be very effective the Herrmann Brain Dominance Instrument® (HBDI®), which is a cognitive style measurement tool and model that helps describe thinking preferences in individuals and teams..

Interestingly, we have found that each of the members of our partnership corresponds to one of the Keirsey Temperaments—our partner Dallas Grundy was a Rational™ (objective oriented; thrives on conceptualization), our partner Raqiba Bourne and Dr. Robinson were each an Idealist™ (people oriented; thrives on harmony), Dr. Pinkett was a Guardian™ (task oriented; thrives on procedure), and our partner Lawrence Hibbert was an Artisan™ (response oriented; thrives on action). We have found the MBTI®, Keirsey®, and HBDI® frameworks (and others like them) to be extremely helpful in understanding one another and identifying potential areas of conflict. We also believe these tools can also be used in determining whether a potential teammate or partnership is a good fit and how to resolve conflict.

UNDERSTAND THE PERSONAL MISSION, VISION, AND VALUES OF YOUR TEAMMATES AND PARTNERS

The previous action steps suggest that as your relationships evolve to become high-performing teams and effective partnerships, the level of communication and understanding should generally increase. Familiarize yourself with the track record and leadership style of teammates. For fellow partners, you should take deliberate and ongoing steps to understand their personal missions, visions, values, and motivations to determine if the partnership is a good fit. It is important to have these conversations because when personal mission, vision, and values do not align, it can lead to some very challenging situations. The only remedy is honest and ongoing dialogue. This is something we have practiced in our partnership through MBS and BCT.

NAVIGATING THE WINDS OF CHANGE WITH TEAMMATES

People change and, accordingly, their personal mission, vision, and values can also change. Furthermore, all things must eventually come to an end. Even the greatest teams must eventually disband as the team members undergo shifting priorities in their lives. By regularly "checking in" to discuss each of the individual partners' direction, you can ensure that the partnership is still meeting everyone's expectations.

Sometimes the mission, vision, and values of what you are trying to achieve must change to reflect changes in the partners. Sometimes the partners have to change to reflect the mission, vision, and values of what you are trying to accomplish. And sometimes, shifting priorities necessitate that a partner must exit or the partnership must dissolve.

For example, Porter left MBS to focus on his career. Bourne and Dr. Robinson never joined MBS or BCT as full-time employees. Bourne is a real estate investor and trains people on how to effectively manage transitions. And, of course, Dr. Robinson is a professor at Rutgers Business School. And while Grundy served as the chief operating officer for both MBS and BCT, he eventually transitioned into higher education as a dean at Rutgers Graduate School of Education.

Pinkett says:

I'll never forget the day Dallas informed Larry and me that he was leaving the BCT Partners. It was a sad day. He and Larry were the first two employees of the company, and together, we had been through thick and thicker. I knew I was going to miss him, and I knew the company would never be the same without him. With Aldwyn having left the company years earlier, and JR never joining the company full-time, that just left Larry and me as founding members working for the company full-time. I naturally started to wonder what would happen if Larry left and I was the only founder to remain with the firm.

After Dallas informed us of his decision, I had a vision that I immediately shared with Dallas and Larry: it was of me, Raqiba, Larry, Dallas, JR, and Aldwyn pulling a very heavy object with ropes. One by one, someone dropped their rope and walked away. First, JR dropped his rope and walked away. Then Aldwyn dropped his rope and walked away, followed by Raqiba and Dallas, leaving only Larry and me to pull the object. Ahead of us in the distance was a very bright light, although I could not make out the source of the light. My vision ended with Larry and I looking back at the heavy object, then looking ahead to the light, then looking at each other as if to say, "Can we make it?"

I later discussed this vision with JR and shared with him my interpretation: the heavy object represented the heavy sacrifices we had made to get the company off the ground, while the light represented the yet-to-be-realized fruits of our labor. The fact that we started pulling the object together but Aldwyn, Raqiba, JR, and Dallas walked away represented my fear of moving forward without my dear friends by my side. I said to JR, "Maybe the object is too heavy for Larry and me to carry *despite* the efforts we've made together." He replied, "There is another way to interpret your vision." I asked, "How?" He said, "Perhaps you and Larry now have enough momentum to make it to the light *because* of the efforts we've made together, and others can now step in to pick up our ropes." Since then, his metaphor of people joining our team at BCT Partners to "pick up the ropes" of those who have moved on has been an indelible image in my mind.

Fortunately, we have remained business partners with Hibbert and Grundy. Like Dr. Pinkett, Hibbert is a full-time managing partner at BCT, while Dr. Robinson and Grundy sit on the company's board of advisers. We all meet at least once each year to have a discussion about our personal missions and how they may or may not relate to our roles in the venture. We recommend having similar, deliberate, and ongoing discussions with your partners about the direction each individual envisions for himself or herself moving forward.

FORM ORGANIZATIONS
WITH A SOLID FOUNDATION

In Strategic Action 1: Exercise Self-Determination, we talked extensively about identity and purpose as your personal foundation. We also discussed the importance of developing a statement of *personal mission, vision,* and *values* to reflect your identity and purpose. It is important to follow a similar process as you prepare to lead institutions that will wield power.

In *The Fifth Discipline,* organizational development expert Peter Senge describes the relationship between great organizations and their *organizational mission, vision* and *values*—as "governing ideas." According to Senge, vision is the "What?"—the picture of the future the organization seeks to create; mission or purpose is the "Why?"—the organization's answer to the question, "Why do we exist?"; and values are the "How?"—they answer the question, "How do the members of the organization want to act, consistent with the mission, along the path toward achieving the vision?" Senge argues that great organizations have a larger sense of purpose and seek to contribute to the world in some unique way, to add a distinctive source of value. Along the same lines, we see mission, vision, and values as representing the very foundation of great organizations, as shown in figure 12.

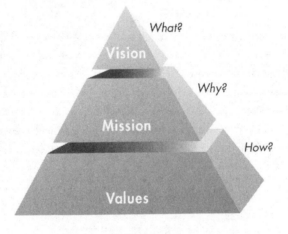

FIGURE 12

When we established Mind, Body & Soul Enterprises, we dedicated an entire weekend working with our partners Porter, Bourne, Grundy, and Hibbert to establish the following governing ideas.

MBS Mission
To empower men and women to fulfill their individual and collective purpose through mental (Mind), physical (Body), and spiritual (Soul) development.

MBS Vision

To create an institution that will

- be a catalyst of positive change;
- empower others to reach their highest potential;
- inspire and encourage people to strive for excellence;
- educate the broadest possible audience through innovative technology, intriguing content, and interactive learning; and
- facilitate an awareness of technology and its role in society.

MBS Values

Integrity, excellence, balance, synergy, community, growth, and innovation.

As college students at the time, we think we did pretty well for our first mission, vision, and value statement! We later modified and improved on these governing ideas when we launched BCT Partners. As Black faces in high places, it is critically important to have the right governing ideas for any organization you start, join, or lead. They represent the organization's core: "why" it exists; "what" difference it seeks to make; and "how" its guiding principles will manifest, regardless of whether the organization exists for a profit or for a purpose.

TRANSFORM MOMENTS INTO MOVEMENTS

The civil rights era was driven by teams who leveraged their might to transform the moment of the Montgomery bus boycott into a movement. The Black Lives Matter era transformed the moment of Trayvon Martin's murder into a movement. Neither movement happened by accident. Both were catalyzed by high-performing teams that formed as a result of very specific moments.

Rosa Parks decided not to give up her seat on a bus in Montgomery, Alabama, which led Jo Ann Robinson and a few associates to call for a one-day boycott, and a movement was born. This movement comprised a large-scale network of people fighting racism and racial injustice.

Racism is still with us. But it is up to us to prepare our children
for what they have to meet, and, hopefully, we shall overcome.
I would like to be remembered as a person who wanted to be
free . . . so other people would be also free. Memories of our
lives, of our works and our deeds will continue in others.
— ROSA PARKS

Alicia Garza posted "our lives matter" on Facebook, which
prompted Patrisse Cullors to reply "#blacklivesmatter," and a movement was born. This movement comprises a large-scale network of
people fighting racism and racial injustice.

Racism infects every part of our society. It infects our laws. It infects
our culture. It is everywhere. It is as pervasive as the air that we
breathe.[18] I think that we are all deeply, deeply committed to the
liberation of Black people. And so, when you put people together
who have and share that commitment, the sky is the limit.[19]
— ALICIA GARZA

We have a responsibility to transform future moments into re-
newed movements that continue the momentum of past ones. As we
shared earlier, Earl Graves once said that "racism" is our greatest challenge and "leveraging our might" is our second greatest challenge.
Interestingly, history has proven over and over again not only that we
can work together but also that by overcoming Graves's second challenge and fully leveraging our tremendous might, we stand our best
chance of addressing his first challenge and dismantling long-standing
and systemic racism.

LEVEL III

Collaborative Action

Keep going, no matter what.
— REGINALD F. LEWIS,
business pioneer and coauthor of
Why Should White Guys Have All the Fun?

Level III: Collaborative Action is defined as actions taken by groups of people that benefit the group and create social and economic value. The mindsets that power Level III are the *intrapreneurial mindset* and the *entrepreneurial mindset,* and the skill sets they naturally cultivate are Strategic Action 7: Think and Act Like an Intrapreneur and Strategic Action 8: Think and Act Like an Entrepreneur. Level III is predicated on two basic truths: (1) intrapreneurship and entrepreneurship are fundamentally about creating value and (2) nothing valuable can be created without two or more people working together.

The Intrapreneurial and Entrepreneurial Mindsets

Intrapreneurs and entrepreneurs do three basic things: *seek* opportunities, *see* opportunities, and *seize* opportunities. According to film producer Will Packer, "When you come into the industry as an outsider, you need to have an entrepreneurial spirit to succeed. In Hollywood, it's very clear that you either play by the rules or make up your own. And I wanted to do it my way." Intrapreneurship and entrepreneurship are a reflection of who you are, what you do, and how you do it. The intrapreneurial and entrepreneurial mindsets are therefore essential to being competitive in the twenty-first century and are grounded in five characteristics:

1. *Creativity*—an inventive or clever approach to generating ideas and solving problems
2. *Resourcefulness*—the belief that they can turn nothing into something
3. *Courage*—a willingness to take calculated risks and the belief that they can achieve whatever their mind can conceive
4. *Resilience*—a strong resolve to persevere when faced with challenges, while maintaining a healthy acceptance of failure as a way to lean and strengthen oneself
5. *Passion*—a boundless enthusiasm for whatever they endeavor to do; a fundamental love for their work; and a desire to create value

Both mindsets take these characteristics and apply them "for a profit" (*intrapreneurship* and *entrepreneurship*) or "for a purpose" (*social intrapreneurship* and *social entrepreneurship*), thus reflecting four distinct pursuits with a range of potential benefits (see table 3). The tool set required to enable each skill set comprises all forms of capital mentioned throughout the book, namely, cultural capital (Strategic Actions 1 and 2), human capital (Strategic Action 3), social capital (Strategic Actions 4, 5, and 6), and intellectual capital (Strategic Action 6). Here, we introduce a fifth and final form of capital—*financial capital*—which is defined as any economic resource used by intrapreneurs and entrepreneurs measured in money. In other words, it is intrapreneurs and entrepreneurs who artfully combine all five forms of capital to grow their ventures or organizations.

THE FOUR PURSUITS FROM AN
INTRAPRENEURIAL/ENTREPRENEURIAL MINDSET

		"FOR A PROFIT"	"FOR A PURPOSE"
THE INTRAPRENEURIAL MINDSET	Pursuit	**1. INTRAPRENEURSHIP**	**2. SOCIAL INTRAPRENEURSHIP**
	Definition	Applying the intrapreneurial mindset to grow an established organization.	
	Context	Established entities such as corporations, nonprofit and community-based organizations, academic institutions, government agencies, school districts, faith-based institutions, and more.	
	Benefits	Career Advancement	
		Power and Wealth	Social, Environmental, Community, and Economic Justice
THE ENTREPRENEURIAL MINDSET	Pursuit	**3. ENTREPRENEURSHIP**	**4. SOCIAL ENTREPRENEURSHIP**
	Definition	Applying the entrepreneurial mindset to create and grow a new organization.	
	Context	New ventures such as lifestyle ventures, growth ventures, civic/community ventures, and social ventures.	
	Benefits	Career Autonomy	
		Wealth and Power	Social, Environmental, Community, and Economic Justice

TABLE 3

THE BENEFITS OF INTRAPRENEURSHIP

The personal benefits of intrapreneurship include career advancement, wealth, and power. For example, nowadays, corporate executives can wield a tremendous amount of power as they shepherd vast multinational resources, and they can amass significant personal wealth through their salary, bonuses, stock options, and other forms of compensation. Several of the action steps we discuss in Strategic

Action 7: Think and Act Like an Intrapreneur can help you to reap these rewards by tying together several previous action steps in the areas of career management (Strategic Action 3), networking and power (Strategic Action 4), mentoring and sponsorship (Strategic Action 5), and leveraging resources (Strategic Action 6).

THE BENEFITS OF SOCIAL INTRAPRENEURSHIP

By contrast, the organizational/community benefits of social intrapreneurship are perhaps not as obvious. Playing an active, socially intrapreneurial role in your organization means ensuring that your organization makes investments to achieve greater social, environmental, community, and economic justice. By directing or redirecting institutional resources in this way, communities and their stakeholders become stronger as a result of your effort. These community benefits can be realized in many ways including volunteerism, monetary and product donations, in-kind contributions, sponsorships, and pro bono assistance.

The organizational benefits of social intrapreneurship are reflected in the fact that when a social investment is made, your organization can realize a range of benefits, such as the acquisition of better talent, the capacity to leverage diversity, the development of stronger suppliers, and the cultivation of untapped markets. Your efforts to realize these benefits can also help advance your career. In Strategic Action 7: Think and Act Like an Intrapreneur, we will discuss how your organization can achieve these and other competitive advantages as a result of your socially intrapreneurial actions.

THE BENEFITS OF ENTREPRENEURSHIP

People pursue entrepreneurship for many different reasons, but the most common ones are the personal benefits of autonomy and the potential to generate personal wealth and power. Entrepreneurs are often widely recognized, influential, and wealthy. By moving from a corporate career or any other job working for other people, you gain autonomy. New entrepreneurs expect to direct their own plans, make their own hours, and have no bosses telling them what to do. For the most part, this is what happens, although our experience is that you go from having one boss to having several bosses: your customers! But, above all, you will hopefully be doing something that you love and are very passionate about so it will never feel like work.

"You know you are on the road to success if you would do your job and not be paid for it."

—Oprah Winfrey

Regardless of whether you aspire to own a business or not, in Strategic Action 8: Think and Act Like an Entrepreneur, we will present ways to embody the spirit of entrepreneurship for employees, new entrants to the job market, and entrepreneurs alike. We will also present the range of entrepreneurial ventures that can supplement your lifestyle or lead to significant wealth creation and action steps to help grow these ventures. Strategic Action 8: Think and Act Like an Entrepreneur in Level III, and Strategic Action 9: Transform Systems in Level IV, will profile entrepreneurs who have created multimillion- and multibillion-dollar business enterprises.

THE BENEFITS OF SOCIAL ENTREPRENEURSHIP

The organizations established by social entrepreneurs have the ability to promote social, environmental, community, and economic justice by creating jobs, ensuring safe drinking water, enacting police reforms, closing the racial wealth gap, and much more. We should also mention at this point that the legal form of your organization (for profit or nonprofit) does not matter for our conception of entrepreneurship. In Strategic Action 8, we will present the range of socially entrepreneurial ventures, including for-profit and nonprofit civic ventures, community ventures, and social ventures. In Strategic Actions 8 and 9, we will profile organizations being led by social entrepreneurs that are making a significant impact locally, nationally, and globally.

A Two-Pronged Approach for Collaborative Action

The strategies presented in the next two chapters are framed within the context of our five guiding principles for intrapreneurial and entrepreneurial collaborative action. They are captured by the acronym V.O.I.C.E., which stands for Vision, Opportunities, Innovation, Capital, and Entrepreneurial Networks, as shown in figure 13. As you will see throughout Level III: Collaborative Action, these five principles apply to both an intrapreneurial and entrepreneurial approach, but in different ways.

Vision
Opportunity
Innovation
Capital
Entrepreneurial Networks

FIGURE 13

In Strategic Action 7: Think and Act Like an Intrapreneur, we explain more fully the intrapreneurial approach—"your inside V.O.I.C.E."—followed by action steps for you to transform established organizations. In Strategic Action 8: Think and Act Like an Entrepreneur, we expand upon the entrepreneurial approach—"your outside V.O.I.C.E."—and provide action steps for you to create transformative new organizations. Suffice it to say that finding your V.O.I.C.E. is a central theme throughout Level III: Collaborative Action. In Level IV: Amplified Action, we describe how these two approaches can and should work together in harmony to achieve both social and economic impact.

Think and Act
Like an Intrapreneur

And even after you so-called have 'made it,'
it's still a fight every single day.
—VIOLA DAVIS,
award-winning actress and producer

When we consider the careers of the successful Black faces in high places, one thing is clear—they have been superb intrapreneurs. They have navigated the various levels of their organization to reach the top and create value inside and outside their organization. They have been clear about where they wanted to go and sought, seen, and seized new opportunities, created innovative teams and initiatives, understood the value of all forms of capital, and leveraged their connections for professional and organizational goals. Ken Chenault, the former CEO of American Express, related a similar sentiment in an interview:

> You can't remain alone in your discipline. What you've got to understand is how things interrelate. What are the connections? And then what are the relevant value drivers for your business? The ability to take in a broad set of facts and knowledge and to see what the connection is to your particular business is critical.
>
> That means that at the end of the day awareness of what is going on in the world and trends and constantly saying, "What does this development mean for my business and my customer?" Because at the end of the day, if you want to be a market leader and innovate, you actually have to come to conclusions that most people don't. And most people don't because they take a conventional view of what they're working on. So, that ability to connect is critical.[1]

For this chapter, we identify relevant commonalities in the career lessons of Black CEOs such as Ursula Burns and Ken Chenault; private foundation presidents such as Lisa Hamilton and Darren Walker; nonprofit executive directors such as Angela Glover Blackwell and Geoffrey Canada; and other Black leaders who made it to the top of their organization, industry, or field. They have been indelible Black intrapreneurs often leading their companies and organizations through challenging times to achieve success.

The Five Principles of Intrapreneurship: Your Inside V.O.I.C.E.

This brings us back to what these accomplished Black intrapreneurs have in common. Intrapreneurship is the first side of the two-sided approach to collaborative action (the second side is entrepreneurship, which we will discuss in Strategic Action 8: Think and Act Like an Entrepreneur). An intrapreneurial approach involves working from "within the system" to change the system for the better and is guided by the following five principles for action:

Vision
Opportunity
Innovation
Capital
Entrepreneurial Networks

VISION: DEVELOP A VISION FOR YOUR PERSONAL LIFE AND PROFESSIONAL CAREER

First and foremost, you must have a vision for what it is you want to achieve in your personal life and professional career. As it has been said, "Without vision, the people perish!"

In Strategic Action 1, we discussed the importance of identifying your mission, vision, and values. In Strategic Action 6, we talked about mission, vision, and values as "governing ideas" for great institutions. We believe they are equally important to great people. Developing your personal mission, vision, and values is fundamental to the intrapreneurship approach because your personal, governing ideas must be in harmony with the governing ideas of your organization. Actively seek employers and prospective employers that offer a natural fit. As you go forward, remember:

- Vision is the picture of the future you seek to create.
- Mission answers the question, "Why do I exist?"

- Values are the actions you take along the path of achieving your vision.

OPPORTUNITY: SEIZE EVERY OPPORTUNITY FOR GROWTH AND DEVELOPMENT

Opportunity is the centerpiece of intrapreneurship. To take advantage of opportunities for growth and development you must push yourself beyond your comfort zone. In Strategic Action 2: Value Exploration, we discussed pushing past your comfort zone and gaining broad exposure. For the intrapreneur, this means

- doing things differently,
- trying new things,
- bridging network gaps by connecting disconnected parts of the organization, and
- actively seeking opportunities for advancement and development.

We should also note that sometimes opportunities arise that allow you to help others. When you are on your way to the top, you do not shy away from opportunities to help others. Not only is it the right thing to do, but using these opportunities to help others will build your social capital (as discussed in Strategic Action 4: Network and Build Power).

INNOVATION: RECOGNIZE THE IMPORTANCE OF PERSONAL, PROFESSIONAL, AND MARKET TRANSFORMING INNOVATION

Innovation leads to transformation. The intrapreneur recognizes that innovation is critical and is willing to change the status quo. Previously we talked about personal innovation and moving beyond your comfort zone (Strategic Action 2). On a professional level, intrapreneurs take those same principles and apply them to how they approach their role in their organization. It means taking risks and being willing to do the unexpected. Those unexpected actions can transform the marketplace and society. The intrapreneur should

* assess where to make a difference,
* look for opportunities for disruptive or transformative change, and
* challenge your organization to do things differently.

Just sixteen months after joining the McNeil Nutritionals division at Johnson & Johnson, Debra Sandler took a bet on a new no/low-calorie sweetener called Splenda when other executives weren't so sure it was a good investment. Since then, the little yellow packets have taken a prominent place on kitchen tables and in restaurants next to Equal and Sweet'N Low, not to mention countless products that have Splenda as an ingredient. Sandler figured the sweetener, which measures and bakes like sugar, would appeal to diabetics—and marketed it to them first. The word of a sweetener that tasted and behaved more like sugar swept through the diabetic community helping Sandler introduce the product into grocery stores and restaurants and niche food and beverage makers like Atkins Nutritionals. Sandler boldly pushed McNeil past its comfort zone, and today Splenda is the number one no/low-calorie sweetener on the market.

But Sandler's bet on Splenda has resulted in more than just profits for McNeil. The sweetener gives diabetics and dieters a tool to help manage their health, and it could be argued that successful blood sugar management helps keep down health care costs—a transformative societal benefit.

CAPITAL: INVEST ALL FORMS OF CAPITAL

As we pointed out earlier in the book, people often think of money when they think of capital. Intrapreneurs recognize that there are five forms of capital—financial, human, social, intellectual, and cultural capital—and leverage all of them. Angela Glover Blackwell did exactly this when she leveraged human capital (what she learned), social capital (the people she met), and financial capital (money from foundations) to launch PolicyLink. "I recognized we needed a new kind of policy organization," she said, "and so from Rockefeller, Ford, and others I got resources to start PolicyLink. . . . [It] includes advocacy, which I learned at the public interest law firm. It includes community building, which I learned at Urban Strategies, it is infused with the respect for community, which I learned as a community organizer, and it understands how to do that in negotiation with partnership and philanthropy, which I learned at the Rockefeller Foundation. . . . It has been a remarkably successful endeavor."

ENTREPRENEURIAL NETWORKS: LEVERAGE YOUR CONNECTIONS

Entrepreneurial networks or connections between people exist within any organization. The intrapreneur's entrepreneurial network should cut across departmental, divisional, ethnic, geographic, and international boundaries.

Intrapreneurs that successfully leverage connections

- cross organizational boundaries to get things done,
- unite disconnected parts of their organization by bridging network gaps, and
- serve as a broker or go-between for disparate entities.

While at PepsiCo, Lawrence Jackson was well aware of the value of entrepreneurial networks. When he headed up manufacturing, distribution, and technical services, he worked with people at all levels, including managers, production line workers, and truck drivers, and was responsible for leveraging their abilities, building team cohesion, and cultivating new ideas. At the time, Pepsi was number two to Coca-Cola, and the culture was focused on outperforming its biggest rival. Doing well meant getting thousands of people at all levels to move in the same direction.

"Though you have differences of opinion and you have different incomes—you may have different points of view and different sports teams you like, but at the end of the day as long as they feel you're a real person and you're honest and trustworthy and you really care about them winning, they care about winning themselves," Jackson says. "I was fortunate to be in jobs most of my life where my results weren't dependent on me; they were dependent on thousands of other people doing well."

Becoming a Black Intrapreneur

We meet many Black professionals when we speak to audiences at organizations, universities, and corporations. Most of them are energized by what we say because our workshops and programs operate from this perspective: if Black professionals can learn how to navigate the organization, more of us can rise to the top. This requires making some strategic moves early in one's career that will set you up for success later in your career. The fact is, we need more Black intrapreneurs thinking strategically about their career, leadership, and community transformation so that they can reach the top and stay there.

But what if you get near the top of the organization and see that the very top slot is not going to be yours? At that point you have some critical decision to make. Do you stay or do you go? Angela Glover Blackwell was faced with this dilemma when, as a senior vice president at the Rockefeller Foundation, she was passed over for the presidency. It was then that she left Rockefeller and started PolicyLink. She exercised her right to leave Rockefeller and leveraged her talents, connections, and resources into one of the most influential social policy innovation organizations in the country. (It was only appropriate that Rockefeller was one of the founding investors in PolicyLink.) The lesson is this: Black intrapreneurs must know their value and know that their talents are useful beyond one organization. To play the game at this high level, you must learn the lessons from those that have mastered the game. In the next section, we offer three action steps for intrapreneurship.

Independent and Interdependent Action Steps for Intrapreneurship

We have repeatedly referenced the work of Thomas and Gabarro in *Breaking Through: The Making of Minority Executives in Corporate America* in the previous chapters. The following is a brief summary of the key takeaways both within and across all three career stages—"Breaking In," "Breaking Away," and "Breaking Through"—that separate minorities who plateau ("minority managers") from minorities who reach the top ("minority executives").

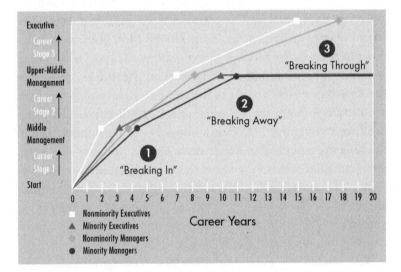

CAREER STAGE 1: "BREAKING IN"

Career Stage 1: "Breaking In" for minority executives represents a period of deepening technical/functional knowledge (such as engineering, accounting, marketing/sales) and fewer departmental changes, lateral moves, and even promotions when compared to minority managers (0.7 average promotions for minority executives compared to 1.9 for minority managers); overlapping and redundant relationships and early mentorship from a nonexecutive (90 percent of minority executives had a mentor within the first three years) both to provide grounding and credibility within a technical/functional area and/or team; and mentoring of subordinates. Black intrapreneurs know the importance of having a network of relationships and mentors. Every one of the Black professionals that we interviewed for this book told us about how important mentors were to their success.

For example, James H. Lowry, the first African American consultant for global consulting firm McKinsey & Company, and senior adviser at the Boston Consulting Group, says, "I deeply appreciated the men and women of all colors, religions, and ethnic backgrounds who mentored me. Thus, throughout my career, I felt a strong obligation to help those coming behind me. Deep down, I have felt a moral responsibility to teach, coach, mentor, and invest in the next generation. Because the stronger and more enlightened the next generation is, the stronger America will be."

Memberships and participation in company-specific and industry-wide organizations also provide networking opportunities with others who are potential mentors, sources of information, and other resources. Black intrapreneurs need the right connections and mentors in the right place at the right time.

CAREER STAGE 2: "BREAKING AWAY"

Career Stage 2: "Breaking Away" for minority executives is characterized by moving beyond deep technical/functional knowledge to developing broad managerial skills and judgment and relationships that span organizational boundaries (such as multiple departments, divisions, offices, locations, and so on).

Cynthia "Cynt" Marshall offers a strong example of breaking away. Marshall developed a very broad set of skills and relationships at AT&T, including positions as far-reaching as operations, network engineering and planning, regulatory/external affairs, human resources, and diversity, equity, and inclusion. The expertise, reputation, and visibility she garnered across her thirty-six-year career caught the attention of Mark Cuban, owner of the National Basketball Association's Dallas Mavericks, in the wake of a scathing report that outlined a culture of sexual harassment against women within the organization. One year after retiring from AT&T in 2017, Marshall became the Mavericks CEO and first African American woman CEO of an NBA team. She has implemented a number of initiatives to transform the Mavericks' culture to be more inclusive, as well as broader initiatives, such as Mavs Take ACTION, which Marshall describes as "a holistic approach to addressing inequities and disparities."

Lisa Hamilton's career followed a similar trajectory in becoming the first woman and first person of color to lead the Annie E. Casey Foundation (AECF). Across her fourteen-year career at United Parcel Service (UPS), Hamilton assumed positions as diverse as corporate tax, package delivery, supply chain management, volunteer programs, and public relations. She was eventually named president of the UPS Foundation and worked alongside then senior vice president of AECF Patrick McCarthy. (Both the UPS Foundation and the Annie E. Casey Foundation were established by UPS founder James E. Casey.) After McCarthy was named president and CEO of AECF in 2010, he hired Hamilton in 2011 as vice president of external affairs. He later promoted her to executive vice president and chief program officer in 2017, en route to Hamilton being named his successor in 2019. In reflecting on her historic appointment to this post, Hamilton said, "I appreciate that my appointment, to many people, symbolizes a reflection of the country.... I represent all those millions of kids in families of color who are looking for a brighter future, and I hold that responsibility very close to my heart."

Career Stage 2 also reflects new and more powerful mentor/sponsor relationships that provide greater visibility and access to opportunities resulting from borrowed (hierarchical) networks stemming from relationships established in Career Stage 1. "It is no surprise that two of those former CEOs who were [at the highest levels of corporate America], Ursula Burns and Ken Chenault, were at American

Express and Xerox, and Vernon Jordan [a prominent Black business executive and one of the most sought-after corporate board directors in America] was their sponsor. As Dick [Parsons, former chairman of Citigroup and former chairman and CEO of Time Warner] says, as he knows so well, you must have sponsors and you must have white sponsors, white people, white men especially, willing to champion your cause, and we do not see enough of that in corporate America," said Darren Walker, president of the Ford Foundation, which is the third-largest private foundation in the United States.

CAREER STAGE 3: "BREAKING THROUGH"

Career Stage 3: "Breaking Through" for minority executives is characterized by stretch and strategic broadening assignments such as task forces, special projects, and provisional assignments; high-consequence/visibility assignments and/or successful assignments with objective measures of success such as a successful product/service launch, a turnaround of a failing line of business or operation, and improved sales. According to Thomas and Gabarro, "A promotion to executive level often requires one or more widely visible and high-impact achievements which serve to distinguish the individual from the many other qualified candidates."

For example, when Ken Chenault took over American Express Travel Related Services in the 1990s, they were losing money. In an interview on *60 Minutes* he said, "They were losing money, and I really was able to put together a team and figure out how to motivate people to do things that they didn't think were possible. And we went from $100 million and losing money to over $700 million in sales, and it was one of the most formative experiences of my career."[2] This success gave him visibility and propelled him up the ladder.

During Career Stage 3, minority executives' networks are characterized by interorganizational ties to other minorities and nonminorities (more numerous than minority managers) and senior-level mentor/sponsor relationships. In fact, not only did minority executives form more developmental relationships on average than both minority managers and white executives across all three career stages, but it was in Career Stage 3 that they formed their highest average number of developmental relationships (2.5) when compared to Career Stages 2 and 1 (2.3 and 1.8, respectively).

ACROSS ALL CAREER STAGES

Across all three career stages, minority executives demonstrated a commitment to excellence and love for their work (that is, passion) (Strategic Action 3); had more diverse and heterogeneous networks (Strategic Action 4) when compared to minority managers who tended to have more homogenous (that is, predominantly Black or predominantly white) networks; had diverse mentors (Strategic Action 5), formal involvement in "partnerships for change," such as affinity groups, employee resource groups, and business resource groups; and informal "minority activism" efforts to advocate for change (Strategic Action 6). A summary of the lessons learned both within and across all three career stages can be found in table 4.

SUMMARY OF KEY STRATEGIC LESSONS
FOR INTRAPRENEURS BY CAREER STAGE

	CAREER STAGE		
	1	2	3
STRATEGIC ACTION 3	"BREAKING IN"	"BREAKING AWAY"	"BREAKING THROUGH"
DEVELOP SELF-MASTERY AND FIND MEANING (Job Assignments and Opportunities for Development)	• Job continuity and deepening technical/ functional knowledge	• Moving beyond technical/ functional knowledge • Developing managerial skills and judgment	• Stretch and strategic broadening assignments • High consequence/ visibility assignments with success
	Commitment to Excellence • Loving the Work		

	1	2	3
STRATEGIC ACTION 4	**"BREAKING IN"**	**"BREAKING AWAY"**	**"BREAKING THROUGH"**
NETWORK AND BUILD POWER	• Dense (redundant) ties and borrowed (hierarchical) networks • Mentoring subordinates	• Spanning organizational boundaries	• Inter-organizational ties to other minorities and nonminorities
	Diverse networks (i.e. heterogenous not homogenous)		
STRATEGIC ACTION 5	**"BREAKING IN"**	**"BREAKING AWAY"**	**"BREAKING THROUGH"**
MAXIMIZE MENTORING	• Early mentors; typically not an executive	• New and more powerful mentor/sponsor relationships	• Senior-level mentor/sponsor relationships
	Diverse mentors (i.e. heterogenous not homogenous)		
STRATEGIC ACTION 6	**"BREAKING IN"**	**"BREAKING AWAY"**	**"BREAKING THROUGH"**
LEVERAGE OUR MIGHT	Partnerships for Change • Minority Activism		

TABLE 4

FIGHT, FLIGHT, FORGO, OR FRIEND

Black intrapreneurs must know that they always have agency and must use it to maintain their own self-efficacy and . . . sanity. When we meet Black professionals who experience challenges or feel as if they don't really fit in their organization, we remind them of the four Fs that summarize the eligible responses to conflict and complicated interactions:

1. *Fight*—Directly address the problem in the short term and take action to correct it.
2. *Flight*—Avoid the situation by leaving the department or organization.
3. *Forgo*—Recognize the problem or issue but take no immediate action. Commit to address it in the future.
4. *Friend*—Educate and address the problem by seeking to change the situation and "friending" the other party.

Each of these tactics has pros and cons, but just having these tactics gives you options to consider when facing challenges of navigating complex organizations.

JOINING A CORPORATE BOARD OF DIRECTORS

One of the most accomplished Black intrapreneurs of modern times was the late Vernon Jordan. He started his career as a civil rights lawyer and gradually became one of the most influential Black faces in high places, ultimately serving as an adviser to President Bill Clinton. Not only did he have influence in the halls of government, but he was also among the vanguard of Black professionals in the 1990s and early 2000s to serve on several corporate boards of directors for major companies such as American Express, Bankers Trust, Revlon, Sara Lee, Corning, Xerox, and RJR Nabisco. Two of those boards should stand out, as Vernon Jordan was on the board when Ken Chenault and Ursula Burns were hired as CEO. That is no coincidence. Jordan was instrumental in getting these companies to diversify their executive suite.

There continues to be an important need for Black faces in high places on corporate boards of directors to influence the direction, resources, and initiatives of large companies. With this great power comes great responsibility. Corporate directors have fiduciary responsibility for the decisions made as members of the board.

Here are some tips from DeForest B. Soaries Jr., who serves on several corporate boards and teaches a masterclass, "How to Become a (Paid) Corporate Director":

1. Learn as much as you can about corporate governance.
2. Conduct a comprehensive assessment of your knowledge, skills, and strengths.
3. Identify a specific category of corporate governance where you believe you can add value (such as audit, governance, compensation, strategic planning, technology, and so on).

4. Connect with people you know who are already on corporate boards.
5. Serve on nonprofit and public boards to gain relevant experience.

Becoming a Black Social Intrapreneur

An article appearing in the *Stanford Social Innovation Review* defines a social intrapreneur as "an entrepreneurial employee who develops a profitable new product, service, or business model that creates value for society and her company."

We need more Black social intrapreneurs who can navigate the internal corporate or organizational bureaucracy and bring resources to communities of color. This means using your position to bridge the network gaps inside the organization and between your organization and the community.

Pushing your employer to become more socially responsible and inclusive can make a tremendous difference for your career. You must determine your organization's or corporation's answers to the questions we pose. The answers will show where your organization or corporation may fall short and where your efforts should be focused.

We describe six action steps to help you think and act like a social intrapreneur, each of which falls into one of four categories we often use to guide corporations and organizations in their diversity, equity, and inclusion (DEI) and community investment strategies:

1. *Workforce*—includes the sourcing, recruitment, and hiring of the people who work in the organization or corporation.
2. *Workplace*—involves the organizational culture—how people treat one another; who advances and is promoted through the ranks and who is not.
3. *Marketplace*—covers activities at the intersection of the company/organization and its customers/clients,

including efforts to work more collaboratively with Black consumers, customers, clients, or other people of color.

4. *Community*—represents all of the strategic community investment, social investment, community engagement, and philanthropic activities that are directed at communities of color. Marketplace and community-related activities often yield some economic return in addition to a social return on these investments.

From our experience, most corporate and organizational DEI investments are directed at the first two categories in the list above and result in increasing the productivity and/or economic value of the company or organization.

Figure 14 depicts the six collaborative action steps for social intrapreneurship and their associated categories. For each area, we offer a question representing a litmus test for whether your organization subscribes to the social intrapreneurship paradigm of the "double

FIGURE 14

bottom line"—doing well (financial returns) and doing good (social returns)—and views diversity, equity, inclusion, and community investment as sources of competitive advantage.

Collaborative Action Steps for Social Intrapreneurship

ADVOCATE FOR DIVERSITY, EQUITY, AND INCLUSION (WORKFORCE AND WORKPLACE)

Diversity is more than an asset to be managed; it is an asset to be harnessed. Inclusion is about more than involvement; it is about empowerment. Equity ensures equal opportunity for everyone to achieve the same outcomes.

In the wake of George Floyd's murder, BCT Partners experienced a tremendous increase in the demand for our DEI products and services. That year, we secured the largest number of DEI contracts and the largest size for a DEI contract in the company's history. Organizations were literally beating down our door to help them facilitate courageous conversations, conduct a DEI assessment, develop a DEI strategic plan, deliver DEI training, and much more.

Based on our experience, a good DEI strategic plan incorporates four key components:

1. The overarching *objectives* the organization seeks to achieve
2. The quantifiable *goals* to determine if the objectives have been met
3. The *strategies* needed to fulfill each objective
4. The *measures* or metrics against which progress can be determined for each strategy

A good DEI strategic plan not only outlines what the organization seeks to accomplish but also outlines how progress will be measured. In addition to the best practices to establish DEI objectives, goals, strategies, and measures, we recommend the gold standard to include:

if a manager or executive meets or exceeds their performance measures on DEI matters, it increases their compensation.

A 2013 study by the Institute for Diversity in Health Management of 1,109 hospitals, titled "Diversity and Disparities Benchmark Survey," found that 50 percent of hospitals allocated resources to DEI, 37 percent set goals for DEI, 27 percent had a plan for DEI, and 18 percent required training on DEI, yet only 13 percent tied a portion of executive compensation to meeting DEI goals.

Facilitating widespread DEI transformation will therefore require bold leadership from social intrapreneurs who can argue the double bottom line for DEI, that is, the social case for DEI ("it is the right thing to do") and the business case for DEI ("it is a strategic imperative").

Several studies have determined the incontrovertible value of DEI to any organization, which includes winning the war for talent, strengthening customer orientation, increasing employee satisfaction, improving decision-making, fostering innovation, enhancing the organization's image, and even improving the financial bottom line. In fact, according to a study performed by McKinsey & Company of 533 companies globally, the organizations that ranked in the top quartile for ethnic diversity financially outperformed the organizations that ranked in the bottom quartile for ethnic diversity by as much as 36 percent. They also found that for every 10 percent increase in senior executive team racial and ethnic diversity, an organization can expect a 0.8 percent rise in earnings before interest and taxes. "Many successful companies regard [DEI] as a source of competitive advantage, and specifically as a key enabler of growth," according to McKinsey. Travis Montaque, one of a few Black tech CEOs in the country, said it best:

> Executives need to take an honest look at their own corporation's identity. It requires stripping away silos. In the process, business leaders should ask themselves how they can make systemic changes at the ground level that will hold everyone in the company accountable for working toward true diversity and equality.
>
> As leaders, we need to reeducate our broader employee base. We can facilitate ongoing conversations about what equity means; ensure

HR departments are well equipped to recognize microaggressions, racism, and unconscious bias; and create more opportunities for communication between departments, seniority levels, and peers. If we cultivate corporate cultures that place education and genuine conversations at the center, we can change our company blueprints. We can make space and normalize diversity.

Black social intrapreneurs should recognize their unique perspective and role in achieving competitive advantage and enabling organizational growth through DEI.

SUPPORT THE DEVELOPMENT OF UNTAPPED AND EMERGING MARKETS (MARKETPLACE)

Today, if you visit Harlem, you'll see a mix of pricey new condos and many more white faces mixed in with the Black and Brown faces who have called the neighborhood home for decades. Even as Harlem's gentrification progressed, however, not everyone was racing to gain a presence there—but it was exactly where the late Anthony Jerome Smalls of the TJX Companies wanted the company to open its next New York store. When we interviewed him, he said, "I had people here and other places say hmm, Harlem, be careful—and there is nothing scary about Harlem at all. We have been so successful in Harlem because we've carried what the people wanted, and we've hired people from the local Harlem community and the local churches to work in that store."

It's a classic example of successful socially intrapreneurial thinking achieving the double bottom line.

Traditionally, products, services, marketing, and advertising efforts have been geared specifically, if not exclusively, to tier one consumers—the hundred million people earning more than $20,000 a year.[3] But in tiers two and three, there are close to six billion people who make less than $20,000, but of course need to purchase goods and services, and who can benefit from jobs and medical coverage. Smalls took advantage of this opportunity.

But penetrating these markets effectively often requires partnering with intermediary organizations such as nonprofit organizations, trade associations, faith-based organizations, high schools, community colleges, affinity groups, and ethnic professional organizations. It is difficult if not impossible to engage residents and be genuinely embraced by the community if you don't work closely with the entities that are connected to residents and represent the community. Obtaining their buy-in and soliciting their input at a more than superficial level are critical steps to developing untapped and emerging markets.

TJX worked with forty local churches, schools, and educational programs; the Abyssinian Development Corporation led by prominent minister Rev. Calvin Butts; and the Apollo Theater to hire the 150 workers who staff the first store and will go back to the same groups to help find workers for the second. Smalls said, "Then we go away and let them run their local business. I think over time we've learned a few things about working with people because we all want the same things. [Everyone wants] the same thing. They all want their families to be taken care of. They want to be treated with dignity and respect, and they want to earn a living wage."

Smalls recognized there is considerable demand for goods and services in these emerging inner-city markets that is not being met. Domestically, retail buying power of inner-city consumers is estimated at approximately $85 billion, which is more than all of Mexico! It represents a tremendous opportunity to establish businesses in these communities, as well as to gear marketing and advertising campaigns toward these populations.

As an intrapreneur, you understand that relationships matter, and as a Black face—or a woman, a person with a disability, or a part of another group that has traditionally been a victim of the glass ceiling or hampered by the ever-changing game—you may have the insight and sensitivity that will help you gain the trust and assistance of community organizations. The demand from corporations and organizations for help from local communities is growing, and as in any supply and demand relationship, you can expect that local communities are becoming increasingly selective about with whom they do "business."

So if your corporation or organization hasn't already done so, it would serve you well to start building those relationships now.

PROMOTE ORGANIZATIONAL/CORPORATE SOCIAL RESPONSIBILITY AND PRACTICES AS A PART OF BRANDING (MARKETPLACE)

In 2001, a survey concerning global public opinion of corporations and social responsibility was performed by Environics International.[4] The results provided insight to those aspects of a corporation's social practices that matter most to the general public.

In wealthy countries such as the United States, *social responsibility makes a greater contribution to corporate reputation than brand image.* The survey asked respondents to rank the factors that influenced their overall perception of a company. The top-ranked response was the social responsibility displayed by the firm, including labor practices, business ethnics, or environmental impacts, and the second-ranked response was brand quality and reputation.

Companies that ignore social responsibility lose customers. If a company is known to display poor social and environmental practices, consumers are likely to "vote with their wallets" and punish those companies by no longer purchasing their products or services. This was found to be particularly true in North America where 42 percent of consumers punished companies for being irresponsible. In the late 1990s, athletic footwear and apparel maker Nike Inc. suffered a great deal of backlash from customers, including protests outside its flashy NikeTown stores, when reports about poor employee treatment in their contractor factories overseas made it back to the Western world.

Today, the company has made changes in an effort to satisfy its critics and periodically issues a corporate responsibility report that not only discusses its efforts to improve conditions in its contract factories, but now talks about its internal efforts to promote environmental sustainability as well as its ongoing work to improve the lives of young people and people of color across the globe.

For example, Nike ran an ad in 2017 featuring Colin Kaepernick, the NFL quarterback who sparked controversy by kneeling during the national anthem. There were consumers who cut the brand's logos off their socks or even burned their sneakers. But there were also those who purchased Nike products in support. A Quinnipiac University study cited by the *Washington Post* in September 2018 revealed that eighteen- to thirty-four-year-olds approved of Nike's decision to feature Kaepernick by a 67 to 21 percent margin. What's more, 34 percent of Millennials were more likely to purchase Nike products following the brand's campaign, according to a November 2018 survey from ROTH Capital Partners

While some critics say Nike hasn't completely solved the problems in its supply chain, the level of public scrutiny and ire has diminished considerably within certain communities, and they have regained goodwill within others.

Investors decide whether to buy or sell shares based on a company's social performance. According to a Environics International survey above, 61 percent of residents in the United States own shares in a public company. Of these, more than one in four had bought or sold shares based on a company's social performance. Naturally, the better the social performance the more likely they were to buy shares, and conversely, poorer social performance made it more likely to sell shares.

The lesson here is that brand image and organizational/corporate citizenship are inextricably linked. When you demonstrate good organizational and corporate social responsibility, consumers and stakeholders take notice, and it ultimately enhances your brand. For a nonprofit organization, branding has a direct impact on fundraising, development, and attracting volunteers; for a for-profit company, branding has a direct impact on sales. In other words, organizational/corporate citizenship is not just good for the community; it is also good for business.

ADVANCE TRUE SUPPLIER DIVERSITY
(MARKETPLACE AND COMMUNITY)

Supplier diversity is more than just maintaining a database and participating in a supplier diversity fair every year or contracting with women and minority suppliers for commodity goods—like cups, drinking water, and office supplies—and services like cleaning that are differentiated only by price. Real supplier diversity is a strategic commitment to contract goods and services that span the entire spectrum of your needs and ensuring that your minority and female suppliers are increasing their revenue.

We need more than supplier-diversity managers. We need supplier-diversity intrapreneurs. People who bridge network gaps and broker opportunities for their suppliers, and not just at their company but at other companies too. This kind of activity can ultimately benefit everyone because it builds the supplier's capacity and grows their company, making them better able to serve their clients' needs as their businesses expand.

These efforts must be positioned as strategic investments in viable markets; not investment because it is the right thing to do, but investment because it is the only thing to do in a society whose diverse populations represent a significant economic base.

If the suppliers aren't growing, then what's the point? When suppliers don't grow, wealth is not being generated, and if wealth is not being generated then there are no real, long-term benefits from supplier-diversity efforts. Instead, companies are merely contracting with unsustainable companies that will either lose money or break even, as opposed to creating institutions that can generate wealth and stand the test of time.

The last generation of supplier diversity efforts tied managers' performance to goals of between 10 percent and 20 percent of total procurement dollars—*at best*. The top companies for supplier diversity average about 22.7 percent; the top fifty average just 9.7 percent, and the national average is a mere 2 percent.[5]

Given the increasing diversity of our society, companies must increase the percentage of dollars spent with minority suppliers. Thirty percent is realistic today, and by 2050, half of dollars spent should be with minority- and women-owned firms.

To reach these goals, companies must invest in suppliers—and by invest we mean more than just maintaining a list of small-business contractors, espousing a commitment to supplier diversity on a website, attending supplier diversity fairs, or any of the things a corporation or government agency can do *before* deciding to work with a minority-owned business.

Instead, companies should take deliberate steps to invest in the capacity and the future growth of its minority business partners *after* they have engaged in a relationship with them. This includes a host of what we consider to be more progressive measures:

- Arranging a favorable payment schedule to minimize cash flow pressures on small enterprises
- Creating opportunities for minority business partners to learn some of your company's best practices
- Providing ample lead time to coordinate internal resources for a new project
- Conducting true joint marketing for new business opportunities and not just those that require a minority business partner
- Actively providing referrals to other customers
- Developing mentoring programs
- Financing receivables
- Assisting those firms in expanding globally

The firms that are willing to make these investments will see a return on that investment—in terms of the quality of the goods and services they receive through mutually beneficial, long-term relationships.

The next generation of supplier-diversity efforts must establish goals and benchmarks to ensure that diverse suppliers are not just obtaining contracts but also achieving growth by tying performance to the growth of the suppliers.

In 1993, Johnson Controls Inc. started its supplier-diversity efforts spending $2 million with seventeen suppliers. By 2006, under Reginald Layton, the company's diversity business development director, that number grew to $1.29 billion spent with Asian, Black, Hispanic, and Native American firms.

Johnson Controls put together a plan that includes monthly reviews of how much it is spending with minority suppliers; a plan that helps companies supplying one location get contracts to supply neighboring regions; mentoring programs with minority suppliers in cities including New York, Detroit, San Antonio, and Nashville; and training to increase understanding among its own employees of its minority-supplier programs.

"Supplier diversity is crucial to our continued corporate success," says Layton. "Not only do our diverse suppliers bring business expertise and a fresh perspective, thus increasing our competitiveness; they also allow us to realize cost efficiencies. In turn, our support helps to strengthen the suppliers and their local economies."

We need social intrapreneurs who facilitate connections between diverse suppliers that can lead to more than just collaborations but to strategic partnerships such as joint ventures, mergers, and acquisitions that can ultimately help their company by building the capacity of the suppliers and growing their companies (both Strategic Action 8 and 9 provide some strong examples). This is the art, not the science, of supplier diversity—it means embodying the same spirit of entrepreneurship that is embodied by the suppliers themselves. Helping your company and helping these businesses to then help your company is an effective way to strike the double bottom line. This is socially intrapreneurial thinking and community investment as a competitive advantage.

• • •

INTRAPRENEURS HELPING ENTREPRENEURS: VHA MENTORS MINORITY BUSINESSES[6]

VHA Inc. is a national health care network that provides supply chain management services and supports the formation of regional and national networks to help more than fourteen hundred member hospitals improve their clinical and economic performance. VHA's membership roster includes some of the best-known hospitals in the nation, as well as hundreds of smaller ones who provide essential care to communities across the US. VHA is working with Novation, its supply contracting company, and Spectrum Health, a member of the VHA alliance, to deepen their corporate support of supplier diversity by playing an active role in mentoring and helping grow minority businesses.

"Traditionally we've been able to identify a sufficient number of minority business enterprises for service requirements; nevertheless, it is almost unheard of to find minority suppliers in the manufacturing space who are producing finished clinical products, which is where the bulk of health care spend lies," said Christopher Baskel, former system director of Supply Chain Management at Spectrum Health. To address this issue, Spectrum Health established a mentoring relationship with two minority businesses, WJG Enterprise Molding Co., an automotive manufacturer, and Veteran Medical Products Inc.

Spectrum sought assistance from VHA's central region to mentor WJG in expanding their business model to manufacture bedside plastic products in addition to their portfolio of automotive products. Donna Clutter, director of Business Development & Marketing for VHA Central, explains, "We were in uncharted territory. We mentored WJG on everything, from the importance of trials to testing new products to establishing relationships with distributors, prescribing literature requirements, and educating their people internally."

During the process, WJG owner Bill Grice hired Ralph Jefferson as vice president to manage WJG's newly created Medical Products Division and to serve as liaison between WJG, Spectrum, VHA, and

Novation. Jefferson says, "They [Spectrum Health, VHA, and Novation] helped us understand how to do business with health care organizations. We couldn't have done it alone."

"When the first product was ready for market," Baskel says, "VHA was instrumental in reaching five states immediately through regional contracts with Novation. Discussions are already underway to take the family of products national."

Spectrum Health's success with WJG was built upon its prior success with Veteran Medical Products. Spectrum worked closely with Veteran Medical Products to expand its manufacturing operations from medical components into the finished medical products arena. "It was a huge leap for our business to go from ingredient components to finished goods," explains Veteran Medical Products owner Roosevelt Tillman. With Spectrum's assistance, Veteran Medical now manufactures several medical products that are offered on a Novation regional contract.

According to Lamont Robinson, former director of Business & Product Development at Novation and a longtime advocate of supplier diversity, "Our work with WJG and Veteran Medical Products is a shining example of a large corporation stepping up to mentor minority businesses in a way that creates a winning outcome for everyone involved. VHA has strengthened its supplier base. The minority firms have advanced their growth. And the economy has benefited through job creation as a result of our collective efforts. I expect to see more and more corporations emulating what we've accomplished by seeing the value of mentoring minority businesses."

ENGAGE THE LOCAL COMMUNITY AS A STAKEHOLDER IN REAL ESTATE AND OTHER DEVELOPMENT (COMMUNITY)

It's important to work with community developers to build new office buildings, manufacturing facilities, and warehouses, which typically constitute up to 30 percent or more of corporate assets. That's where folks like Dudley Benoit come in. When he was vice president of intermediaries lending for JPMorgan Chase's Community Development Group in New York, Benoit helped direct resources to projects in communities that otherwise may have a hard time getting funding—with an expected below market rate of return.

For more than twenty years, JPMorgan Chase has committed more than $2 billion to support financing and investments for the construction or rehabilitation of affordable housing, special-needs facilities, and commercial projects, including more than forty-one thousand units of housing for both renters and homeowners.

Benoit fused his professional interest in policy and urban development with a deeper desire to make conditions better in urban communities.

"I was born in Newark, New Jersey, so I am from the hood, from the city, and I have always had an interest in why things weren't working right [in the city]," Benoit says.

He studied policy and urban development at the University of Michigan, and in his studies zeroed in on the flow of capital out of cities. As money flowed out, many cities suffered. He continued his studies learning about tax, housing, and other public policies.

"But at the end of the day I always thought it was about capital and resources. So for me the best way to learn about capital was to go work at a bank," he says.

Benoit continues to be deeply involved in directing that capital and resources to communities of color. "I am working with organizations all around the country who are developing urban areas. That brings me full circle."

JPMorgan Chase and other banks are indeed mandated by the Community Reinvestment Act to do the kind of lending that Benoit oversaw. And while it is a requirement, we assert that some banks might only do the bare minimum in these areas if not for people like Benoit, who not only cares about the redevelopment of urban areas, but who can personally relate to the need for the work. In 2007,

JPMorgan Chase's CRA activities earned the highest possible rating from its regulators.

Doing real estate, construction, and other development activities in a way that truly benefits the company and the community means giving local residents and leaders a seat at the table. They could have a seat on redevelopment boards; provide input to site selection, zoning, or related issues; participate directly as construction workers; or simply be a part of forums and hearings to foster open dialogue. This keeps the "community" in community development.

ACHIEVE FINANCIAL AND SOCIAL RETURNS ON DOMESTIC AND GLOBAL PHILANTHROPIC INVESTMENTS (COMMUNITY)

Social investment is subtly but distinctly different than philanthropy:

- Philanthropy is giving to causes because they are worthy. Social investment is supporting causes because they are worthy *and* aligned with your strategic goals and objectives.
- Philanthropy typically involves giving money and perhaps engaging employees in volunteer efforts. Social investment creates opportunities to leverage the expertise of your organization *and* using employees, products and services, office locations, proprietary knowledge, and other resources.
- Philanthropy is charity with an expected social return on investment. Social investments are designed to meet a societal need *and* generate a financial return.
- Philanthropy is a single bottom line; social investment is a double bottom line.

A number of organizations, particularly corporations, have moved toward more strategic giving and have aligned their philanthropy in some way with their core business activities or programs. In doing so, they are creating social and economic value simultaneously.

During his tenure at American Express, Ken Chenault said, "So, for me, for our company, what I said is: 'I've got two aspirations for the company.' I want us to be one of the most successful companies in the world. [The] second aspiration [is that] I want us to be one of the most respected and admired companies in the world." Along the same lines, he also said, "Business exists because society allows us to exist. And in exchange for that permission to pursue profits, business must behave and act in ways that protect and enhance the world we live in. In other words, a business exists to serve its customers and the communities in which it operates. You can't just look at the bottom line. There is an impact on society that goes far beyond the products or jobs it creates."

Some companies are now seeking opportunities for a true financial return on investment along with the social benefit—which entails monitoring how their efforts increase sales, advance strategic goals, achieve improved outcomes, and whether they are sustainable long term. Sometimes, while doing social good, there is an immediate or eventual spillover to the financial bottom line.

Alignment with organizational goals, objectives, and proprietary resources is a critical component to creating economic value, as your organization is much more likely to achieve financial ROI when your social investments are in some way tied to your core business areas and strategic goals and objectives. Naturally, the expected rate of return on a social investment is typically not expected to rival that of a pure financial investment, but some kind of economic return is expected nonetheless.

There is nothing wrong with traditional philanthropy. We are great believers in philanthropy and its benefit to communities. But in the context of the double bottom line and community investment as a competitive advantage, true social intrapreneurs recognize that through social investment, the results once achieved through philanthropy can be multiplied and can even lead to a financial return for their organizations. With the underlying tools introduced with Strategic Actions 1 through 6, the social intrapreneur can help transform institutions to be more responsive and more responsible to the communities from which they benefit.

Think and Act
Like an Entrepreneur

The hustle that gets you there doesn't always
serve you when you're at the summit.
—LIN-MANUEL MIRANDA

Entrepreneurs make a difference in our neighborhoods, communities, and regions by building businesses that create jobs and invest in the organizations and institutions that we discussed in Strategic Action 6. However, according to a Brookings Institute analysis, "Black people comprise approximately 14.2% of the U.S. population, but Black businesses comprise only 2.2% of the nation's 5.7 million employer businesses."

Black faces in high places must be among those either starting or supporting the growth of viable Black-owned businesses. As pointed out by Andre M. Perry, senior fellow, and Carl Romer, research assistant at the Brookings Metropolitan Policy Program, strategic investments in Black businesses have an economic and social impact "for individual business owners, local communities, and the overall economy."

In fact, in a research study by Dr. Karen Parker of the University of Delaware that appeared in *Urban Affairs Review*,[1] a rise in Black business ownership in urban neighborhoods during the 1990s into the 2000s led to a decrease in youth violence in those same neighborhoods. And it wasn't a coincidence. After controlling for other possible variables (poverty, unemployment, etc.), Dr. Parker found that as the number of Black businesses rose in these neighborhoods, Black youth violence decreased. Why? Dr. Parker speculates Black businesses bring three things to a community: role models, reshaping, and resources.[2] Black entrepreneurs become role models for young people who are trying to figure out what they want to do. Black entrepreneurs cause all residents, but especially youth, to reshape their perceptions of their community. Black entrepreneurs bring resources to the community that strengthen it.

And yet, only 3 percent of Black-owned companies are making more than $1 million in revenue. Now don't get us wrong, we respect anyone who can create a business and make a go of it. But there is a difference between "lifestyle" businesses and "growth" businesses. Lifestyle businesses are businesses that people do as side hustles or to replace income that they would have in a job. We have written in our other books about how important start-up companies and being in business is for our community. From our perspective, it is the top 3 percent of companies, the growth ventures, that are positioned to make long-lasting, wealth-creation, and generational change. We want to see more multimillion-dollar and multibillion-dollar Black-owned businesses.

Tyler Perry put our modern entrepreneurial efforts into historical perspective when he said, "[Tyler Perry Studios] was once a Confederate army base, which meant that there were Confederate soldiers on that base plotting and planning for how to keep 3.9 million Negros enslaved. Now that land is owned by one Negro." To put this further into perspective, when the *Black Enterprise* BE 100s list was created in 1973, the combined revenues for the list was $473 million. In 2020, the BE 100s companies combined revenues totaled $25 billion, and these companies employed more than seven hundred thousand people. That is the power of Black-owned million-dollar and billion-dollar businesses.

In 2019, the company we cofounded, BCT Partners, made the BE 100s list for the first time at number ninety-two! We were humbled to join the list of distinguished entrepreneurs who have shown us the way. When we were in college at Rutgers University, it was the dream of our fledgling partnership to one day grow a company to high enough revenues that we would be listed on the BE 100s! It was hard work and we celebrated.

At the same time, we were disappointed that only a relatively few Black-owned, privately held companies reach a level where they are growing and expanding with revenues of more than $10 million per year. When we looked around at the top companies on the BE 100s, we wanted to know more about how companies like World Wide Technology (1), ActOne Group (2), Urban One (9), Diversant (24), IMB Development Group (42), and McKissak and McKissak (64) made it to the top and stayed there. These lessons are detailed in this chapter so you, too, can think and act like an entrepreneur and see opportunities to support entrepreneurs as you ascend to the top.

Lessons Learned from the Most Successful Black-Owned Businesses

To create a future that has more Black-owned multimillion- and multibillion-dollar companies, we must learn from the success of others. For Black entrepreneurs, we suggest three books as starting points for the journey. The first one is *Lessons from the Top: Success Strategies from America's Leading Black CEOs* by Derek Dingle. In this book, he profiles eleven legendary Black CEOs of companies that appeared for many years on the BE 100s list. Three stood out to us: John H. Johnson ("The Pioneer"), Herman J. Russell ("The Builder"), and Bob Johnson ("The Brand Builder"). And, if we were writing Dingle's book today, we would add Cathy Hughes and Oprah Winfrey to this list. Their stories teach us lessons on how successful Black businesses are important to society.

John H. Johnson, the legendary publisher of *Ebony* and *Jet* magazines, taught us about using business to uplift the image of Black America and how valuable those images can be to advertisers. Herman J. Russell taught us how to build a business empire that also supported civil rights, equality, and wealth creation. (In fact, it has been widely reported that Russell often paid for the bail of Dr. Martin Luther King Jr. and other civil rights leaders when they were jailed after protests.) Bob Johnson and Cathy Hughes taught us the value of our media companies in portraying positive images of Black people. In all of these cases, the underlying lesson of these growth businesses is to continuously innovate and seek new opportunities for growth. When they innovated, they succeeded in their markets. When they did not innovate or pursue new opportunities, each of these businesses declined and in one case (Johnson Publishing) disappeared.

Lessons Learned from the Fastest Growing and Most Successful Businesses

We also became interested in another list of companies we admire and respect: the *Inc.* magazine 500 list (the *Inc.* 500). This annual list represents the five hundred fastest growing, privately held firms in the United States. That led us to the second book, titled *The Breakthrough Company* by Keith McFarland. McFarland studied seven thousand companies that have appeared on the *Inc.* 500 list. He studied these companies systematically to gain insights into their growth, trajectory, financing, and management styles.

The major lesson of the book is that every small business that becomes a breakthrough company is able to overcome several "breakthrough dilemmas"—two are worth mentioning at this point. Breakthroughs can come from building on structural advantages as opposed to relying upon nimbleness and "smallness" to be competitive in your industry or market. Breakthrough can also come once a company decides to build a culture that empowers employees and endears customers to the products and services they provide. A final breakthrough dilemma we have experienced is finding balance between relying upon your own internal ideas and incorporating the best outside ideas.

To arrive at these and other characteristics of breakthrough companies, McFarland used a systematic approach to study the *Inc.* 500. He used the methodology of Jim Collins from his book *Good to Great: Why Some Companies Make the Leap and Others Don't*, the third book we suggest to entrepreneurs looking to reach the top and stay there. In *Good to Great*, Collins is trying to answer one fundamental question—how do *good* companies become *great* companies? As we grew BCT Partners, in the mid-2010s, we had the entire company read this book. Our most valuable lessons learned had to do with being deliberate about leadership, strategy, recruiting, and culture. Ultimately, it caused us to shift direction and make some tough decisions about mergers, acquisitions, hiring, and firing.

The Five Principles of Entrepreneurship: Your Outside V.O.I.C.E.

In Strategic Action 7, we used the acronym V.O.I.C.E.—vision, opportunity, innovation, capital, and entrepreneurial networks—to present the underlying principles of intrapreneurship and how to be entrepreneurial within an established organization (your "inside voice"). Here, again, we look to V.O.I.C.E. to frame how you should approach entrepreneurial endeavors (your "outside voice"). Again, the "inside voice" and "outside voice" represent different sides of a two-sided approach, namely, Black faces in high places working "inside the system" and "outside the system."

Vision
Opportunity
Innovation
Capital
Entrepreneurial Networks

VISION: DEVELOP A VISION FOR YOURSELF AND YOUR BUSINESS

As an entrepreneur you should have a *vision* for what kind of business venture you want to create. Are you trying to leave your job and replace your income? Are you creating a venture to follow your passion and make some extra income? Are you trying to build wealth or make a social impact or both? These are important questions for every entrepreneur to answer before making major investments of time or money. To develop your vision, you should write down the values you want to integrate into your business, the impact you want the business to have on you, your family, the community, the industry, and society. Having a vision of where you want to be will help you make strategic decisions easier because you can evaluate them based upon where you want the company to go. This is an essential first step.

OPPORTUNITY: IDENTIFY, EVALUATE, EXPLORE, AND PURSUE A VENTURE OPPORTUNITY

Opportunities are the lifeblood of the entrepreneur. Entrepreneurs must be able to *identify*, *evaluate*, *explore*, and *pursue* a venture opportunity. Ask yourself, *What is the business opportunity that I see? What market need am I seeking to address?* Remember, every idea is not a business opportunity. If you are going to spend money and time to set up a business, you should determine if a real opportunity exists. This means identifying and evaluating a business idea for its potential to generate money and/or make a social impact. Exploring a business opportunity means developing a business plan that describes how you will pursue the opportunity. Pursuing the business opportunity is where the execution takes place. How you target and address the opportunity is just as important as the planning. How you go about executing your plan will determine your success.

INNOVATION: CULTIVATE, MANAGE, AND PROTECT INNOVATION

Entrepreneurship is about *innovation*. Innovation takes a business into new and different directions—new markets, new industries, new applications, and so on. Many argue that this is the most important aspect of a new venture, because without it you will have a difficult time distinguishing what you do from the competition. To establish and maintain a competitive edge, entrepreneurs must be innovative. They must be able to cultivate, manage, and protect innovation and innovative practices. But don't think that the only way to be innovative is to create new products or technology. The design consultants at Doblin (a Deloitte Company) write about ten types of innovation when it comes to business. The list includes innovations in business models (profit model, network, structure, and process), product offering (product system, product performance), and experience (customer engagement, brand, channel, and service).[3] Uber, Calendly, and SoFi are examples of companies that don't make anything but are innovative in their approaches to customers and business models. When you think about innovation, remember that there are many ways to be innovative in entrepreneurship. Creative approaches to business issues are also innovative. Without innovation, the potential for growth is limited because there is little to differentiate you from the pack.

Innovation in your business may be the unique way that you put the components of your business together, or the exact combination of services or locations that you offer.

———

God created you with creativity

so you could be creative in your creation.

—Bishop George C. Searight Sr.,

senior pastor at Abundant Life Family Worship

Church, New Brunswick, New Jersey

———

CAPITAL: INVEST ALL FORMS OF CAPITAL

As mentioned previously, capital is anything that can be acquired, exchanged, converted, or invested. All five forms of capital have an important role to play within an emerging business venture. You will need

1. *Financial capital,* meaning money that you have, acquire, or borrow, in order to launch and grow your business;
2. *Human capital*, meaning the skill, training, education, and experience that you bring to a venture;
3. *Social capital,* meaning the collection of meaningful relationships that you and your team have;
4. *Cultural capital,* meaning the knowledge of cultural norms and values, and the social resources that you have cultivated; and last
5. *Intellectual capital,* meaning the capital that resides in your teams of people and is often the source of innovation and intellectual property.

It is important for those engaging in entrepreneurial ventures to consider how each of these forms of capital has value—and to leverage all of them—when building a business.

ENTREPRENEURIAL NETWORKS: LEVERAGE ENTREPRENEURIAL NETWORKS

Entrepreneurial networks connect people within and between organizations. Entrepreneurs must leverage their personal, professional, and organizational networks to be successful because they connect entrepreneurs to capital, innovation, and opportunities. As we discussed in Strategic Action 4: Network and Build Power, you must make sure that you work for your network and your network works for you. Entrepreneurs leverage their networks toward gathering resources and opportunities for their ventures.

We talked extensively about working with others in Strategic Action 6: Leverage Our Might, but we cannot emphasize this enough. The benefits of having a team include:

- Leveraging more than just your own capital (human, social, financial, cultural)
- Having more hands to do the work
- A higher survival rate than companies with one person[4]

We should note that your team is not always inside your organization. Sometimes, you will need partners outside of your company to be part of your team to get large projects done. Your network of professional advisers is critical for your businesses. Lawyers, accountants, financial advisers, human resource specialists, and others should be part of your team.

But there are challenges to having a team:

- If the new venture was your idea, you must make sure that everyone is on board with your vision.

- Many entrepreneurs tend to micromanage their team. You must be willing to delegate and give others on the team some autonomy.
- Leadership and management skills are critical when you have a team working with you. We know many innovative entrepreneurs who were horrible managers and didn't know how to lead their companies.

If you want to create high-growth ventures, you must be able to work with a team.

Independent and Interdependent Action Steps for Launching Businesses and Social Ventures

DEVELOP A SOLID BUSINESS MODEL AND PLAN

Every entrepreneur should know the answers to these questions: How does your venture operate? How does it create the products or provide the services? What are the sources of revenue and income? What is the cost structure? The answers to these questions are critical to your new venture. Without good answers to these questions, your business will not achieve its potential. We have found the Business Model Canvas (www.strategyzer.com/canvas) to be an effective tool for mapping, interrogating, and pivoting your business model. To get some assistance with business planning, you can contact your local SBA, SCORE, SBDC, or the entrepreneurship program of a nearby college or university.

MANAGE BUSINESS OPERATIONS AND GROWTH

Once you have established your business, it is important to manage the operations and growth of the business. We reveal several action steps for growing your company in this chapter. But many companies neglect to work on the processes that will make their companies better. It is important to establish strong administrative, operations, and financial processes. In some cases, it may be necessary to have professionals from a business incubator program or coworking space to assist you on this. For example, BCT benefited tremendously from the full range of new business services offered by New Jersey Institute of Technology's VentureLink business incubator, including office space and start-up support within a community of entrepreneurs.

Collaborative Action Steps for Growing Businesses and Social Enterprises

Not everyone desires or is able to create a multimillion-dollar business enterprise or social enterprise. Once again, vision is important here. But if you are a Black entrepreneur who seeks to create an *enterprise*—a *business enterprise* (for a profit) that creates intergenerational wealth or a *social enterprise* (for a purpose) that makes a profit and makes a lasting difference in society—then you should concern yourself with whether your venture is on the trajectory to achieving this goal. Often, the greatest challenge for organizations that want to make the leap from a small business to a business enterprise, or a small organization to a social enterprise, is to overcome challenges in three categories:

1. *Money* goes back to the idea of financial capital. Your organization needs financial capital to grow and expand. Investors want to put money into organizations that want to grow. In the for-profit arena, it is often the growth-oriented types of business enterprises that have the best chance of attracting bank financing or angel investors—wealthy individuals who are interested in investing in start-up companies, inventions, and businesses that are early in their growth life cycle. In the for-purpose arena, it is often the growth-oriented types of social enterprises that have the best chance of attracting investors such as government, foundations, corporate philanthropy, and individual donors.

2. *Marketing* is a big challenge for businesses. It is similarly important for social purpose organizations to increase awareness of their work and accomplishments, particularly to the stakeholders whom the organization depends on for support. You may have the best product or service available, or do the best work, but if no one knows anything about it, your growth will be limited. Marketing challenges include branding your image, positioning your product/service in the marketplace, pricing, and promoting your business or organization to the right people at the right time so that they will support you.

3. *Management* is critical. You really have to know how to get people to work for you and with you to maintain effective and efficient operations, whether it is a business enterprise or social enterprise. Having the right team is paramount.

Money, marketing, and management are among the core challenges that limit a company's ability to transition from a small business to a business enterprise or from a small organization to a social

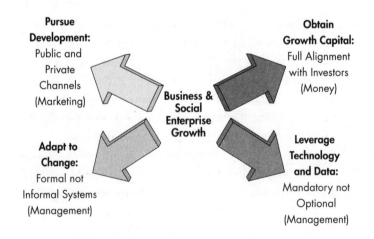

FIGURE 15

enterprise. Next, we present action steps that are core to both business enterprises and social enterprises in the areas of *money, marketing,* and *management,* as shown in figure 15. They are followed by game-changing strategies that are specific to each type of enterprise.

OBTAIN FULL ALIGNMENT WITH GROWTH CAPITAL INVESTORS (*MONEY*)

Obtaining growth capital is an important strategy for entrepreneurial ventures because launching new products or services, expanding operations, purchasing new equipment, and opening new locations require money. Knowing where to find the financial and other capital that is necessary to make these moves is critical if you are going to grow and reach scale.

Full alignment means that you and your investors are on the same page with respect to your vision for your venture and how their resources will be used to get you there. More specifically, you must think carefully about the *sources* and the *uses* of investment money. For growth ventures, with respect to sources, you want investors with specific expertise in your industry. With respect to uses, you want to reach an agreement concerning your business plan and the returns on investment you can realistically deliver. For social ventures, with respect to sources, you want to align yourself not only with investors who are familiar with your work but, in the case of corporate supporters, who have a positive reputation that complements yours. A social venture to reduce lung cancer probably shouldn't accept investment from a cigarette company because cigarettes can lead to lung cancer!

Generally speaking, the sources of growth capital for business enterprises include debt lenders and equity investors such as family, friends, angels, private equity firms, and venture capitalists. Sources of growth capital for social enterprises include debt lenders and social venture philanthropists, including social venture capitalists, community development venture capitalists, individual investors, and social venture funds.

Are You Ready for Growth Capital?

Obviously, not every organization, company, or entrepreneur is ready for an investment of growth capital. Here is how you know you are ready:

You have a solid business plan. The first thing a potential investor or bank loan officer will ask you for is a business plan. Lenders and investors in for-profits want to know how the business will make money, grow its operations, and repay the loan or generate a financial return on investment. They want to understand the financial outlook and how you will attract customers. Lenders and investors in nonprofits want to know how the organization will utilize the money to build capacity and generate a social return on investment (and, if applicable, repay the loan). If you don't have this document, you will not be taken seriously.

You are clear about your vision for your venture. Is your vision for the venture accurately reflected in your business plan? It is important for you to know what your vision is for the venture. This may change over time, so it is wise to revisit it periodically to see where you stand. Your vision for growth should align with an investor's in order to maximize the potential for all parties.

You have a strategy for growth. Within and beyond your business plan, do you have, and can you articulate, a strategy for growing your company? Are you clear about how you will spend the financial capital? These are key questions because it must be explained to lenders and investors. They'll want to know if you are going to use the funds to buy new inventory, develop a new product, expand service delivery, or purchase more plant, property, or equipment. Each of these may be a way of expanding capacity, but they each have different implications for growth.

You've thought about an exit strategy. An exit strategy is a formal way of thinking about what you ultimately want to do with your venture. If you are a for-profit, do you want to sell your company in the short term or will you try to keep this company as a family business that is passed on to the next generation? If you are a nonprofit, are there alternative sources of revenue or financing that exist or can be cultivated to support your organization into the future? The answer here can help you determine the type or the source of investment you should pursue.

We encourage you to obtain growth capital for your business or social enterprise. If you use debt, you should realize that there may be a limit to what you can borrow. As long as you make your payments to the bank, they will leave you alone. One of the major benefits of having an equity investor or a social venture philanthropist, as opposed to a bank loan, is that you gain more than the financial capital. The best investor is one that actually can help you grow your venture. They should have contacts or expertise or perhaps both. This is another dimension of what we mean by your investors having full alignment with your vision for the company. The right equity investor will bring more than money (often referred to as "smart money").

Eden Organix was an eco-conscious beauty store and spa founded by Robinson and his wife, Valerie, in 2008. The long-term goal was to create a business enterprise with multiple locations and create a recognizable brand for eco-conscious beauty products. Start-up costs for doing the construction of the leased space, buying equipment and supplies, and all the other costs were more than $170,000. In order to open the doors, Dr. Robinson and Valerie applied for a government-backed Small Business Administration loan through local banks, used money they saved up, and raised money from family and friends including Dr. Pinkett. The next step would be to open a second location, and that would require more funds. To go to that next step, Dr. Robinson and Valerie could go back to the same people who invested the first time, identify other investors, or take on more debt. With the long-term goal to create a business enterprise, it makes sense to meet and court investors who have interest in eco-conscious companies. Unfortunately, Eden Organix didn't make it that far. Valerie and Dr. Robinson weren't making any money with the business and decided to close it down in 2015.

The illusion is that any money is good money. The reality is that you only want money from investors who are fully aligned with your vision for growth.

LEVERAGE TECHNOLOGY AND DATA:
MANDATORY NOT OPTIONAL (*MANAGEMENT*)

It is nothing short of amazing when you consider how technology has and continues to transform our society, from mobile devices to social media to virtual reality/augmented reality. Moreover, the emergence of big data, machine learning, and artificial intelligence has opened up new possibilities that were once considered science fiction. Along these lines, any business or social enterprise must embrace technology and data as integral, strategic, mandatory tools for conducting business in the twenty-first century, not optional ones.

As it applies to your venture, this could include using technology and data to enable your company to manage customer relationships; finance and accounting; electronic communications; enterprise resource planning; supply chain management; marketing and advertising; knowledge management; and sales force automation.

Technology and data cannot be regarded as a necessary evil or even as an optional investment to build business and social enterprises. They must be regarded as mandatory. Even a modest, but appropriate, investment in technology and data capabilities can help your company increase revenue and achieve cost savings that enable you to compete with much larger entities. BCT uses technology to manage our accounting, timekeeping, calendars, and communications. Online tools allow us to host virtual meetings and perform demonstrations remotely, which lightens our travel budget. We also use web-based customer relationship management tools to track and manage sales leads, which helps us to capitalize on business opportunities. We leverage descriptive, predictive, prescriptive data analytics, and our proprietary Precision Analytics, to deliver value to our customers.

The illusion is that technology and data are optional. The reality is that they are mandatory, especially to become a business or social enterprise.

ADAPT TO CHANGE: FORMAL NOT INFORMAL SYSTEMS (*MANAGEMENT*)

The only thing constant is change, and the only thing you can count on is change and more change. Society is evolving rapidly and so is the landscape for private and nonprofit organizations. Along these lines, growth ventures, civic ventures, community ventures, and social ventures on the path to becoming enterprises must have an ongoing, systematic mechanism for tracking market trends and forecasts within their industry and adapting their organization to respond to these changes. This doesn't have to be anything elaborate, but it does have to be formal and deliberate, not informal and happenstance.

This could involve any of the following tactics performed on a regular and ongoing basis: attending conferences in your industry; subscribing to trade publications and industry reports; conducting informational interviews with academics or other thought leaders; conducting an environmental scan or SWOT (strengths, weaknesses, opportunities, and threats) analysis; revisiting your company's strategic plan; or simply searching the internet for the latest information. Above all, it must involve some form of *succession planning*, or planning for changes in leadership, by clearly defining roles and responsibilities and cultivating new leaders.

At BCT, we constantly adjust to the realities of the marketplace by encouraging intellectual curiosity and continuous learning for our staff; reassigning or shifting roles and responsibilities; and modifying the organization's structure as needed. As one way of promoting organizational learning at BCT Partners, we have held what we call a "Knowledge Review," which is essentially an opportunity to discuss current issues and trends, their impact on the company, and what the company must do to adapt to those changes.

In his number one bestselling book, *Who Moved My Cheese?*, author Spencer Johnson artfully uses the story of four mice to make clear the following basic principles for effectively dealing with change: (1) accept that change happens, (2) anticipate change, (3) monitor change, and (4) adapt to change quickly. The illusion is that you can survive by simply adapting to changes as they present themselves. The reality is that organizations that fail to regularly reevaluate their position in the marketplace are organizations that fail.

PURSUE BUSINESS DEVELOPMENT OR FUNDRAISING AND DEVELOPMENT: PUBLIC AND PRIVATE CHANNELS (*MARKETING*)

In many cases, relationships aren't everything; they are the only thing. Organizations that want to grow, however, must leverage existing relationships while constantly exploring ways to establish new ones. Therefore, revenue-generating opportunities are best cultivated through both what we refer to as *private channels* (the "back door" of existing relationships) and *public channels* (the "front door" of marketing to the general public).

For entrepreneurs who seek to create business enterprises, revenue-generating opportunities specifically refers to your business development, marketing, and sales efforts to secure customers and contracts. For social entrepreneurs who seek to create social enterprises, it specifically refers to your branding, marketing, awareness, and fundraising efforts to secure grants and donors, and other development activities to secure volunteers and in-kind contributors.

Public channels and the "front door" refer to opportunity channels that are publicly available to everyone such as cold calling, attending conferences or opportunity fairs, subscribing to mailing lists, registering at informational websites, conducting marketing and advertising campaigns, and publishing an organizational brochure or website. If your products and services are highly differentiated and your competitive advantage is significant, you can be reasonably effective when you go through the front door. For example, if you have an advanced technology product, such as a mobile telephone that clearly outperforms the iPhone, then you may have a much easier time selling through front-door channels than if you're selling website design services, which are far more commoditized.

Private channels and the "back door" symbolize opportunity channels that stem from your contacts, your relationships, and your network, which we discuss in Strategic Action 4: Network and Build Power. For-profit entrepreneurs and social entrepreneurs should always pursue both public and private channels. But our message to for-profit entrepreneurs is the following: in your efforts to secure deals, you can waste a lot of time trying to get in through the front door. Your time is *always* better spent by exploring the back door first! If you focus only on the front door, you can be assured that meanwhile deals are getting done through the back door and you don't even know it!

For example, let's say you're running a business and trying to convince a large corporation to purchase your company's goods or services. You would be much better served by searching out your network, or your network's network, or your network's network's network, to determine if you know anyone with any connection to that corporation *first* (the private channel) than to deal with a relative stranger at the company's next procurement fair (the public channel). The ideal scenario is to make the private connection, followed by the public connection. During our first year of operation, 100 percent of BCT's business came through private channels and relationships, and the percentage still remains high to this day.

As another example, let's say you are the executive director of a community-based organization. As you seek to raise awareness and market your organization's work and accomplishments, you will be in the best position to grow your pool of investment dollars and volunteers by targeting philanthropic organizations and donors who have invested in your organization in the past (the private channel) than by targeting philanthropic organizations and donors that are new to your organization (the public channel).

Social entrepreneurs should *always* consider ways to diversify their organization's income stream between philanthropic organizations who make investments via grants and individual contributors who make investments via donations. Not neglecting one at the expense of the other means targeting your marketing, awareness, and branding efforts at each stakeholder. This can also enhance your ability to engage volunteers who are interested in supporting your work.

The illusion is that the front door *or* the back door is a way to find opportunities for business development or fundraising and development. The reality is that you are always best served by pursuing the front door *and* the back door.

Collaborative Action Steps for Growing Business Enterprises

For business enterprises, in addition to *money, marketing,* and *management,* we further address the areas of *mentoring* and *mergers, acquisitions, and other strategic partnerships*, both of which are often underutilized or underexplored:

- *Mentoring* programs are business-to-business relationships between larger, experienced firms and relatively smaller, emerging firms. These programs provide technical assistance, training, capacity building, and procurement opportunities to help Black-owned businesses grow and address the challenges of money, marketing, and management.
- *Mergers, acquisitions, and other strategic partnerships* represent the most sophisticated of business-to-business relationships. By joining forces with other firms in creative ways that increase their size and scale, Black-owned businesses can bolster their capacity to obtain money, market their products and services, and build a strong management team.

With these two additional considerations, we present the six action steps for business enterprises, as shown in figure 16. We discuss the remaining two action steps specifically for entrepreneurs to create business enterprises.

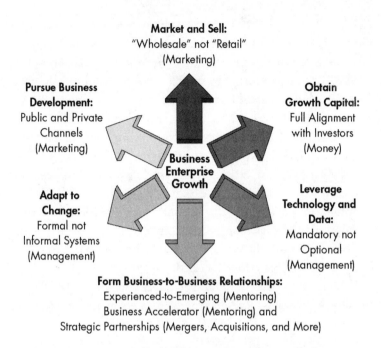

FIGURE 16

MARKET AND SELL:
"WHOLESALE" NOT "RETAIL" (*MARKETING*)

It's more efficient to target wholesalers or intermediaries who can sell your products or services to your target customers than for you to use a customer-by-customer, organization-by-organization, or company-by-company (retail) approach. Seek out entities that represent, gather together, or aggregate several of your target customers to expand your marketing and sales reach.

You will make far more efficient use of your time by (1) marketing to membership organizations whose members are your target customers, or (2) attending conferences and trade shows typically attended by your target customers, or (3) establishing a partnership with a larger firm already working with your target customer base (wholesale), than by going door-to-door trying to reach those same customers (retail).

You may recall that the first company we founded was MBS, which provided educational services and training. One of our first clients, the National Action Council for Minorities in Engineering (NACME), was supported by several corporate sponsors. Many of these corporations later hired MBS based on being exposed to us at the NACME conference. This was a far better and more efficient way to generate sales than knocking on each company's door and pitching our services cold. Today this strategy serves BCT well. Many of our strategic partners have existing relationships with federal clients and far exceed the connections we've been able to establish so far. Our association with our strategic partners makes it easier for us to develop relationships with even more potential customers. In other words, one of the best ways to establish a "wholesale" partnership is through the aforementioned "back door" of existing relationships.

The illusion is that you should go target your customers directly. The reality is that it is more efficient to target an intermediary instead.

FORM BUSINESS-TO-BUSINESS RELATIONSHIPS (MENTORING AND MERGERS, ACQUISITIONS, AND OTHER STRATEGIC PARTNERSHIPS)

In Strategic Actions 4, 5, and 6, we discussed the critical importance of relationships between people who have a complementary individual agenda (Level II: Interdependent Action). Similarly, relationships between businesses are critically important to organizations that have a complementary collective agenda (Level III: Collaborative Action). Such relationships should be pursued along three lines: (1) mentoring relationships between large, experienced firms and relatively smaller, emerging firms, (2) business development programs specifically geared toward growth ventures, and (3) strategic partnerships between companies, such as joint ventures, mergers, and acquisitions.

Mentoring:
Experienced-to-Emerging Business Relationships

One of the more widespread and prevalent strategies that emerged for intrapreneurs was mentoring programs that paired experienced, senior-level executive mentors with less experienced protégés, as we discussed in Strategic Action 5. While corporate mentoring programs are numerous and commonplace, business-to-business mentoring programs are few and far between. They shouldn't be. Experienced companies can teach, coach, counsel, sponsor, and provide model practices for less-experienced Black-owned businesses, in the same way corporate mentors do for their protégés. Fortunately, there is a growing list of programs that pair large, experienced companies with less-experienced Black-owned businesses so that the latter can grow and reach scale.

BCT Partners, and our affiliates, have participated in several mentoring programs, such as Accenture's Diverse Supplier Development Program (DSDP), EY's Entrepreneurs Access Network (EAN), and the US Small Business Administration's (SBA) All Small Mentor/Protégé Program for federal contractors. BCT has been a protégé to FEI Systems and ICF International. In fact, not only has BCT been formally mentored by these larger firms, but we have also formally mentored smaller firms, such as The Brunswick Group and N-Touch Strategies by forming joint ventures in the federal 8(a) business development program.

These and other experienced-to-emerging business mentoring programs represent an intrapreneurial *and* entrepreneurial way of creating wealth (see the callout box "Intrapreneurs Helping Entrepreneurs: VHA Mentors Minority Businesses" for a great example). The role of intrapreneurs is to make the business case within their companies as to why it is important to establish such programs and become willing mentors. The role of entrepreneurs is to show their willingness to learn and grow as a protégé. Perhaps more importantly, entrepreneurs must also demonstrate that their companies' capabilities can add value to a larger firm at scale, if they receive the appropriate support. Much like the double bottom line discussed in Strategic Action 7, business-to-business mentoring can be a win-win:

expanding corporations' supplier diversity efforts and facilitating the growth of Black-owned businesses.

Mentoring: Business Accelerator Program

In addition to these mentoring programs, there are also a growing number of business accelerator programs that are specifically focused on helping already established minority-owned firms become growth ventures, as opposed to being focused on start-up firms. These programs provide assistance in some or all of the following areas: marketing, business development, financial management, structuring of joint ventures, mergers, acquisitions, capitalizations, and identification of procurement opportunities. Some programs also include a goal in terms of the amount of money the corporate members should spend in contracting with the minority-owned business participants. But all of these programs represent the nascent vanguard of much-needed initiatives to help minority small businesses become minority business enterprises.

BCT has participated in several of these programs including New Jersey Institute of Technology's Enterprise Development Center, the National Minority Supplier Development Council (NMSDC) "Centers of Excellence" program, and NMSDC's Advanced Management Education Program at Northwestern University's Kellogg School of Management. Other capacity-building programs for minority-owned businesses include Rutgers Business School's Entrepreneurship Pioneers Initiative, Maryland Small Business Development Center–Central Region's "CEO Accelerator," Interise's Streetwise MBA, Chicago United's "Five Forward" initiative, the Minority Business Accelerator of the Cincinnati USA Regional Chamber, the SBA's Emerging Leaders program, Goldman Sachs's 10,000 Small Business Program, and the various mentor-protégé programs of the federal government (the SBA program is the most used).[5]

While there are indeed several programs that support minority start-up companies and minority small businesses, there is an alarming dearth of programs specifically designed for minority firms and minority business enterprises. Given the success of the minority small business development movement, we are long overdue for a concerted effort to build minority business enterprises.

———

Entrepreneurship does not have to be a

zero-sum game where business owners always

fight for their piece of the economic pie.

Strategic Actions 6 and 8 can make the pie bigger.

———

Mergers, Acquisitions, and More: Strategic Partnerships

Over the past few decades, we have witnessed several mergers and acquisitions among long-standing, multinational corporations such as Disney and Marvel, Google and Android, AOL and Time Warner, and Exxon and Mobil, to name a few. Now, certainly, there are a variety of market forces that led to the consolidation of these publicly traded companies, and these forces do not necessarily exist among Black privately held firms. But there is still a lesson to be learned from the trend: if large, complex companies can figure out how to join forces and work together, then business owners in the Black community should be able to do the same. We should be able to put aside any pettiness, posturing, politics, and personality differences and figure out how to align our efforts just like the big boys and big girls!

If there ever was a time when large corporations or government agencies could say that they can't find any "qualified" Black-owned firms or that there are no Black-owned firms out there, those days are long gone. We cannot just look to corporations and government agencies to open their doors to us. That is only part of the solution to building business enterprises. Entrepreneurs must also look to one another—our peers—to leverage our might vis-a-vis Strategic Action 6. This is the other part of the solution, and this is the ball that lies in our court.

It puzzles us how challenging it can sometimes be for Black-owned businesses to work together. This is something we have experienced firsthand at BCT Partners: *some business owners would rather be captain of a tugboat than the lieutenant of a cruise liner*. We don't get it! We have started five companies over the course of our careers, and we have had nine different business partners along the way. It never ceases to amaze us that discussions about equity and ownership can get so complicated and contentious. At certain points we have had to say, "People! People! We have nothing. So, understand that 50 percent of nothing is nothing!" We're fighting over scraps, relatively speaking, while the big girls and big boys are busy merging, acquiring, and consolidating to create even larger entities to more effectively compete with our firms, which only puts us further behind in the race.

We are *not* suggesting that Black business owners cannot work together. As we discussed in Strategic Action 6, time has proven that we can and do work together effectively. We are suggesting, however, that there is always room for us to work together more. Furthermore, Strategic Action 4 clearly articulates the value of joining forces with people across the entire spectrum of diversity including whites, Latinos, Native Americans, Asians, Pacific Islanders, and so on. You should not confine your strategic partnerships, such as joint ventures, mergers, and acquisitions, solely to other Black-owned companies. You must develop relationships with firms representing other ethnicities, nationalities, and geographies that share similar values and are pursuing complementary objectives.

Where appropriate, there are a range of strategic partnerships that must be explored and implemented by Black entrepreneurs that go beyond mere cooperation to include coalitions, consortia, joint ventures, and ultimately, mergers and acquisitions. We will discuss these options in even greater detail in Level IV: Amplified Action.

The illusion is that you should go it alone in business and that there is some kind of badge of honor by building your business from scratch. The reality is that business success is fundamentally built upon business-to-business relationships and, nowadays, a sophisticated composition of relationships.

Collaborative Action Steps for Growing Social Enterprises

For social enterprises, in addition to *money, marketing,* and *management,* we further address the areas of planning *methods* and outcomes *measurement*:

- *Planning methods* refers to the activities that determine how your civic, community, or social venture develops its overarching strategy and its approach to implementing that strategy. For example, the board of directors is best to make certain planning decisions, while other planning decisions are best made by staff or other stakeholders. A solid planning approach is one that involves the right people at the right levels of the organization in the right discussions about the right issues.
- *Outcomes measurement* refers to how your organization evaluates and measures progress toward its stated goals, objectives, and/or intended impact.

These two additional areas lead us to the six game-changing strategies for social enterprises shown in figure 17. We discuss the remaining game-changing strategies specifically for social entrepreneurs to create social enterprises.

COMBINE PLANNING ACTIVITIES: STRATEGIC PLANNING AND BUSINESS PLANNING (*METHODS*)

Strategic planning is a centralized, high-level process that establishes your organization's governing ideas—mission, vision, and values—as discussed in Strategic Action 6, as well as your organization's key objectives, focus areas, and performance indicators. Most nonprofit organizations do this type of planning. In many organizations, strategic planning is a facilitated discussion among board members that charts out where the organization wants to be in five or ten years.

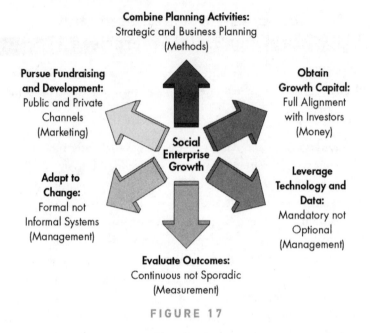

Combine Planning Activities:
Strategic and Business Planning
(Methods)

**Pursue Fundraising
and Development:**
Public and Private
Channels
(Marketing)

**Obtain
Growth Capital:**
Full Alignment
with Investors
(Money)

**Social
Enterprise
Growth**

**Adapt to
Change:**
Formal not
Informal Systems
(Management)

**Leverage
Technology and
Data:**
Mandatory not
Optional
(Management)

Evaluate Outcomes:
Continuous not Sporadic
(Measurement)

FIGURE 17

Business planning is a decentralized, lower-level process that assumes the mission, vision, and values are established and carries the strategic plan to each level and functional area of the organization. A well-constructed business plan includes sections such as your theory of change; business model; products/programs/services; market analysis including competitors, strengths, weaknesses, opportunities, and threats analysis; operations plan; financial plan; and other sections that may be unique to your organization. Business planning is important as a tool for implementation and outcomes evaluation (discussed in the next section). A business plan can be used to evaluate an opportunity to expand operations or services. And once the decision has been made to move forward, it can easily be turned into a tool for implementing the new project, program, service, or business. A summary of the difference between the two processes is shown in table 5.

STRATEGIC PLANNING VS. BUSINESS PLANNING

	STRATEGIC PLANNING	BUSINESS PLANNING
KEY QUESTION	What should we do in the future?	How do we get this done?
ORIENTATION	Objective orientation	Action orientation
SPAN OF OBJECTIVES	Organization-wide key objectives and focus areas and key performance indicators	Department- or program-specific objectives, operational plan, and financials, which tie back into the Strategic Plan.
LEVEL OF SIGN-OFF	Board Level	Executive Level
FREQUENCY IT IS REVISITED	Revisited less frequently; minor changes	Revisited more frequently; multiyear

TABLE 5

For the purpose of capacity building, the reason why business planning is an integral "next step" to strategic planning is that it makes the business case for pursuing a given opportunity and should answer questions such as: What is the business model? How can such an effort be sustained and expanded over time? How can such an effort foster the organization's growth? The illusion is that strategic planning is sufficient. The reality is that strategic planning without business planning is incomplete planning.

EVALUATE OUTCOMES: CONTINUOUS, NOT SPORADIC (*MEASUREMENT*)

Jack Welch, the lauded former CEO of General Electric, is credited with saying, "If you want something to improve, measure it!" We wholeheartedly believe this statement. If you can't measure it, you can't manage it. To move toward becoming a social enterprise, you must perform outcomes measurement on a continuous and ongoing basis, not an occasional or sporadic one. It must be part of your organization's regular activities and must be used to improve your organization's operations.

What does measuring outcomes do for an organization? A proper outcomes-evaluation approach can do four things:

1. *Empower staff and other stakeholders* to be more informed and make better decisions.
2. *Generate new and better information* to improve programs, products, and services.
3. *Demonstrate value* by determining what kind of impact your efforts have on your target community, clients, or issue.
4. *Build organizational capacity* by ultimately improving the processes, systems, and overall work of the organization.

The metrics your organization will use to measure outcomes will vary depending on your organization and the type of work that you do. The key is to make sure that the metrics make sense for what you are doing. You may need to talk to an expert in the social or economic issue you are working on to make sure that you are measuring the appropriate things to track your outcomes. The following are overarching evaluation objectives that may be helpful in this regard:

- *Participatory*—You should involve all relevant stakeholders in your evaluation activities, such as staff and partners, as well as potential beneficiaries such as students, residents, families, and so on, where appropriate.
- *Comprehensive*—You should consider whether your evaluations will measure both *process* indicators or "intermediate" outcomes—such as relationship building, meetings, and collective goal setting that are building blocks—and *product* indicators or "final" outcome measures—such as increases in the number of jobs, reductions in carbon emissions, improved student performance, and so on. Once again, taking some time to think about which of these types of indicators is important for your work will go a long way toward moving your

organization from a sustainability paradigm to an enterprise paradigm.

- *Rigorous*—You should quantify and qualify your outcomes for both social outcomes and the financial resources needed to achieve those outcomes (such as $1 million to create one hundred jobs; $500,000 to reduce carbon emissions by 50 percent; $2 million to increase student SAT scores by one hundred points) in conducting your evaluations. An appropriate level of rigor allows you to know the social and financial value of staff time to produce outcomes for both you and your investors. In doing so, you are also in a better position to know what kind of money to say no to because it is not enough to achieve the desired impact.

Regularly conducting outcomes measurement along these lines promotes "lifelong" learning for your organization.

From Entrepreneurship to Intrapreneurship

Throughout this chapter, we've made repeated references to "enterprises" within the context of growth and reaching scale. Looking back to Strategic Action 7: Think and Act Like an Intrapreneur, it should now be clear that as your entrepreneurial venture becomes larger and more established, the collaborative actions for intrapreneurship and social intrapreneurship become more and more relevant to your organization. Once your organization has reached some semblance of scale, it must now assume greater responsibility for developing untapped markets, establishing its own supplier-diversity program, engaging in social investment, and all of the intrapreneurial strategies we discussed in the last chapter. We cannot assume that Black-owned or Black-controlled means community oriented. Black entrepreneurs and social entrepreneurs must ultimately hold themselves to the same standard of accountability to communities as the intrapreneurs we discussed in Strategic Action 7.

Institution Building

In light of the several questions we posed in this chapter under the action steps, the ultimate question to entrepreneurs and social entrepreneurs alike is the following: *If the founding members or key leaders of your organization were to step down tomorrow, would your organization continue to grow?* If the answer is no then there is more work to be done for your organization to be considered an *institution*. If the answer is yes then your organization is likely to be there. One of the primary reasons certain government organizations, corporations, and nonprofits are institutions is because they have *institutionalized* the action steps in this chapter and their ability to replace their leaders. To the extent that you want your organization to have staying power, you must do the same.

As you can see, our definition of *institution* equally applies to public, private, community, educational, philanthropic, and faith-based organizations. Strategic Action 9: Transform Systems will make clear how to work across all of these sectors—intrapreneurs and entrepreneurs alike—to empower people and build institutions that have longevity and create lasting change.

LEVEL IV

Amplified Action

Individually, we are one drop. Together, we are an ocean.
—RYŪNOSUKE AKUTAGAWA

T o make clear what we mean by *amplified action*, we will use a box as a metaphor, whereas the height you can lift the box is representative of the impact you can have on society.

From Independent Action to Amplified Action

Person or Organization = "Small" Impact

FIGURE 18

The most ineffective way to lift the box as high as possible is to do it alone. The same is true for people or organizations endeavoring to make an impact on society. While you can make a difference by working alone, it will only be in proportion to your individual or *independent action* $(1 + 0 = 1)$, as shown in figure 18.

An effective approach to lifting the box as high as possible is to work with someone else. Similarly, people and organizations desiring to make an impact on society will be far more effective working together via *interdependent action* $(1 + 1 = 2)$ than apart, as shown in figure 19.

People and Organizations = "Moderate" Impact

FIGURE 19

Synergy is created when the whole is greater than the sum of its parts. Dr. Stephen R. Covey, the renowned leadership authority, once said, "Synergy is better than my way or your way. It's our way." Synergy is the bonus that is achieved when things work together harmoniously. Therefore, an even more effective approach to lifting the box is to create a *system* that enables people to work together in harmony.

The *resources* necessary for this system are the tool sets that people and organizations can use to facilitate change, which are the five forms of capital we have discussed previously: human capital (skills and abilities), cultural capital (insight and understanding), social capital (relationships), intellectual capital (team-based assets), and financial capital (money).

The *processes* are how these resources, people, and organizations work and relate to one another. For example, harmony can be achieved by defining a process that governs the interactions between the parties involved. This could be as simple as a shared understanding or as elaborate as documented policies and procedures. In the example of lifting the box, a process to achieve harmony could be as informal as saying "One, two, three, *lift!*" or it could be as formal as drafting a handbook explaining exactly who should lift the box in what specific location to ensure that the box's weight is evenly distributed.

Synergy is collaborative action.

The synergy for Black faces in high places is driven by *collaborative action*, or people and organizations working together in a way that is "mutually beneficial," and leverages their collective resources harmoniously to produce more than what they could have produced independently or interdependently. Under these circumstances, their efforts are synergistic in achieving an impact that is larger than the sum of all parts (1 + 1 = 3), as shown in figure 20.

Reaching *scale* means going from "each one, reach one" to "each one, reach *one hundred,*" or "each one, reach *one thousand,*" or "each one, reach *one million,*" or even more! You reach scale by amplifying collaborative actions.

Using the box as a metaphor again, the most effective approach to lifting the box as high as possible is to *transform systems* by amplifying the collaborative efforts of people and organizations, as shown in

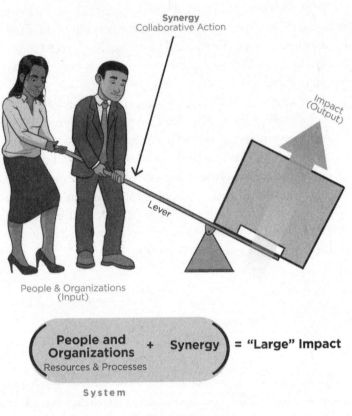

FIGURE 20

figure 21. Similarly, the most effective way to make the greatest differ-ence in society is to create a system that incorporates aspects of both synergy and scale in amplifying the collaborative efforts of people and organizations.

Figure 21 shows how people, organizations, resources, and pro-cesses are the "inputs" to the system. As mentioned previously, *syn-ergy is collaborative action: a harmonious configuration of people, organizations, processes, and resources working together toward a goal of social and/or economic impact.* What translates their collaborative action into *amplified action* is the use of *scale*. As shown in figures 21

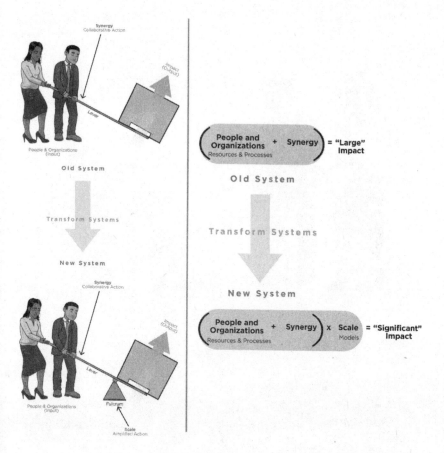

FIGURE 21

and 22, by engaging synergy (the lever) *and* scale (the fulcrum) we transform the old system into a new system that can have significant impact. Much like a lever and fulcrum can significantly amplify the collaborative efforts of people to lift a box, an effective "model" for social and/or economic impact can significantly amplify the collaborative efforts of people and organizations to create the effect of scale. *Scale is a multiplier: it is an effect that translates collaborative action into amplified action* or action that achieves the broadest or deepest possible impact.

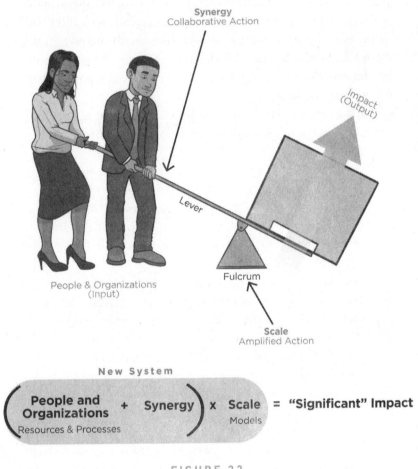

FIGURE 22

Scale is amplified action.

The "model" for increasing social and/or economic impact is the fulcrum in figure 22. An effective model allows you to amplify action through the skill sets, strategies, tactics, programs, policies, and approaches to change that have already proven effective. This includes skill sets such as Strategic Actions 1 through 8. And much as the size, shape, and location of the fulcrum can dramatically increase (or decrease) the height the box is lifted, the effectiveness of a given model can dramatically increase (or decrease) the potential for positive, lasting, widespread change.

A few examples of effective models for change (that is, fulcrums) to create social or economic impact at scale include the following:

- A charter school that has demonstrated its ability to help underserved youth attain a quality education in one city expands to the fifty largest urban metropolitan areas.
- A profitable for-profit business at a single location franchises its business model and grows its footprint to encompass an entire region.
- A social program that has successfully helped low-income families accumulate wealth and gain access to quality health care is replicated from a state program to a federal program.
- A commercial product that has proven its ability to measurably reduce domestic carbon emissions to the environment broadens its customer base to other nations around the world.

All of the above led to the "output" from the system of *impact* or the positive difference that can be made in society. Impact speaks back to your bottom line: social or economic or both (the double bottom line). If you are a statewide elected official, it could mean reductions in crime. If you are the executive director of a national youth program, it could mean increased graduation rates. If you are the founder and CEO of an international public relations and event-planning firm, it could mean increased awareness of a worldwide issue.

Systems that combine synergy and scale can lead to the "broadest" possible social and economic impact, that is, an impact that is wide ranging and far reaching or the "deepest" possible social and economic impact, that is, an impact that is targeted and penetrating.

A broad impact could be felt regionally, nationally, or globally, while a deep impact could be focused on a specific neighborhood, community, or issue (such as poverty elimination or environmental justice). When people and organizations work together to create systems that combine synergy and scale, they can have a significant impact $(1 + 1 = 100)$.

Actions speak louder than words.

Amplified actions scream louder than words.

Changing the Game

The mindset that is required to achieve amplified action is the *game-changers mindset*, that is, a mindset that is geared toward making fundamental changes throughout an industry, sector, or "game" that achieve a lasting social and economic impact.

The fundamental building blocks of changing the game are people and organizations. People are the most *important* building blocks along with the relationships that are formed between them. Ultimately, it is through the actions of people that change is facilitated. Informal and formal organizations are perhaps the most *influential* building blocks. Because they comprise groups of people and leverage their might, organizations (and, more important, collaborations between organizations) have the greatest power and potential to facilitate widespread change.

What distinguishes an organization from a collection of individuals is the establishment of roles, responsibilities, and processes such as status reports, team coordination, succession planning, and administrative, financial, and operational tasks, just to name a few. We can think of very few examples of an individual who changed the game that did not have an organization or some kind of formal organizational infrastructure supporting her or him.

You are most effective in changing the game as a member, an affiliate, or a part of an entity that is greater than yourself over which you exert some measure of decision-making authority: your own business, a community group, a membership association, a faith-based organization, a corporation, a network, and so on. In this capacity, you not only bring your personal resources to the table, but you also bring the resources of your organization, including its organizational memory and relationships and its human, financial, and technological wherewithal. Preferably, the entity with which you are affiliated is an *institution*.

Institutions are organizations that stand the test of time. Institutions are establishments or organizations that will exist long after we have left this world and will continue to uphold their governing ideas, mission, vision, and values over time. Institutions can make sure that the social and economic change you are advocating stays in place for years to come.

In essence, Strategic Action 7 challenged today's intrapreneurs to compel their institutions to be more responsive to the needs of Black people. Why? Because by changing their institutions for the better, the changes they've made have greater potential to become *lasting* changes. But remember that our definition of *institution* doesn't just apply to businesses. It equally applies to community, educational, philanthropic, and faith-based organizations too. Strategic Action 8 essentially challenged modern entrepreneurs to work together strategically to build for-profit and nonprofit institutions. Why? Because by creating institutions, the positive efforts of the institution become *lasting* work. Scale and scope are the technologies that empower people to build institutions in ways that create *lasting* change.

Strategic Action 9: Transform Systems will challenge both intrapreneurs and entrepreneurs to go even further and become game changers. Why? Because game changers strive to ensure lasting changes not only within their institutions but also throughout society.

9

Transform Systems

Since we know that the system will not change the rules,
we are going to have to change the system.
—REV. DR. MARTIN LUTHER KING JR.

Level I provided the foundation for any *relationship*—knowledge of
self—and highlighted the paramount importance of self-determination

(Strategic Action 1), exploration (Strategic Action 2), and self-mastery and meaning (Strategic Action 3). Level II provided some powerful tools for *interpersonal relationships* via networking (Strategic Action 4), mentoring (Strategic Action 5), and leveraging our might (Strategic Action 6). Level III provided the foundation for any *organization*—for a profit or for a purpose—to achieve both intrapreneurial (Strategic Action 7) and entrepreneurial (Strategic Action 8) pursuits. In Level IV and here in Strategic Action 9, we provide some powerful models for *interorganizational relationships*, which we will simply refer to as *strategic partnerships,* or formal relationships between at least two organizations to achieve a mutual purpose that benefits both organizations.

The Continuum of Strategic Partnerships

If you desire to make changes at a broader or deeper level through for-profit companies and nonprofit organizations, the continuum of strategic partnerships comes into play (see figure 23). Strategic partnerships can be formed both within sectors (for example, between two nonprofits) and across sectors (for example, between a business, nonprofit, government, and faith-based organization). They represent the building blocks of systems that combine synergy and scale to achieve social and economic impact.

The Continuum of Strategic Partnerships

Competition	Co-Opetition	Cooperation*	Coalition	Consortium	Joint Venture	Merger/ Acquisition
Configuration 0 COMPETE Function independently		**Configuration 1** COOPERATE Work closely together		**Configuration 2** COALESCE Align mutual objectives		**Configuration 3** COMBINE Unite to form a single entity
None		Low		Medium		High

Level of Integration

* Cooperation = Coordination/Collaboration/Colocation

FIGURE 23

THE EIGHT FORMS OF STRATEGIC PARTNERSHIPS

RELATIONSHIP	INTEGRATION	FORMALIZATION	DURATION	DESCRIPTION
	What is the degree of integration?	How is it formalized?	How long may it last?	When is it appropriate?
TIER 0: COMPETE – FUNCTION INDEPENDENTLY				
Competition	None	-	-	Organizations have no relationship or act independent.
TIER 1: COOPERATE – WORK CLOSELY TOGETHER				
Co-opetition	Low	Contract or MOU	Situational	Conditions exist for cooperation and competition between organizations.
Cooperation	Low	LOI or MOU	Temporal	Short-term relationships or resource sharing between organizations.
TIER 2: COALESCE – ALIGN MUTUAL OBJECTIVES				
Coalition	Medium	Contract or MOU	Temporal	Both organizations have complementary needs and objectives.
Consortium	Medium	Contract or MOU	Semi-perpetual	Member organizations have complementary needs and objectives.
TIER 3: COMBINE – UNITE TO FORM A SINGLE ENTITY				
Joint Venture	High	Joint Venture Agreement	Semi-perpetual	Complementary assets can be better leveraged through a single organization.
Merger/ Acquisition	High	Asset Purchase Agreement	Perpetual	Value of merged/acquired assets can be increased by the combined/parent organization.

TABLE 6

Each of the eight forms of strategic partnerships—*competition, co-opetition, cooperation, coalition, consortium, joint venture, merger,* and *acquisition*—can be categorized according to three considerations (see table 6):

1. *Integration*—What is the degree of combined effort, shared resources, and mutual objectives that characterize the relationship?
2. *Formalization*—How is the relationship made "official" and legally binding?
3. *Duration*—How long may the relationship last?

We describe each tier and its corresponding form(s).

TIER 0: COMPETE

Organizations "compete" when they have no relationship and advance their interests independent of one another.

Competition

Tier 0 and its sole form—*competition*—is characterized by rivalry, opposition, and even antagonism. Competition between two organizations operating in the same space may arise over resources, customers, markets, products, services, clients, ideas, and even over the media. Competition is the basis of any free market economy and is central to the idea of capitalism. The idea that competition provides incentives for self-improvement emerged as a theme in economics as early as Adam Smith's eighteenth-century treatise *The Wealth of Nations*. Competition is the status quo and is the opposite of cooperation.

TIER 1: COOPERATE

Organizations "cooperate" when they work closely together toward a common goal. The basic element for cooperation is trust. Cooperation uses trust to overcome many obstacles. Therefore, you cooperate with those you trust. As we explained in Strategic Action 4, trust is built up via deposits to the emotional bank account and through ongoing interpersonal interactions.

Naturally, you must build trust among the people within your organization. But this is often not enough. Trust is built *interpersonally* and *interorganizationally*. For the latter, the people within your organization must also build trust with people in other organizations. This is how relationships become "institutionalized" and not just "personalized."

Years ago both of us presented seminars to the Weinberg Fellows Program sponsored by Weinberg Foundation of Baltimore, Maryland. The Fellows Program brought together directors of nonprofit agencies serving disadvantaged residents in the Baltimore metropolitan area for executive leadership training and networking. During the retreats, these leaders interacted and built relationships with one another. That was a great first step toward building trust, especially among organizations that could work together toward common goals.

These two degrees of trust—interpersonal and interorganizational— are built over time and go a long way toward cooperation. Trust is built because the organizations know what to expect from one another. Even in the best situations of cooperation, however, there is still the possibility of misunderstanding what each other means by cooperation. We are reminded of a phrase that President Ronald Reagan used regarding US-Soviet relations: "Trust but verify."

Cooperation

Tier 1 corresponds to two forms: *co-opetition* and *cooperation*. Since cooperation is a broader concept, we describe it first and then go back to describe what we mean by co-opetition.

Cooperation can actually manifest itself in three ways, *coordination*, *collaboration*, and *colocation*:

1. *Coordination* is showing up at the "same time, same place" and completing some assigned tasks. It does not take any shared resources or much shared responsibility. There is a common purpose, but generally it is easy to facilitate. In fact, coordination doesn't take much trust, making it ideal for new organizational relationships. An example of this is when organizations "cosponsor" events that are organized by another organization (the "sponsor"). Your role might be to show up and to encourage others to be there. As long as you believe in the common purpose of the event, it is fairly easy to facilitate.

2. *Collaboration*—When organizations truly *collaborate*, they share resources and responsibilities for events, projects, initiatives, or programs. Collaboration requires trust and commitment. An example of this is the collaboration that has taken place between home improvement retailer Home Depot and Kaboom, a social venture that builds playgrounds in underserved communities. Home Depot provides significant funding, but its biggest contribution is the volunteers that it provides from its stores and headquarters to participate in the builds. When this collaboration passed the one thousandth playground milestone, it was noted that more than ninety-nine thousand people had participated as Team Depot Associates and donated more than 954,000 volunteer hours on these builds. Of course, Home Depot benefits from this collaboration too. They have an active partnership with a national nonprofit organization that does great work. Home Depot is associated with positive community work and uses this as part of its "cause marketing" activities—associating a marketing campaign with a significant cause to promote both the company and a cause, which appeals to its socially conscious customer base. This is an intrapreneurial approach to the double bottom line of making a profit and making a difference.

3. *Colocation*—An additional way to cooperate is to join forces with another business or organization to share the physical space for your operations. By forming *colocation* or cooperation relationships, you may also be able to share certain resources, such as administrative staff, computers, conference rooms, phones, photocopiers, and so on, thus reducing the cost for these resources to both parties. We used this relationship form when we moved our first business, MBS Enterprises, into a garage with two other businesses. We shared many resources and helped one another as often as we could with business leads, referrals, and joint projects. This is the essence of what business incubators do for new businesses. Colocation can help minimize costs and lead to opportunities.

Cooperation can lead to wonderful partnerships, but we advise you to document the terms of more complicated arrangements explicitly. This may mean writing a letter of intent (LOI) or a memorandum of understanding (MOU) to detail how you will operate this strategic partnership. Cooperation is ideal for *temporal* (short-term duration) relationships or when resource sharing between organizations is important for meeting your objectives.

Co-opetition

Co-opetition is a word that authors Adam Brandenberger and Barry Nalebuff use to describe the arrangements between organizations that cooperate and compete simultaneously. Their research demonstrated the pattern of co-opetition between companies that realize there are some situations requiring cooperation between rivals to increase the size of the total pie.

This approach demands mature leadership and a big-picture view. It encourages organizations to compete in situations when their independent agendas are best served by doing so, and to cooperate in situations when there are common goals that can be best achieved by working together. Therefore, these types of relationships and their duration are *situational*. And, because of the open nature of the network, this model encourages new and innovative ideas to come out of the strategic partnership. Co-opetition should be formalized on a case-by-case or project-by-project basis using memoranda of understanding (MOUs), or contracts (that is, a teaming agreement). This allows for an explicit agreement about expectations and actions of the organizations.

One example of co-opetition is in the education reform movement. Many organizations are working in the same space. Charter schools, urban school reformers, after-school programs, and organizations focused on teacher, principal, or educational leadership development are all working toward the goal of addressing deficiencies in the educational infrastructure in the US. It is very easy for these organizations to compete for the limited resources that exist for education, especially in urban areas. The challenge is to recognize that the default mode of competition assumes a zero-sum game where "if I win, you must lose."

Mature leaders recognize that if the true goal is education reform, there are many instances where it is more effective for organizations that usually compete with each other (either directly or at the very least with their different approaches) to cooperate. In the New York City area, charter school organizations KIPP, Achievement First, and Uncommon Schools are working together according to the co-opetition model to increase the number of charters available in the state and to advocate for favorable policies for all charter schools. KIPP also works closely with Teach for America to identify teachers in urban school districts. While these organizations continue to compete for resources such as grants, they have decided to cooperate along the lines of reform.

TIER 2: COALESCE

To "coalesce" is to align mutual objectives. For Tier 2, we are particularly concerned with how organizations form strategic partnerships to achieve common goals. At this midpoint of integration, organizations have to learn to combine efforts in more intense ways. These strategic partnerships take on two forms: *coalitions* and *consortia*.

Coalition

A *coalition* or *strategic alliance* is a closed network of organizations working toward the same goals. These arrangements share three characteristics. First, the partners work together for a specific purpose. That purpose is clear and unequivocal. Second, the partnership is closed to others once it is established. Third, the partnership has its own established set of rules, norms and values via contracts, MOUs, or letters of partnerships that formalize the relationship. These documents lay out how the strategic alliance is going to work and explain the control and distribution of resources. Strategic alliances are appropriate when both organizations have complementary needs and objectives over a specific duration.

When your efforts are geared for a purpose, this kind of structured partnership can occur both within a sector (that is, business-to-business) and across sectors of the economy (that is, social sector, government, and business). An example of this would be the strategic alliance between the Kauffman Foundation and the National Urban League, the White House and the Business Roundtable for the Urban Entrepreneurship Partnership (UEP) that took place during the Obama administration. The UEP program provided one-stop economic empowerment centers to offer business training, counseling, and procurement opportunities to minority and urban business owners. It is significant that no one organization thought it could take on this task alone. Partnering made more sense than going alone.

Consortium

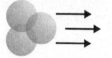

When organizations unite for a common shared purpose and conduct joint marketing campaigns or events or make purchases together, we call these arrangements a *consortium, federation*, or *cooperative*. A consortium is an alliance formed for a common goal. Because of the degree of integration necessary for a consortium to function well, it requires some formalization using contracts or MOUs.

Members of consortia have complementary needs and objectives over the foreseeable future. There are multiple examples of this in the airline industry, including the Star Alliance (approximately twenty-one airlines), the SkyTeam Alliance (approximately eleven airlines), and oneworld® (approximately ten airlines).

The goal of these consortia is to make international travel easier by bringing member airlines under one roof and by coordinating connections across airlines. They also make it easier for customers of their alliance to use frequent flyer miles between and across airlines around the world. For complex travel plans, customers have an advantage because of the network of airlines that are working together. This benefits the customers and, as a result, benefits the network of airlines that are members of the consortium.

Consortia can be formal or informal in nature. In the case of the Star Alliance, since 1997, it has not been an independent entity although recently there has been talk of formalizing the Star Alliance by creating a jointly owned venture with the member airlines. The point here is that a formalized consortium will create a new business or organization to carry out the common goals.

A wonderful example of a formal consortium was evident among the membership organizations representing ethnic journalists. It began in 1994, when the Asian American Journalists Association, the National Association of Black Journalists, the National Association of

Hispanic Journalists, and the Native American Journalists Association convened a joint conference to promote the following common goals:

- Improving the industry's coverage of communities of color
- Increasing opportunities for young and prospective journalists
- Promoting diversity and helping others to understand its value
- Fostering better race relations

That same year, they established UNITY: Journalists of Color Inc., "a permanent, not-for-profit, strategic alliance of journalists of color acting as a force for positive change to advance their presence, growth, and leadership in the fast-changing global news industry." Unfortunately, the Black journalists left UNITY in 2011, and then the Hispanic journalists left in 2013, due to "financial disorganization."[1]

TIER 3: COMBINE

Organizations "combine" when they unite to form a single entity. At Tier 3—the highest form of integration—the resources of two or more organizations are completely joined together using one of the following forms: *joint venture*, *merger*, or *acquisition*.

Joint Venture

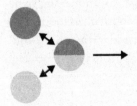

A *joint venture* between organizations creates a new (semi-)autonomous organization using the resources of the partners. In a joint venture, the partners must contribute resources to create the new entity and take on the risk jointly for a common purpose. They are most appropriate when complementary assets can be better leveraged through a single organization. They also last until both parties decide to dissolve them (semiperpetual duration).

BCT Partners and One Economy Corporation set up a joint venture called Access One Corporation. Access One's mission was to equip affordable housing with broadband and telecommunications solutions. This was an opportunity each partner was interested in pursuing, but each lacked some of the necessary expertise. Together, however, the market could be pursued by capitalizing on the expertise each organization brought to the table.

Most people are unaware that Verizon Wireless is actually a joint venture between Verizon Communications, the second-largest telecommunications company in the United States, and Vodafone, the second-largest mobile telecommunications company in the world behind China Mobile. Verizon Communications owns 55 percent of the venture while Vodafone owns 45 percent.

Joint ventures require some sophistication to set up and are formalized through a joint venture agreement. Therefore, we advise you to engage legal, accounting, and finance experts who specialize in joint ventures to assist you in setting one up. Some of the challenges to forming joint ventures include determining the following: the degree of participation, ownership, and control of each joint venture partner; valuation of investments; allocation of all rights to jointly developed intellectual assets; protecting intellectual property, know-how, and trade secrets; linking decision-making structures; developing financial models that allow both firms to share the risks as well as rewards of the joint venture; and termination/liquidation of the joint venture. The potential for profits may outweigh the challenges.

Merger

In a *merger*, two organizations become one through formal, legal, and financial proceedings that govern the transfer of assets.

While there can be many economic benefits to mergers, there are also many things to consider. Merger deals often fail because the two organizations are not compatible. The sources of the incompatibilities can be a result of the mismatch of cultures, operations, or corporate strategies. Since a merger is ostensibly a joining of two organizations, there should be many things that make the newly merged organization better than if the organizations continued to operate independently.

A primary success factor for mergers lies in whether the merger was well-formed strategically. There should be some complementary aspects that bring two organizations together, and these reasons should make sense to customers and stakeholders. And then there are the people—a merger is really a merging of two sets of employees. The entire process is about change, and if the people are not properly communicated with and are not taken care of, there will be challenges.

Mergers require a significant amount of expertise to complete successfully. We will discuss some of these considerations after we describe acquisitions.

Acquisition

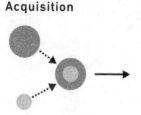

An *acquisition* is a way to acquire the assets, talent, and market of an organization that is competing or complementary to your organization. It differs from a merger in that your organization is literally acquiring the assets of the other organization to expand the wherewithal of your organization.

For example, if your company has done great work within the United States but has limited experience abroad, it might be smart to acquire a company with a large number of international clients or is based outside of the US. This is precisely what FedEx did in China. Over a twenty-year period, they acquired three companies who serviced the Asian market and formed a fifty-fifty joint venture with DTW, a Chinese domestic shipping company. In 2005, FedEx was given permission to acquire DTW's 50 percent ownership and become the sole owner of a company based in China. The FedEx-DTW joint venture and previous acquisitions provided FedEx with the experience that allowed it to expand its capacity to serve an area of enormous potential.

In 2006, Carver Federal Savings Bank, the largest Black-operated, publicly traded bank in the US, bought Community Capital Bank in an effort to diversify its business as larger national banks encroached on its base in New York's Harlem neighborhood.

Whereas Carver had a deep mortgage-lending business and built a niche lending to churches, the buyout of Community Capital catapulted the bank into commercial lending with a group of bankers already experienced and actively working in the area.

"Our bank is quite small relative to the institutions we are competing against in our marketplace," Carver chairwoman and CEO

Deborah Wright told *Black Enterprise* magazine at the time. Carver needed to increase its scale and needed opportunities to expand profits, she explained. "This transaction hits both objectives," she said.

As with mergers, it is important to consider the impact of bringing new people, processes, and markets into your organization. In many cases, the acquiring organization is the dominant entity and ultimately makes the decisions concerning how to leverage (or retire) the acquired organization's assets, including its brand. This may lead to minor consolidation, or it may lead to massive changes, including layoffs.

Acquisitions tend to be far more commonplace in the private sector than in the nonprofit sector. Even when a struggling nonprofit is acquired by a stronger nonprofit, it tends to be treated and referenced as a merger. Unlike corporations, nonprofit organizations are not traded on public markets, so there is no-bidding process to acquire a nonprofit. For nonprofits, such a transaction would have to be approved by each organization's board of directors, leading to a merger. But to the extent that there may be an imbalance in their respective strengths, although it is called a merger it may feel like an acquisition!

Mergers and acquisitions are not to be taken lightly. They represent the only two forms of strategic partnerships that are *perpetual*, meaning there is no turning back once the transaction has been completed. Furthermore, perhaps not surprisingly, mergers and acquisitions are perhaps the most complex type of strategic partnerships to implement. They are formalized through legal proceedings that govern the transfer of assets. Therefore, we advise you to obtain legal, accounting, and finance assistance from experts who specialize in mergers and acquisitions to assist you in implementing one.

Finally, while the potential for profits from a joint venture, merger, or acquisition can be tremendous, these strategic partnerships should be pursued only on the basis of whether it makes sense in terms of the value that can be exploited and the alignment it has with your company's core competencies, corporate values, and corporate culture.

THE THREE "B'S" OF GROWING A
BUSINESS OR SOCIAL ENTERPRISE

Another way of framing the strategies for growing a business or social enterprise are as follows:

1. **Build** the organization or company from the ground up.
2. **Borrow** the capabilities of another organization or company via strategic partnerships up to and including joint ventures.
3. **Buy** the capabilities of another organization or company via merger or acquisition.

Black faces in high places understand that it behooves entrepreneurs and social entrepreneurs to explore all three approaches.

GUIDING PRINCIPLES
FOR STRATEGIC PARTNERSHIPS

The following are guiding principles to keep in mind as your organization pursues strategic partnerships with other organizations:

1. *Only pursue higher tiers of strategic partnerships when you have established the necessary capacity to implement them.* As you move from left to right on the continuum of strategic partnership in figure 23, not only does the degree of integration generally increase, but so does the degree of complexity and sophisication to implement the strategic partnerships. For example, a merger between two companies is far more complicated and requires greater sophistication to implement than a cooperative agreement between two companies.

2. *Your organization should only explore more sophisticated strategic partnerships to the extent you have the capacity to implement them.* For example, if your nonprofit does not have a functioning accounting system, then it will be difficult to merger it with another nonprofit's accounting system. If neither company has a functioning financial system, then it will be a nightmare! Particularly as it relates to consortia, joint ventures, mergers, and acquisitions, make sure your organization has solid systems, processes, and procedures in core areas before looking to combine them with those of another company.

3. *Don't just create organizations; combine them.* While higher tiers of strategic partnerships tend to be more complex, more sophisticated, and require greater capacity to implement, do not allow that to preclude or disuade you from exploring them. If the last generation of Black entrepreneurs was in a strong position to *create* businesses and social ventures, this generation is in a strong position to *combine* businesses and social ventures.

4. *You must combine the old-school solidarity of finding strength in numbers and working together with your new-school sophistication.* Use your education, training, and acumen to combine a limousine company in Atlanta with another limousine company in Washington, DC; or combine a local youth organization with another youth organization serving the same neighborhood; or combine an emerging law firm with an experienced law firm, so you can collectively synergize and reach scale.

5. *Sacrifice a little to gain a lot.* Much like we discussed in Strategic Action 6 in the context of *ubuntu*, in order to form more strategic partnerships successfully, every one of us is going to have to sacrifice something individually in the short term—control, ownership, money, or power—to achieve something greater collectively in the long term. If no one is willing to sacrifice, then the entire landscape devolves into a tragedy of the commons. *Sacrifice* is the operative word here.

6. *Understand the importance of size and scale.* In Strategic Action 8, we talked about the need for more Black-owned *business enterprises* or growth ventures that reach scale. In the twenty-first-century business landscape and its age of consolidation, where big companies are getting even bigger, *size matters.* A comparable argument could also be made as it relates to organizations operating in the social sector. It is becoming increasingly necessary for organizations to reach a certain size and scale in order to compete, sustain themselves, and continue to grow.

We transform systems by finding synergy and reaching scale with the goal to have the broadest and deepest possible impact. On the following pages, we offer amplified action steps that will help entrepreneurs and intrapreneurs find synergy and reach scale.

Collaborative Action Steps to Find Synergy

SEEK DIVERSE PARTNERSHIPS TO INCREASE IMPACT AND FIND INNOVATION

Much as your interpersonal relationships should be diverse, as we discussed in Strategic Action 4, your strategic partnerships should be diverse. Black-owned or -led organizations should build strategic partnerships with organizations owned and led by people of similar and different backgrounds who have common interests. When building these strategic partnerships, seek quality over quantity. We have found it is better to develop deep relationships with a small group of partner organizations than to develop thin relationships with several partner organizations.

For example, David Steward's World Wide Technology (WWT) has built a sizable business of more than $13 billion by forming quality, strong, and strategic partnerships.

In 1987, Union Pacific Railroad needed to audit three years' worth of freight bills and hired David Steward's company Transport Administrative Services to do the job. Steward had previously worked for Missouri Pacific Railroad, which was now Union Pacific. Steward's experience, combined with his reputation and relationships, resulted in Union Pacific giving him a contract to review $15 billion in bills for undercharges.

Just three years before, Steward, a railroad industry veteran, who had also worked for Federal Express, convinced the previous owner to sell the transportation audit company to him for no money down.

"I had no money, all the trappings of the two kids and a wife and a mortgage and all the other things that go along with it, and I didn't have any resources to be able to do it, but I was determined to buy a company," he said.

Once he had control of the company, he borrowed against some of its assets to give the previous owner a down payment and to get working capital so that he could get the business going.

The acquisition was a good fit. Having worked in the industry, Steward was familiar with the errors that often appeared on transportation bills. He leveraged some of his previous business relationships to land contracts to audit freight bills for overcharges for companies like McDonnell Douglas, General Motors, Chrysler, Ford, Campbell Soup, and Abbott Laboratories.

To handle all of that data, Steward's company put together a network of computers and developed its own software that could handle the information faster than the railroad's own computers. The system worked so well that he began to rethink his business plan.

"So was I in the business of analyzing and reviewing freight bills or was I in the business of using technology in a unique, different way to find solutions for companies?" The answer was the latter, and so in 1990, he and friend James Kavanaugh, an executive at Future Electronics Inc., a Canadian seller of chips and electronic components, founded World Wide Technology.

Kavanaugh contributed experience in sales and management as well as his knowledge of electronics distribution, software development, and component manufacturing. Both had valuable relationships with previous colleagues and customers.

Steward and Kavanaugh executed an effective "inside/outside" strategy with Steward being the "outside" face of the organization doing deals. Kavanaugh focused on "inside" operations. Steward gave Kavanaugh a 15 percent stake in the company on just a handshake.

WWT is primarily a reseller of information technology products from large equipment manufacturers such as Cisco, Dell, and Hewlett-Packard. WWT then provides the associated services to install and maintain these products, including network design and installation; systems and application integration; and procurement. Their clients include government agencies and companies in the automotive, retail, and telecommunications industries. The company also offers web-based products and services including e-commerce systems development, order tracking, and catalog development.

Over the years they developed more than twenty-five strategic partnerships with companies like Cisco Systems, Dell Computer, HP, Sun Microsystems, Novell, Lexmark, Symantec, VMWare, and Sony Electronics to resell, install, and service their products like computers, servers, routers, switches, storage, and software. In 2001, WWT spun off a new venture, Telcobuy.com, to focus specifically on equipment sales in the telecommunications market. In 2002, they merged Telcobuy.com back into WWT so the company could focus all of its energies on five markets: federal, telecommunications, commercial, state and local, and health care. Its client list includes the states of Missouri and Alaska. It's the largest Black-owned company in the US.

PURSUE STRATEGIC PARTNERSHIPS ACROSS THE ENTIRE CONTINUUM WITH PEOPLE AND ORGANIZATIONS YOU TRUST

Your organization should generally explore only higher tiers of strategic partnerships with organizations with whom you have established an appropriate level of trust. It is like dating. As your trust and familiarity with a potential partner increases, and mutually shared values are identified, only then should you consider taking the relationship to another level. Test the waters with simpler relationships. This will help avoid the headache of having to dismantle a complicated, dysfunctional relationship that could have been foreseen. For example, if a strategic partnership is not working out it can serve as a red flag not to proceed to a joint venture, merger, or acquisition. At BCT Partners, we have experienced both the pleasure and the pain of developing strategic partnerships across the entire continuum.

Tier 1: Cooperation—When BCT first launched with only Pinkett, Hibbert, and Grundy as full-time employees, we colocated the company with two sole proprietors we trusted and knew well—a mutual friend Hibbert grew up with, Baron Hilliard, and a college classmate, Anthony Emmanuel—sharing office space in a modest carriage house with no air-conditioning or heat that could barely fit us all.

Tier 2: Coalition—One of our first collaborations was with One Economy Corporation, a nonprofit organization founded by Rey Ramsey and Ben Hecht. Dr. Pinkett had formed a mentoring relationship with Ramsey, which established a solid foundation for trust. As result, One Economy became one of BCT's early clients, and both organizations later formed a coalition named Access One Corporation to bring high technology into low-income communities. BCT also formed a coalition with Red Fern Consulting to launch the first virtual reality solution intended to mitigate unconscious bias. The founder of Red Fern, Steve Mahaley, was a former colleague of Dr. Robinson's wife's aunt, Cheryl Stokes, which made for a trusting relationship between both organizations. Lastly, BCT formed a coalition with the Omaha Empowerment Network in launching the Redefine the Game Institute, a leadership development program for Black professionals based on the ten game-changing strategies in our first book, *Black Faces in White Places*. BCT and the Omaha Empowerment Network had established a long-standing and trusting relationship based on years of working together on various community and economic development initiatives before launching the institute.

Tier 3: Joint Venture—After graduating from the federal government's 8(a) business development program for government contractors, BCT established three small-business joint ventures—the Brunswick-BCT Group, NTouch-BCT Strategies (founder and managing partner, Natasha Williams-Pinkett), and BCT-FEI Partners—to maintain eligibility and competitiveness for certain federal contracts. Each joint venture was formed in partnership with people and organizations with whom BCT had already been doing business and had already established trust.

Tier 3: Merger/Acquisition—Dr. Pinkett met and became good friends with Janet Reid, Vincent Brown, and David Hunt when Dr. Pinkett's neighbor, Milton Anderson, was working at RWJBarnabas Health and hired BCT to deliver unconscious bias training for their leaders. Anderson recommended that BCT develop a collaboration with Reid and Brown whereas Hunt had previously conducted training at RWJBarnabas Health. Training almost a thousand people together formed trusting relationships among all the parties that would later blossom. Reid and Brown, who previously founded Global Novations, the largest Black-owned diversity, equity, and inclusion (DEI) consulting firm (which they sold to Korn Ferry), became mentors, sponsors, and strategic advisers to BCT Partners. BCT would eventually close its first acquisition by purchasing Hunt's company, Critical Measures, which further expanded BCT's DEI work into the health care industry.

Clearly, trust has always been a cornerstone to our successful strategic partnerships across all tiers. But not all of our efforts have been successful, as we have had several failed attempts. The most significant occurred after more than one year of planning discussions and drawing up legal documentation, when a potential merger partner walked away from the deal at the eleventh hour as a result of personality clashes. The failed merger was a major setback. We learned some valuable, albeit painful and costly, lessons from the experience about the importance of trust among all parties at the table. We were able to apply those lessons to subsequent deals, including the aforementioned acquisition of Critical Measures.

It is undoubtedly because BCT has formed strategic partnerships at every tier with people and organizations we trust that the company has grown to be proudly recognized by *Black Enterprise* as one of the nation's largest Black-owned businesses, by *Forbes* as one of America's Best Management Consulting Firms, and by *Inc.* as one of the five thousand fastest-growing private companies in America, and as the EY Entrepreneur of the Year.

FIND A UNIQUE POINT OF LEVERAGE

When amplifying action for synergy, duplicating what others have done may not be effective. Finding that unique point of leverage to increase economic or social impact is a key aspect to getting synergy to work for you. Once you identify that unique point of leverage, you can join your own skill set and tool set with the skill set and tool set of others to make new businesses and organizations that make an even greater economic and/or social impact.

A good example of this action step comes from the social sector. Dr. Cheryl Dorsey, the longtime president of social entrepreneur funder Echoing Green, wanted to diversify who was supported as a social entrepreneur. In most cases, young, white, Ivy League–educated fellows were funded to address social problems outside of the United States. These social entrepreneurs were doing amazing work, but where were the people ready to address the pressing needs of the Black community? Too often, they were not represented in the final list of Echoing Green fellows.

To address this challenge, Echoing Green formed a strategic partnership in 2012 with the Open Society's Campaign for Black Male Achievement. Echoing Green was known for identifying social innovators who work on the world's most pressing problems. The Campaign for Black Male Achievement (CBMA), led by Shawn Dove, was known for its pioneering work to address the challenges facing Black men and boys. Together they developed a new fellowship program that was specifically dedicated to improving the life outcomes of Black men and boys.

This type of strategic partnership had never been tried before in the multi-decade history of Echoing Green or, for that matter, anywhere in the United States. The result has been a new wave of Black social innovators and other social entrepreneurs who are focused on issues in Black communities around the US. From 2012 to 2018, Echoing Green invested $6 million in eighty-six CBMA fellows through the fellowship. These eighty-six fellows collectively have earned more than $53 million for their impactful work over the same period. That's amplified action!

For Echoing Green and CBMA, the unique point of leverage was found at the intersection of social innovation and programs that increased Black male achievement. The combination of tool sets, skill sets, and capital from all parties were best suited for harnessing social innovation to affect the Black community.

Amplified Action Steps to Reach Scale

DEVELOP SYSTEMS THAT TRANSCEND PEOPLE AND PERSONALITIES

Black intrapreneurs and entrepreneurs must build internal capacity that does not rely upon specific people being present to make the company work. Many organizations and companies crumble after the founders leave. This often happens because the founders did not infuse a culture of excellence, effectiveness, and efficiency that would outlive their engagement in the company or organization.

There are some success stories that remind us of the importance of developing systems that transcend people and personalities. When Bert Mitchell left his job as managing partner at Lucas Tucker & Co. in 1972, he wanted to lead his own accounting firm on his own terms. He worked for a year on his own and then in 1974 invited a colleague to join him, Robert Titus, who was working as a sole practitioner. He shared his books with Titus, and an alliance was born. "I was sold on the partnership when Bert showed me his financial statements," Titus told *Black Enterprise*. "He had a good set of clients, and he was making money."

Fast-forward thirty years, and Mitchell & Titus, LLP grew to become the largest minority-controlled accounting firm in the US., with offices in the Northeast and Chicago. The firm's growth strategy has included going after not-for-profits, municipalities, government-funded organizations, small businesses, and building strategic partnerships with bigger firms on large projects and acquiring other firms. They grew through strategic partnerships with larger accounting firms and acquisition of smaller ones.

As the firm grew, it also kept a keen eye on building the firm in a way that it would live on beyond its founders. "One of the great joys of working in a new firm like this is to watch it grow as you turn it over to a new generation," Titus told *Ebony* magazine in 1991. "We want Mitchell/Titus & Co. to outlive Mitchell and Titus, and we're on our way to providing for that."

At that time, nearly half of its sixteen partners were still in their thirties. The company deliberately recruited young talent and shared a financial interest in the business with them so they could hold onto them.

"We were willing to share interest in the business with young Black professionals at a very early stage," Mitchell told *Ebony*, "because we were concerned about harnessing talent. Sometimes we would say, 'Well, maybe this person needs another year or two before letting them into the partnership ranks.' But we would decide to err on the other side and gave people an opportunity as early as possible. And I think that strategy has prevented our best people from being stolen."

Today, that strategy has resulted in exactly what Mitchell and Titus wanted. Titus retired in 1995 and Mitchell retired in 2010 with a new CEO and full team in place to take the firm forward. In 2017, Mitchell Titus became an independent member of the BDO Alliance USA, which allows "access to the specialized resources and capacity of this national network, which is 500 member firms strong."[2]

Without succession planning

your organization will successfully die.

BE DELIBERATE ABOUT ALIGNING ORGANIZATIONAL CULTURE WITH YOUR SCALING STRATEGY

Organizational culture is one of the keys to creating companies and organizations that can scale up. Every organization has a culture—even when they don't try to create one. An organization's culture is all of the unwritten rules, policies, and norms that hold the organization together. Every organization has a way it hires employees, rewards managers, develops talent, makes decisions, and competes with other companies or organizations. Our advice is to be deliberate about the culture and make sure it matches your scaling goal.

This alignment takes place internally and externally. Internally, you'll want there to be alignment between your organizational culture and your scaling strategy. When a company is small and new, it is much easier to set and maintain the culture. But as the number of employees and the complexity of the organization increases, it becomes much more challenging. Empowering the executives to take risks and propose new strategic directions requires a different culture than a company that is very conservative in its approach to growth. If you want your organization to take risks and be innovative, then you must organize it with this in mind. If risk taking is not right for your organization, then don't build a culture that rewards it. Be deliberate about creating your own organizational culture.

Organizational culture should also influence who will engage when you want to scale up through merger or acquisition. The founder of Urban One (formerly known as Radio One), Cathy Hughes, told us in an interview that corporate culture made a difference in each of the partnerships she has considered. When she reflected upon the merger discussions that took place between BET and Radio One back in 1989, she believes that the two companies had two different cultures and different points of view. She told us, "Syndicated Communications sat us down and said, listen, both of you are going great guns, but look how powerful you would be if, in fact, you had a cable network, Cathy and Alfred. And how powerful you'd be, Bob, if you had a radio network. So, since you know, we're responsible for the both of you, why don't we put the two of you all together?" (Note: Syndicated Communications is a private equity firm that had invested in both BET and Radio One to get them started in 1980.)

Clearly, both companies were seeking strategic partnerships to increase the scale of their economic impact. But it didn't happen. For a merger to work, more than markets and economics must be aligned. The executives and the culture of the two companies also have to be complementary

Hughes definitely had a mindset that was about growth and entrepreneurship. Within ten years of those merger discussions, Radio One was valued at $950 million, and in 1999 it was traded publicly for the first time on the New York Stock Exchange. This made Hughes the first Black woman to head a publicly traded firm in the US. Her son, Alfred Liggins III, became the CEO, and she moved over to the chair of the board of directors.

The merger with BET didn't happen, but in 2003, Radio One formed a joint venture with the Comcast Corporation and its owners, the Roberts family, called TV One, which launched in January of 2004. Initially, Radio One owned 36 percent of the joint venture and had creative control. Hughes says that that joint venture worked because "they're a family operation just like us." By 2011, Radio One had acquired a 50.8 percent share of the joint venture and controlled the company. By 2015, Hughes had bought out Comcast's share and brought it together with Radio One to create Urban One. Finding the right partner led to an increase in the scale and economic impact of the Hughes/Liggins empire.

In 2015, Urban One acquired 53 percent and then 80 percent of Reach Media. Reach Media had the biggest syndicated radio shows in urban America, and bringing these assets into Urban One expanded the market reach of the company. She told us, "Our merger with Reach Media, Tom Joyner's company, turned out to be very, very profitable for everyone involved." She attributes this to the ease of working with a company with similar values and culture as well.

PUSH THE ENVELOPE ON STRATEGIC PARTNERSHIPS BY PUTTING PRIDE ASIDE

Black entrepreneurs seeking to create long-lasting institutions for the Black community beyond personal family gain must put aside any family pride, personalities, and politics to build strategic partnerships with fellow Black entrepreneurs and non-Black entrepreneurs. We must push the envelope and explore the entire continuum of strategic partnerships—especially Tiers 2 and 3—more so than the more commonplace I'll-call-you, you-call-me collaborations at Tier 1. Do not make the mistake of assuming that Tier 2 and 3 strategic partnerships are only at the discretion of large companies! But to do this in the spirit of Strategic Action 8 and *ubuntu*, all parties must put their egos aside, because the larger and more complicated the deal, the more susceptible it can be to becoming derailed. We experienced this firsthand with our failed merger.

We interviewed Bob Johnson, the founder of BET, about the merger discussions with Radio One, and he eloquently explained the nuances involved that often prevent Black entrepreneurs from merging with other businesses. Here is an excerpt from our interview:

> **Bob Johnson:** What I learned, and it was just not Radio One, we attempted to do an assets merger and even one with the great John Johnson, a joint venture and a magazine. To this day, I do not know of a major company that came about as a result of a merger of Black business owners. And it's not just ego. First of all, most Black businesses are family-run proprietary businesses that were created as a result of

segregation that prevented Blacks from doing business in the broader community . . .

That's why Black businesses would never merge, because if I'm an owner of a business, I own that business for my family. It's almost like a family heirloom. In fact, when I sold BET to Viacom, I was accused by a number of people of selling almost a Black legacy or a Black heirloom. And they felt that it should be perpetually and eternally Black owned. They saw it as you're selling out, not only a Black business but a Black voice.

So, if you're going to merge a business, and there are five family members on one side and five family members on the other side who are, if you will, receiving their financial well-being off of that business, you got to be damn careful in who you imagine you're coming together with. If that business doesn't work, then both families suffer. Or if some family members are in the business that don't really pull their weight but are there because they're family members, and the other guy coming in says, "I'm going to be the CEO, and the first thing I'm going to do is fire your cousin or your brother." It's really complicated to bring about a Black merger. These businesses suffer from that and plus, they have difficulty getting to scale.

And Johnson is correct. There are no major large-scale Black business mergers. We have seen several successful Black-owned companies that have been acquired by much larger corporations. For example, Shea Moisture was acquired by Unilever, Carol's Daughter was acquired by L'Oréal, Bevel by Proctor & Gamble, and before being acquired by Sundial Brands, *Essence* magazine was owned by Time Inc. But we cannot name one large-scale multihundred-million-dollar merger between two Black-owned businesses.[3]

The lesson we take from our failed merger and the BET and Radio One story is that company culture matters as much as the intentions of the founding executives in charge. When we come together while uplifting the principles of collectivism over individualism, we cannot only leverage our might but can do so at tremendous size and scale leading to significant social and economic impact. We need to think broader, beyond our independent strength or our family's interdependent strength.

Innovate locally. Scale globally.

FIND THE RIGHT MODEL FOR REACHING SCALE

Finding the right model for reaching scale is critical in any company or organization. Strategic Action 9 has described many different types of strategic partnerships that can be the "right" model for reaching scale for economic or social impact. When scaling for economic impact, finding the right model will also tell you how much financial capital or what kind of strategic partnerships you'll need to make it happen. You'll need to make decisions about who will be the partners or investors in your business. You'll need to figure out if having multiple business units or franchising is your path to scale.

These were the questions that Lisa Price, the founder of beauty and skin-care company Carol's Daughter, had to wrestle with as the company grew from something she did as a side hustle to a multimillion-dollar business.

When Price started Carol's Daughter in 1993, she says she never imagined that it would turn out this way. Price literally was making body butters and other skin-care products in her Brooklyn kitchen. She sold her products at local festivals and church events. Eventually, customers were coming to her house to purchase and pick up their orders. Somewhere along the way, she realized that her lifestyle business could become a high growth venture that could generate wealth for her and others. By 1999, she had opened up her first storefront location. In 2004, she took on a business partner, music mogul Steve Stoute. Stoute brought business chops and connections to the table. With his guidance, Price was able to "go big." (To hear Price tell the full story, check out her interview with Guy Raz on the podcast *How I Built This*.)

The investors of 2005 put in $10 million to expand Carol's Daughter into multiple locations across the country, including a flagship store in Harlem. The funding allowed the company to expand its reach beyond New York and increase production.

Carol's Daughter was not a perfect play for economic impact. They made some mistakes along the way, and the financial crises didn't help matters. But as the CEO, Price was able to change her model for economic impact by reconfiguring the partners, investors, and processes for every stage of the business. At its height, the company had eighteen hundred employees nationwide.

Ultimately, Price and her partners exited the business when L'Oréal acquired Carol's Daughter in 2014 in a deal reported to be worth $27 million. That's large-scale economic impact from a business that started in Price's kitchen!

Models of social impact will also involve strategic partnerships and financial capital. In Chicago, Brenda Palms Barber created Sweet Beginnings as the for-profit social enterprise spin-off from her nonprofit, North Lawndale Employment Network, and as an extension of their community job training program. Using a hybrid social venture model (a for-profit company owned by a nonprofit organization) to provide a narrow, deep impact, Sweet Beginnings provides job opportunities for formerly incarcerated men and women from the local neighborhood. Since 2004, they have built a line of all-natural skin-care products and organic honey under the brand name BeeLove (www.BeeLoveBuzz.com).

By providing job training and employment and developing an intensive work preparation program called U-Turn Permitted, Sweet Beginnings has employed nearly five hundred people.[4] Amazingly, the recidivism rate for these five hundred people is just around 4 percent. Her model of change is to give these men and women a chance to work, and once they have proven themselves in this setting, they are able to find work in other places. Her work has made a big impact on each of the men and women who have worked as beekeepers, in manufacturing, or in sales and customer service. And to achieve this goal of community transformation, Barber formed several strategic partnerships with the City of Chicago, the Chicago O'Hare Airport, the Department of Corrections, and even Whole Foods. Ultimately, the entire community is affected by this model of social impact.

By contrast, KIPP creates schools that provide an alternative to the public school system. Through its unique educational model, it establishes high academic standards, focuses on useful behavioral patterns, and implements rigorous teaching techniques to develop well-educated students throughout the country. KIPP pursues school charters and partners with school districts in urban areas. KIPP's model of change is scalable as it expands the number of schools it runs across the country through partnerships, establishing a network of similar social ventures, and through increasing the capacity of its school leaders.

Both of these social impact examples use different models of change based on the scale intended by the individual organizations. Both used collaborative actions that resulted in amplified action to increase the ultimate output.

TRANSFORMING SYSTEMS
FOR YOUTH IN HARLEM

The story of Harlem Children's Zone (HCZ), formerly known as Rheedlen Centers for Children and Families, is a story of scaling strategically to transform systems.

HCZ was founded by Geoffrey Canada, who grew up in the South Bronx and studied education at Harvard. In the late 1990s while working at Rheedlen, he grew frustrated that its after-school, antiviolence, and truancy prevention programs weren't doing enough to decrease the low graduation rates, criminal activity, and youth unemployment that afflicted the community.

"There wasn't one thing going wrong for our children in Harlem; it was everything that they came in contact with. Our children ended up in the worst schools, they had the worst health care," Canada has said.

The HCZ team put together a program that connects education, health, and youth development issues. Its comprehensive cradle-to-college philosophy includes programming for babies and parents, preschoolers, and older students. And it appreciates the complexity of the urban environment and running a thousand-student school.

Today, HCZ has fifteen community centers serving more than thirteen thousand children and adults, including more than nine thousand children considered "at risk." The emphasis of HCZ's work is not just on education, social services, and recreation but on rebuilding the very fabric of community life. It seeks to combat truancy and the breakdown of families in less economically successful neighborhoods (primarily in Harlem).

"We had to create a pipeline, starting at birth, that ensured our children came into the world healthy and happy and that stayed with these children through every developmental stage of their life until they graduated and then went into college. And then we would stay with this group of children through college," Canada said. "And instead of having so many of our children dropping out of school and getting involved with drugs and crime, we would have the next generation of successful parents, of successful taxpayers. We would have a generation of young Harlem adults prepared to take their places in this new global economy and compete successfully with children any place in America, and indeed in any place in the world."

HCZ's strategy for scaling up its efforts was written in the organization's ten-year business plan. In 1997, the agency began a network of programs for a twenty-four-block area—the Harlem Children's Zone Project. In that same year it spread to an almost one-hundred-block area serving seventy-four hundred children and more than forty-one hundred adults.

HCZ has partnered with many different organizations and institutions in New York City, including Harlem Hospital and the Harlem

Health Promotion Center, to monitor and treat asthma patients. It has worked with corporate, family, and private foundations and various agencies and departments in New York City and New York State government. This approach to scaling up begins with a pilot project to make sure the model works and then partners with people and organizations to expand the footprint of that impact. Each of these strategic partnerships allowed HCZ to increase the scale and scope of their social impact within the one hundred blocks of the zone.

In 2009, two Harvard University researchers released a study that showed that children educated in the Harlem Children's Zone made exceptional gains. They found that math test scores for eighth graders jumped 35 percentage points from where they were two years earlier when they entered the Children's Zone's charter middle school, Promise Academy. English language scores rose 14 percentage points.

But what about other communities in other cities? One way to scale up the social impact of the Harlem Children's Zone would be to establish HCZs in other places around the country. But Canada and the executives of HCZ did not use this approach. Canada believed that the model worked well for New York but wasn't convinced that it could be adopted wholesale in other places. Furthermore, Canada was concerned about burdening his staff with the hundreds of individual requests for technical assistance.

The alternative was to periodically allow leaders from any community around the nation to come to HCZ and experience how it works. Then, these leaders could take what they learned back and modify it for their own community. HCZ essentially created a model and gave it away to anyone who could use it. They established the HCZ Practitioners Institute to address the demand from other communities to learn the HCZ way.

In 2010, President Obama announced that HCZ would be used as the model for a national program to create programs in twenty "Promise Neighborhoods" and allocated $10 million toward the planning of the initiative, which could lead to an expansion of HCZ's approach to communities throughout the US. This strategic partnership with the federal government led to many communities developing HCZ-like initiatives in communities that needed help. A major part of the new initiative was the establishment of the Promise Neighborhood Institute, a strategic partnership with PolicyLink led by Angela Glover Blackwell.

HCZ transformed community systems by using every tier of strategic partnerships. They scaled strategically to significantly expand their social impact both locally and nationally.

Transforming Systems and Leaving a Legacy

Transforming systems can lead to different degrees of impact and is a result of the efforts of entrepreneurs and intrapreneurs who are seeking social and economic impact.

Thinking back to the stories of some of the social impact in the last few chapters, we can see some fantastic examples of transforming systems. Angela Glover Blackwell's PolicyLink seeks to transform policy systems for social justice. Geoffrey Canada and Harlem Children's Zone seek community transformation through youth development. Brenda Palms Barber and Sweet Beginnings seek to transform a Chicago neighborhood by expanding the job and economic opportunities for formerly incarcerated men and women. Cheryl Dorsey and Echoing Green with Shawn Dove and the Campaign for Black Male Achievement invest in innovative solutions to transform the outcomes of Black men and boys. These Black faces in high places demonstrate how people and organizations can fight government, corporations, and community leaders and use whatever power they have through systems transformation and strategic partnerships to push for changes in society.

The same could be said for the stories of economic impact. Companies that grow their businesses into institutions take on expanded roles in society as well. The larger they become, the more that society expects from them. Companies can affect citizens and customers on a large scale. Mitchell Titus grew to become the most successful minority-owned public accounting firm and changed the perceptions of the accounting community about minority-owned enterprises. In Strategic Action 7 we explored the importance of social intrapreneurs who challenge their corporations to continuously improve their marketing efforts in the Black community. And then there are the examples of Black CEOs like Ursula Burns, Ken Chenault, and Ken Frazier who have guided multibillion-dollar corporations to new economic heights while also leaving a legacy of speaking truth to power and speaking up for social justice. Entrepreneurs like David Steward labored to grow WWT into a multibillion-dollar business enterprise that has changed the landscape of the information technology industry. The same could be said for Cathy Hughes and Bob Johnson. These Black faces in high places transformed systems leading to economic impacts.

To make long-term change you must wrestle with the things that make institutions, institutions. If you are ready to transform systems, you are working to change, if not completely reform, the status quo. This means you are growing an entrepreneurial venture; fighting to redirect resources within an existing corporation; advocating for new public policies that can make a lasting difference; or permanently changing people's behaviors or perceptions.

Once you do this, you are not only transforming systems, you are also reshaping the circumstances of Black people and all people in America. And in doing so, you are making America a better place. We believe that leaving a positive legacy is an important part of doing work that makes a social and economic impact. In fact, our final chapter, Strategic Action 10: Seek Significance, typifies what it means to do work that is meaningful and lasting and that transcends helping oneself to helping others.

Seek Significance

The key to realizing a dream is to focus not on success
but significance—and then even the small steps and little
victories along your path will take on greater meaning.

— OPRAH WINFREY

The wisdom of Oprah; bestselling author, speaker, coach, and pastor John Maxwell; and Christian educator, entertainer, and entrepreneur Clancy Cross are powerful in portraying the distinctive difference between seeking success and seeking significance (quotes are courtesy of media mogul and entrepreneur Necole Kane's website):

With success, my motives may be selfish; with significance, my motives cannot be selfish. Success asks, "How can I add value to myself?" Significance asks, "How can I add value to others?" If I pursue success, my joy is the result of my success; if I pursue significance, my joy is the result of others' success. With success, my influence is limited; with significance, my influence is unlimited. Success can last a lifetime; significance can last several lifetimes.

I know a lot of people who believe they are successful because they have everything they want. They have added value to themselves. But I believe significance comes when you add value to others—and you can't have true success without significance.
— JOHN MAXWELL

Being significant means living an unselfish life that puts others ahead of self. The result is a legacy defined by the number of lives impacted, rather than the size of a bank account. Fame and fortune don't define success. Even in the dictionary, "significance" precedes "success." I wonder how much better the world would be if more people focused on leaving a legacy of significance.
— CLANCY CROSS

In *The Go-Giver: A Little Story About a Powerful Business Idea,* authors Bob Burg and John David Mann similarly flip the script on how significance can even lead to greater success. The book centers on an ambitious young man named Joe—a "go-getter"—who desperately seeks success only to learn that stratospheric success is achieved by being a "go-giver"—someone who puts others' interests first and adds value to their lives. In other words, both the secret to success and the secret to significance are not found in working harder to *get more* but to *give more.*

Success is selfish and significance is selfless. Seeking significance is a skill set that flows naturally from the *servant leader's mindset* or the belief that the role of leaders is to think less about themselves and more about the well-being of others. According to leadership guru Ken Blanchard, "Self-serving leaders think leadership is all about them—but servant leaders know that leadership is about others. It's about *serving first* and *leading second.*"

Success is a societal standard, whereas significance is a spiritual one. "If you don't believe in anything else, you know, you have to believe in this principle of love. The more you give, the more you receive. Every book, regardless of the religion: the Buddhists teach it; the Muslims teach it; the Jews teach it; the Christians teach it. If you give out, you get back. It's just how God set things up. It is very wise," says Cathy Hughes.

Success, no matter how large, is temporary.

Significance, no matter how small, is timeless.

Seeking Significance: Strategic Giving and Philanthropy

Significance can be achieved by service to others, giving, and philanthropy. Figure 24 gives you an overall framework for strategic giving and philanthropy.

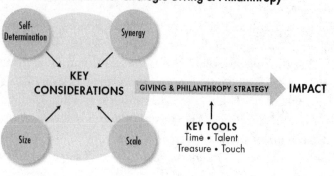

FIGURE 24

KEY CONSIDERATIONS: SELF-DETERMINATION, SYNERGY, SIZE, AND SCALE

Your giving and philanthropy strategy should be guided by three key considerations, which we have discussed previously:

1. *Self-Determination*—In what ways are your identity and purpose reflected in your giving and philanthropy? If you identify as a Black woman and one of your purposes is to empower Black girls, then how are you aligning your efforts to benefit Black women and girls?

2. *Synergy*—How are you combining your efforts with others to have a greater impact together than you could apart? Who are the like-minded and like-hearted individuals and groups you are joining forces with?

3. *Size and Scale*—Is your intended impact deep (impacting a few people) or broad (impacting many people) or both? How can you achieve the greatest possible impact?

Angela Glover Blackwell and the nonprofit organization she founded, PolicyLink, provide a strong example of how the pieces of a giving and philanthropy puzzle can all fit together for a Black face in a high place.

Advancing your career is success;

empowering your community is significance.

Among PolicyLink's many national accomplishments are implementing "Promise Neighborhoods" in twelve communities with more than $800 million in programming to improve educational outcomes for three hundred thousand children; delivering more than $1 billion in resources to create access to healthy food in low-income communities; piloting the Affirmatively Furthering Fair Housing rule to ensure fair housing and create communities of opportunity with $250 million in support; and designing and launching "My Brother's Keeper," the nation's premier boys and men of color initiative now shepherded by the Obama Foundation, and supported by more than fifty cities to advance programs for boys and men of color. In addition to this national impact, Blackwell shared the following reflections on her personal giving and philanthropy with us:

> I think my whole professional life is about giving back and giving forward. I'm generous with my contributions; at least I try to be to organizations that I'm not a part of but I think are doing good work. . . . I'm always taking time to talk to people in my office who come to see me, particularly young activists. I always will take a couple of hours to meet with people and tell them anything I know. Even though I do a lot of speaking at very visible, high-powered venues, I also will speak at a high school or community group every now and then just because I want to make sure that I'm always doing that. I'm on an advisory group for a small high school right here in Oakland just to help that small school. I'm conscious of the fact that in the community I'm viewed as someone who is very visible, and therefore I know that it means a lot to be able to go to a high school, to be able to go to a church, to go to a neighborhood function, and so I feel that's giving back. I try to give back by

providing access to young people, by speaking in places one might not necessarily think that I would speak, by giving money to organizations that are working on tough issues that are getting to people who are poor and struggling and might not be part of the work that we're doing. I think that giving back is important.

In the introduction to his book *Doing Business by the Good Book: 52 Lessons on Success Straight from the Bible,* David Steward, founder and chairman of World Wide Technology, the largest Black-owned business in America and number one on the *Black Enterprise* BE 100s list, discussed his outlook:

I can attest that when you do business by the Good Book, you get results. It works like this: Adhering to the principle of loving and caring for others, my company focuses on providing the best value and service we possibly can. Companies that do this are generally successful. Likewise, we're interested in attracting and retaining the right people. Once they come aboard, our objective is to provide them with opportunities to succeed. This is what gives me the most satisfaction. Nothing is more rewarding to me than knowing that our people are prospering and able to provide their families with such things as a fine education and new homes—all of which result from the leap of faith we took when we began this company.

My company is also my ministry. It provides not only an opportunity for me to conform to the lessons of the Bible, but also a platform on which to serve God by being an ambassador in the business world.

Steward also shared the following during an interview with us:

I spend an awful lot of time in our community with charities. I chaired the United Way, the first person of color ever to chair the United Way of Greater St. Louis. We raised . . . $68 million . . . the fifth largest campaign in the country. And I ran the United Way campaign, and I spent a lot of money, resources, and time to do that. Before that I ran

SEEK SIGNIFICANCE | 297

the African-American Giving Initiative here in St. Louis, and it's the largest in the country. My wife and I did that.

I use influence that helps move the needle to help improve the quality of life for people. And I think there is a huge return on that kind of investment. And so if you talk about power, I guess, the only power I really know, the source I know that really and truly has power, is my faith in God Himself and Jesus Christ, and that's been a reservoir of power, and there's a set of principles around that that just work.

These and other examples of strategic giving and philanthropy reflect entire lifetimes of work. Oprah, Hughes, Glover Blackwell, Burns, Steward, Chenault, Johnson, Canada, and other Black faces in high places demonstrate what can be accomplished when all ten strategic actions are put into practice. They established a great foundation of self-determination (Strategic Action 1), exposure (Strategic Action 2), self-mastery and meaning (Strategic Action 3). They built solid personal relationships (Strategic Action 4), developmental relationships (Strategic Action 5) and leveraged the power of strength in numbers (Strategic Action 6). They carried out illustrious careers as social intrapreneurs and social entrepreneurs (Strategic Actions 7 and 8). And then they figured out ways to bring people, organizations, synergy, and scale together to achieve a social and economic impact (Strategic Action 9). Their legacies are further amplified by their strategic giving and philanthropy (Strategic Action 10).

The golden rule is

"Treat others the way you want to be treated."

The platinum rule is

"Treat others the way they want to be treated."

Key Tools:
Time, Talent, Treasure, and Touch

The key tools for giving and philanthropy:

- *Time*—Dedicating your time to worthy causes and initiatives
- *Talent*—Contributing your skills and abilities to efforts that can benefit from them
- *Treasure*—Donating money, goods, and other resources to people and organizations
- *Touch*—Doing the little things that can mean a lot

We believe the purpose of giving and philanthropy are to make contributions back to our community, our nation, our society, and our world. Your *giving and philanthropy strategy* therefore defines how you will use your tool set of time, talent, treasure, and touch to achieve the greatest impact.

GIVING AND PHILANTHROPY THROUGH TIME AND TALENT

If you have already decided to give of your time or your talent, then you should also ask the question, *What approach will I take to giving and philanthropy?* There is a difference between spending time delivering food baskets to needy families during Thanksgiving and mentoring a student through high school. The food delivery is a onetime event, and mentoring is ongoing. Balancing these two approaches brings some depth to your giving and philanthropy. If all of your giving and philanthropy are on a onetime basis, you'll never have the chance to understand an issue or the concerns of others with any depth. You also may never know the impact of your service. Providing ongoing support or sustained efforts allows you to see how they change over time.

There are several models of giving and philanthropy through time and talent:

- *Join Community Volunteer Programs*—It's been said that "volunteers are not paid—not because they are worthless, but because they are priceless." There are many organizations that need volunteers to get their good works done. If you are already involved in organizations, then you'll have plenty of opportunities to volunteer. But what if you don't know where to volunteer? There are several organizations and websites that can help you find volunteer opportunities. Organizations like the United Way and the American Red Cross provide local opportunities for volunteering. You can search online databases on the Volunteer Match, Mercy Corp, and Idealist websites. Some workplaces host "volunteer challenges" or other competitions to see which unit will have the highest number of volunteer hours. Certainly, religious and faith-based institutions, such as churches, mosques, temples, and so on, offer plenty of opportunities through their various ministries, fellowships, and community outreach. These are all great ways to get involved.

- *Join Corporate Volunteer Programs*—Most corporations give of their employees' time and talent as a social responsibility to the community where the corporation is based. Your company may be willing to give you time off for community service or allow you to provide pro bono services to organizations that can leverage your expertise.

- *Practice Mentoring*—In Strategic Action 5 we discussed the value of being a mentor. Mentoring young people is a great way to give back to the local community. There are formal programs set up to mentor young people during critical times in their lives. Both of us have participated in these types of programs. When Dr. Robinson worked at Merck in the Philadelphia area, he was a mentor for a program called Sponsor-A-Scholar, an initiative run by the community organization called Philadelphia Futures. A young man named Tyrus was his mentee from his first year in high school until his first year in college at St. Joseph's University. Dr. Pinkett still considers himself a mentor to Tuwisha Rogers-Simpson, who previously worked as his public relations manager for several years. Even though she has moved on to bigger and better things, they have maintained a relationship, and he continues to teach, coach, and counsel her on personal and professional matters.

- *Explore Voluntourism*—This adds a significant volunteerism component to a vacation. Former New Orleans mayor and Louisiana lieutenant governor Mitch Landrieu helped to promote this idea as a response to the needs in the Gulf Coast after Hurricanes Katrina and Rita. As "voluntourists," many people used their vacation time and traveled to New Orleans and the surrounding areas to help out in any way they could. This is a nice combination of exposure (Strategic Action 2) with giving and philanthropy.

- *Support Missions and Missionary Work*—Mission trips are run by faith-based organizations to do good works in needy areas. They take on many different forms. Janeen Uzzell, who was instrumental in getting General Electric's Africa Project off the ground, was inspired to do work on the African continent because of a mission trip she took to Kenya in 2006. Some mission trips focus on providing medical care with a team of medical professionals and volunteers. Rev. Paul J. James, senior pastor of Careview Community Church in Lansdowne, Pennsylvania, takes a "Dream Team" of skilled African Americans committed to improving the continent of Africa on mission trips. They donate their time to make cultural connections, empowering partnerships, and long-term relationships with local communities while evangelizing and ministering to them. Most people think of these as foreign mission trips, but there are also many mission trips to inner cities and rural areas in the US that are in need.

- *Join a Nonprofit Board of Directors*—This is a great way to use your time and talent for a nonprofit organization or foundation. Nonprofit organizations can benefit from having people with various backgrounds on their board, especially if they bring skill sets and expertise that they need. An unfortunate trend in this area is the disconnect between the demographics of the boards of directors of foundations and poverty-serving nonprofit organizations and the populations they serve. A report by the Greenlining Institute concluded that 25 percent of the board members at the forty-six wealthiest foundations were people of color. Thirteen of these forty-six foundations had no people of color on their boards. A different study of youth-serving organizations also concludes that diversity of boards of directors is an issue.

  - ▸ To address this challenge, the United Way of Bluegrass in central Kentucky has collaborated with the National Conference for Community and Justice and the Urban League of Lexington-Fayette County to launch "Get On Board," a program designed to increase diversity on boards of nonprofit organizations by providing training and matching boards with qualified individuals. We encourage anyone who wants to give back generously to consider joining with organizations as board members.

- *Enlist in Public Service*—Public service is a broad category of giving and philanthropy through time and talent. In general, if you are involved in public service, you are helping to address social and economic issues that are important to our nation. Rutgers University's School of Public Affairs and Administration launched a new undergraduate major in public service that gives students "deeper understanding of their roles as public servants, broadly defined: Employees of government and not-for-profits, elected officials, members of boards and communities at the local level, volunteers, philanthropists, etc., in the context of civic engagement." Starting salaries are sometimes low in these types of careers, but the longer you do it and the more expertise you bring to the table, the more you will be rewarded. And, of course, there is the reward that comes in providing vital public service as an elected official, educator, community organizer, or one of the many other jobs that are part of the public and social sectors.

LEGACY GIFTS

Legacy gifts are a major source of income for many nonprofits. A legacy gift is a financial donation (a sum of money) or an appreciating asset (business, real estate, jewelry, and so on) left to an organization after the death of a donor to help the organization continue its operations. This is a great way to leave some of your treasure for others. Here are some considerations:[1]

1. *Prepare a will.* Only 40 percent of those who pass away have one. Without a will, you may lose control over your personal possessions.
2. *Leave a gift in your will for any nonprofit organizations that made a difference in your life.* Americans are generous—80 percent of us give to charity each year. Surprisingly, less than 6 percent of Americans have included nonprofits in an estate plan. Imagine the positive impact on our community if everyone made a donation to their favorite nonprofits. Leave a specific dollar amount or a percentage of the assets in your will to the nonprofits of your choice.
3. *Encourage family and friends to leave gifts in their wills to nonprofits that service the Black community.*
4. *Consider using appreciated assets to fund current charitable gifts and planned gifts.* These include, but are not limited to, stocks, bonds, securities, certificates of deposit, real estate,

SEEK SIGNIFICANCE | 303

SEEK SIGNIFICANCE | 303

SEEK SIGNIFICANCE | 303

SEEK SIGNIFICANCE | 303

SEEK SIGNIFICANCE | 303

SEEK SIGNIFICANCE | 303

SEEK SIGNIFICANCE | 303

SEEK SIGNIFICANCE | 303

SEEK SIGNIFICANCE | 303

SEEK SIGNIFICANCE | 303

vehicles, art, and jewelry. Such gifts may even provide tax savings. Contact a professional adviser for advice.

5. *Name organizations as the beneficiary of your pension plan, IRA, or retirement plan.* Doing so can avoid estate and income taxes (up to 70 percent) that might otherwise be due on your plan. Be sure to seek the advice of an attorney or accountant when designating a charity as partial beneficiary of a retirement account.

6. *Name your designated nonprofit as the owner or beneficiary of a new or existing life insurance policy, a bequest of property, or a charitable trust.*

7. *Ask your financial adviser to include charitable giving as part of their counsel to clients.*

GIVING AND PHILANTHROPY THROUGH TREASURE

The African American community has a long history and tradition of philanthropy. As a people, we have proudly used many different models of giving our treasure through churches and other organizations. One of the unfortunate patterns we see in African American communities, however, is a reactive approach to giving and philanthropy. Here is a scenario we have seen before: There is an extreme need this week and we raise some money to address it. Then that money is used up and then the need comes back again six months later. A proactive approach would be the endowment approach: let's raise enough money to create an endowment or foundation that will be able to address the issue well into the future. This approach considers the long term while the reactive approach looks only at the short term.

There are several models of giving and philanthropy through treasure, including proactive approaches:

- *Donate to Charities and Charitable Organizations*—The most straightforward way to give of your treasure is to donate directly to a charity. Since there are so many charities established, how do you know which ones to give to? You should certainly give to organizations that you believe in or whose work you believe is making a difference. If you want to check out an organization, you can read their annual reports or visit websites that rate charities according to fundraising efficiency, administrative costs, and capacity like Charity Navigator (www.charitynavigator.org) and GuideStar (www.guidestar.org).

- *Leverage Online Platforms for Donations*—While many are familiar with microdonation sites such as GoFundMe (www.gofundme.org) and know that many charities accept donations online, there are other ways to donate to charities via the internet. Several websites have emerged in recent years that allow the user to participate in online fundraisers. This takes the time out of going to a specific event or gala, for instance. Examples of this include First Giving (www.firstgivigng.org), where you can make your own fundraising page to raise money for a nonprofit organization and accept donations online, and Bidding for Good (www.biddingforgood.com). A second set of websites facilitates donations or financial transactions with people around the world or in a local community. An example of this is Donor's Choose (www.donorschoose.org), where the donors are able to select specific requests, and Modest Needs (www.modestneeds.org), which offers grants directly to individuals and families in temporary crisis and to promote their self-sufficiency. Lastly, Snowball (www.snowball.it) and OneCause (www.onecause.com) are platforms that support donations via text message.

- *Create a Foundation*—Foundations are organizations that exist to give money away to other organizations or individuals. They are the traditional approach to giving one's amassed treasure away over a long period of time. Some wealthy individuals take a portion of their wealth and create foundations to fund the activities of organizations that fit the mission or purpose of the foundation. Some of the largest examples of foundations are organizations named after the wealthiest families in business— Rockefeller Foundation, Ford Foundation, Kellogg Foundation, Kauffman Foundation, and Gates Foundation. But you don't have to be a billionaire to start a foundation. In 2005, Karen Proudford and her family started a foundation named after their father. The William E. Proudford Sickle Cell Fund is charged with raising money to research a cure and assist people living with sickle cell anemia. Creating a foundation is a great example of what you can do to create a vehicle that will keep on giving.

- *Participate in Giving Circles*—Giving circles are a form of giving that brings people together for organized giving. A giving circle is funded by a circle of individuals who agree to put in a minimum amount into the "giving circle" each year. Members of the circle then bring recommendations to the group for grants. The giving circle votes on who to give to until the funds are gone. Then they repeat the process for the next year. According to the Forum of Regional Associations of Grantmakers, giving circles have raised more than $100 million over the past four years, and the number of giving circles doubled to four hundred from 2004 to 2006. For example, the Black Philanthropic Alliance of the greater Washington, DC, area has established the Black Benefactors giving circle to "address the social ills plaguing Black communities in the region." For more on giving circles, visit unitedphilforum.org or www.philanthropytogether.org.

- *Create or Support Endowments*—An endowment is a sum of money that is set aside for a specific person. When it is set up properly, an endowment can last for many years into the future because the principal is invested in a vehicle that provides enough interest to achieve its charitable goals without touching the principal. Many university scholarships are endowments because the actual scholarship funds are paid out of the interest of the endowment. If you are seeking a way to make a longer-term impact with your treasure, consider setting up an endowment.

- *Create Donor-Advised Funds*—Donor-advised funds are the fastest growing charitable giving vehicle in the nation (according to The National Philanthropic Trust). A donor-advised fund allows an individual to place wealth into a managed account that will identify and fund the types of causes that the donor wants to fund. This approach is similar to that of foundations, but it has fewer administrative costs associated with it because the fund is managing the donations for many different clients.

- *Contribute to Political Campaigns*—Political campaign contributions are a form of giving your treasure that allow you to endorse the policies and values of a political candidate. Alternatively, you could support a political action committee, or PAC, which is a private group organized to help elect political candidates. There are strict rules regarding these types of donations, so check them out before you donate.

- *Enlist Matching Funds*—Many corporations want to support the giving of their employees. They will match any donation that you give to a qualified organization. Most of the time, this requires that you fill out some forms to alert your company that you have given a donation already to an organization. They will verify the detail and eligibility, and your donation amount just doubled!

- *Practice Venture Philanthropy*—Venture philanthropy combines the ideas of venture capital with philanthropic giving (discussed in Strategic Action 8). The term *venture philanthropy* emerged during the late 1990s to describe the approach many former internet entrepreneurs who had recently become millionaires used to perform their giving. They gave to organizations that could demonstrate a social return on investment (SROI). This meant that organizations had to adjust their way of explaining their outcomes. New organizations also emerged during this time, led by or influenced by this idea of measuring (not just evaluating) the impact of these social ventures. Examples of venture philanthropists include the investors associated with Social Venture Partners International (www.svpi.org), Social Venture Circle/American Sustainable Business Council (www.svcimpact.org), and Acumen Fund (www.acumen.org).

- *Donate Goods*—There are several options for donating goods beyond traditional and worthwhile donations of clothes, food, furniture, and canned food to organizations such as food banks, the Salvation Army, and Goodwill Industries. You can also donate more expensive goods such as cars, boats, and real estate. Be sure to familiarize yourself with the prevailing rules for tax deductions and obtain a receipt in order to maximize the benefits to the charity and minimize the risk to yourself.

- *Practice Corporate Social Responsibility*—As we discussed in Strategic Action 7, we believe corporations also have a social responsibility when it comes to giving and philanthropy. Corporations can share their resources by allowing groups to use office space in their buildings or host events for nonprofit or public service organizations.

GIVING BACK TO THE EARTH: SUPPORTING ENVIRONMENTAL JUSTICE

The Flint, Michigan, water crisis brought more attention to how environmental issues can directly affect the Black community. As a result, environmental justice has become a vital part of the modern social justice conversation because it connects the quest for equity to environmentalism. Robert Bullard, the father of the environmental justice movement, tells us that "environmental justice embraces the principle that all people and communities have a right to equal protection and equal enforcement of environmental laws and regulations."[2] As we think about how Black faces in high places can support environmental justice, we consider two levels of action: personal and professional.

On a personal level, it is important to reduce your carbon footprint and reduce your waste, recycle as much as possible, and reuse as many things as possible. If you feel underinformed on these issues, find out more about Black environmentalists and activists who have focused on environmental justice such as Bullard, Majora Carter, Omar Freilla, Van Jones, Wangari Maathai, and Lisa Jackson. Their organizations and social enterprises form a sturdy foundation for the work of today's environmental justice activists. Robinson's daughter, Gabriella, is one of those activists. She volunteers with environmental justice organizations, participates in sustainable fashion practices, and has led environmental cleanups in our local watershed areas as a part of her Girl Scout Gold Award project. In addition to giving to environmental justice efforts, the Robinson family has taken on many other efforts to reduce the carbon footprint of the household (such as hybrid and electric cars, aggressive recycling, composting, and purchasing renewable energy and sustainable products).

As a Black face in a high place, it is also important to think about how your professional activities can advance the cause of environmental justice. For example, from 2008 to 2015, Valerie Robinson was the CEO of an eco-conscious day spa and green beauty store called Eden Organix. She wrestled with many questions about the environmental sustainability of her operations as she designed the store and launched the business. The result was a business that had a much lower carbon footprint than similar businesses in the area. She also purchased from manufacturers who made sustainability a priority and made contributions to local social and environmental justice organizations that were in alignment with her mission and values. It was intentional and required thinking and rethinking business processes and operations.

For Black faces in high places, one approach to developing an environmental justice agenda is to ask critical questions of your organization or company. Here are some examples:

- What has been our history when it comes to environmental impact and communities of color?
- How can we reduce the carbon footprint of our business or organization?
- How can we purchase services and products from companies that prioritize sustainability?
- How can we improve the environmental integrity of the communities where we operate? How can we help create more open spaces, gardens, and green spaces?
- How can our business provide philanthropic support to organizations promoting environmental justice?

No matter how you approach it, actively addressing your environmental impact is an important way to practice environmental justice and give back to the earth through time, talent, and treasure.

GIVING AND PHILANTHROPY THROUGH TOUCH

There are many ways to practice giving and philanthropy through touch. Here we list a few ways, but this is one of the places where you can be the most creative:

- *Offer Words of Encouragement and Appreciation*—You should give people their roses while they are above ground. Along those lines, people often underestimate the power of words of encouragement and appreciation. It could be as simple as saying, "Thank you," or giving someone a compliment; or as thoughtful as telling someone, "I love you," or offering someone a kind word to acknowledge something they have done well; or as elaborate as staying on top of someone to do something positive and new that you believe they can accomplish. For example, were it not for the encouraging words of Dean Don Brown and Professors William Mayo and Christopher Rose at Rutgers University, Dr. Pinkett would have never considered applying for (and winning) the Rhodes Scholarship.

- *Practice Peer Counseling*—We put peer counseling in the touch category because listening and giving advice to another person in an informal way is a great way to help. Listening to someone who is having a hard time is one way to touch them in that moment.

- *Join with Prayer Partners*—We believe in prayer and know its power. When people take time to pray for each other, it can make a difference in both lives. Connecting in this special way is important for faith communities because it brings the community together and creates a place of peace for the subject of the prayers. When you have a prayer partner for a moment or for a longer period of time, you are investing your time in a way that can touch them in positive ways.

- *Perform Random Acts of Kindness*—We often hear about "random acts of violence" in our modern society—senseless acts that injure or kill people. Why can't the forces of good do something random that brings about happiness, healing, and love to others? These "random acts of kindness" are especially poignant when you know that the other person cannot repay you. For example, when Joanna Lee-Lo was diagnosed with acute lymphoblastic leukemia, she had to undergo treatments all alone in the hospital due to the COVID-19 pandemic. She chose to shave her head so the treatments would be easier, and as a sign of solidarity, her twin sister, Joella, chose to shave her head too. "I love you so much, my beautiful sister. You are a fighter, and we'll fight this battle together," she wrote in a Facebook post. As another example, when a group of Howard University students could not afford to attend a prestigious theater program at Oxford, their teacher, Phylicia Rashad, asked fellow actor Denzel Washington for help. Washington paid for it, and one of those students was Chadwick Boseman. Random acts of kindness like this are incredible ways to change the atmosphere and make the way for more kindness, gentleness, mercy, and compassion in the world.

- *Recognize "Unsung Heroes"*—A website run by the Foundation for a Better Life (www.PassItOn.com) highlights the activities of people who are doing good works to improve society. Some are famous people who are using their celebrity to bring attention to worthy causes, but most are regular people like soup kitchen volunteers or Sunday school teachers, who are committed to making changes in their local communities. The site is an attempt to change the dialogue of everyday life from focusing on tragedy to focusing on the triumphs of the human spirit.

Time, talent, treasure, and touch are the key components of giving and philanthropy. We encourage you to bring your own innovation to the models we have described above. Whenever, wherever, and however you give, the ultimate goal is to figure out ways in which you can be *strategic* in your giving and philanthropy. This next section breaks down the specific action steps to accomplish this.

BLACK WOMEN TRANSLATE PAGEANT VICTORIES INTO PLATFORMS FOR PHILANTHROPY

In 2019, history was made when Black women were crowned as the winners of the top five beauty pageants for the first time. All of the winners used their victories to establish a platform for philanthropy and social activism:

- Miss Universe, Zozibini Tunzi, fought gender-based violence.
- Miss World, Toni-Ann Singh, advocated for women enrolled in medical school.
- Miss USA, Cheslie Kryst, worked on behalf of offenders to reform America's prison system.
- Miss America, Nia Franklin, advocated for the arts with an emphasis on children.
- Miss Teen USA, Kaliegh Garris, launched a nonprofit to help people with disabilities.

AMPLIFIED ACTION STEPS FOR STRATEGIC GIVING AND PHILANTHROPY

Up to this point, we have given you many options for giving and philanthropy. Now it is important for us to give you specific action steps to be strategic in doing so. Figure 25 defines our four steps to strategic giving and philanthropy—*prepare, plan, execute,* and *evaluate.* It is a cycle because we are suggesting that you repeat the steps periodically as you think about your next steps in giving and philanthropy.

FIGURE 25

PREPARE

Preparation is the first step of the cycle. This is where you will have to make sure you are clear about your own objectives with regard to giving and philanthropy (see figure 26). The specific steps are:

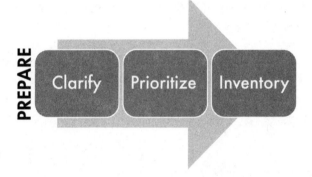

FIGURE 26

Clarify. You should begin by clarifying your personal mission, vision, and values that we asked you to create in Strategic Action 1. How do giving and philanthropy factor into your personal mission, vision, and values? How do you envision giving and philanthropy will factor into your personal mission, vision, and values? This is the perfect time to revisit your statement and see what it says about how you will support your community and society. If it doesn't include any words about how giving and philanthropy matter to you, then this is the time to incorporate them into your statement. Organizations and corporations can evaluate their statements in the same manner.

Prioritize. You should think of all the issues that you are concerned about and then prioritize the ones where you can make a significant impact as the highest on the list to tackle first.

Inventory. As you prepare for giving and philanthropy, you should take inventory of your available time, talent, treasure, and touch—take stock of your available resources. Here are some starter questions:

- How much time do you have during the week to volunteer? What about weekends?
- What talents do you have that could be donated to a charitable cause or organization?
- Are you able to give 10 percent or more of your income toward charitable activities?
- What are you committed to doing in everyday life to help others?

The answers to these questions will help you know what is realistic for your giving and philanthropy strategy. In some cases, it is important to set stretch goals or make sacrifices toward completing a goal.

PLAN

Planning allows your giving and philanthropy to be proactive as opposed to reactive. How do you plan what you are going to do with your time, talent, treasure, and touch? We suggest that you take the following steps (see figure 27):

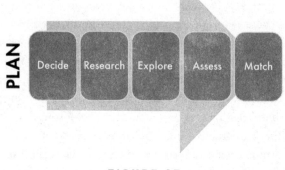

PLAN · Decide · Research · Explore · Assess · Match

FIGURE 27

Decide. During the preparation step you should have revisited your personal mission, vision, and values statement. Now that you've done that, you can decide how much of your time, talent, treasure, and touch you will use at this time to do good works. For example, you may realize that you have $5,000 that you want to donate over the year to charitable organizations. During your planning, you should decide how much you are prepared to give at various points in the year. Make some goals for yourself so that you know what you are working with while you plan out your giving and philanthropic activities.

Research. Do your homework. Identify organizations that do the kind of work you want to support. You'll find out about these organizations from various media sources, or you may ask your friends what kind of giving and philanthropic activities they are doing. This is a very broad search. It will be guided by the priority list you developed in the preparation step. As you find out more about each of these organizations, some will be more interesting to you than others.

Explore. Find out more about the organizations that are interesting to you. Narrow the list down to a set of organizations that care about the same issues or communities that you are interested in affecting. Compile a list of them as a starting point for your exploration. Go to their websites or gather information about these organizations and find out what kinds of activities they do and how those activities may match what you are able to give in terms of time, talent, treasure, and touch.

Assess. Once you have narrowed down the list to a handful of opportunities and organizations, you should take some time and assess each of the options. Evaluate each organization to determine if they are a responsible shepherd of their resources. Consider the work that they do when evaluating their budget. Some organizations are involved in work that may have high overhead, so it is not fair to penalize them for that if that is the reality; others may simply be inefficient. Similarly, some organizations may operate in areas that receive less funding than others and, therefore, may have a smaller budget (such as sickle cell anemia versus cancer). Lower funding doesn't mean they are not effective or needed; it may just be a function of the number of people interested in supporting certain causes.

QUESTIONS TO ASK A NONPROFIT ORGANIZATION BEFORE INVESTING (FROM GUIDESTAR)

- How are you collaborating with similar organizations on a local, regional, or national level?
- What are the main obstacles that inhibit the fulfillment of your mission? How are you planning to overcome them?
- What are your annual goals, needs, and results? How do they compare to similar organizations in your community?
- How much turnover have you experienced of employees and board members in the last two years?
- To what degree have you attracted new people and new ideas to your organization and board?
- How well have you utilized your funding? Describe how efficiently you have fulfilled your goals of recent years in relationship to the amount of funds you have raised.
- Most for-profit organizations have recently restructured themselves in recent years to become more efficient and productive. How, if at all, are you considering (or have you implemented) some version of this approach?
- How efficiently is your organization run? To what degree have you assigned day-to-day management responsibilities to a tightly run executive committee instead of relying upon your full board?
- Who are your main competitors and how do your results in recent years compare to theirs?

Match. The final step to planning is to match what you have figured out with a few opportunities for giving and philanthropy based on your preparation work. Ultimately, you are trying to find alignment between your mission and their mission; their values and your values; your inventory of available resources and their needs; and so on. That is the match you've been looking for. Once you've made a decision, make a commitment to that organization. Figure out all the ways you can be helpful to the organization.

EXECUTE

Execution is where the action takes place. Here is where you transition your giving and philanthropy from designing it to actually doing it. The following are principles to keep in mind:

Make It Fun. Always remember that giving and philanthropy can be enjoyable and that "God loves a cheerful giver" (2 Cor. 9:7). Explore ways to turn your philanthropic efforts into social events: invite others to join you for a charity marathon, involve family and friends in creating a giving circle, organize a sporting event that donates money to a nonprofit, or volunteer with coworkers at the same soup kitchen.

Take It Seriously. When practicing giving and philanthropy through your time and talent, the key is to be responsible: be on time, meet expectations, and give advanced notice for absences. When pledging money, be sure to honor your commitments.

Remain Focused Yet Flexible. The last action step stressed the importance of planning. And while planning is very central to strategic giving and philanthropy, you should also be willing to explore emergent or spontaneous opportunities and be flexible in your approach. For example, there may be an unexpected pandemic such as COVID-19 or tragedy akin to Hurricane Katrina that could benefit from your immediate contributions. Alternatively, on the day you show up to help build an affordable house, you may learn that they have plenty of volunteers for your assigned task and are lacking volunteers for other tasks. If you're flexible, you'll be willing to pitch in wherever you're needed most. The lesson here is to not adhere so rigidly to your plan that you're unprepared to change course and miss out on other, great opportunities to help others.

Leverage Your Contributions. You can maximize your giving and philanthropy by finding creative ways to achieve synergy across your contributions. As an example, you can combine different models, such as donating money and time, to the same cause or donating goods and services to the same organization. You should also be sure to explore how your charitable activities can be leveraged into tax savings. We advise consulting with a tax accountant or financial planner to get the most accurate and up-to-date advice.

Leverage Others' Contributions. You can also leverage might through your giving and philanthropy. Leveraging your network of relationships is one way to bring additional value to your efforts. For example, you could reach out to friends via Facebook, Twitter, or Instagram to pledge money to your walkathon. Involve your family, neighbors, and coworkers—and of course your employer through matching funds programs.

EVALUATE

Take the time to evaluate if and how your efforts are making a difference. Three principles to keep in mind are as follows:

Evaluate Performance and Outcomes. If you're going to take the time to contribute your time, talent, or treasure to an organization, you should also take the time to evaluate its performance and outcomes. When and where appropriate, you should review financial statements, annual reports, program evaluation reports, and IRS Form 990s to evaluate how the organizations are performing. By doing so, you can begin to determine the answers to the following questions: Are you getting the best leverage for your efforts? Are your resources being used in the way you intended? Are your contributions really making a difference?

Set Appropriate Expectations. You should expect any organization that you support to provide some form of documentation that demonstrates their performance in terms of their operations, finances, and how donated resources are being used. But you may not see an immediate return on your investment in a start-up charitable organization. Keep in mind that the organization's capacity will partly determine the depth and the extent of their documentation, much like the short track record of a start-up business venture. That shouldn't stop you from lending your support. Conversely, just because an organization has been in existence for several years does not mean you should take their effectiveness for granted.

Reassess Your Giving and Philanthropy Strategy. Once you have completed your evaluation of performance and outcomes, you should compare this information against your personal mission, vision, and values to determine whether there is indeed alignment between the two. This is an important step because it will suggest either that you are on the right track to making the kind of impact you desire—contributing to, changing, or reshaping America, society, and the planet—or whether you need to make adjustments, or perhaps even revisit your core beliefs. It is very possible that—by circumstance or by design—your personal mission has changed or your personal vision has been recast or your values or priorities have shifted. Based on these findings, the process loops back to "Prepare" to reassess your giving and philanthropy strategy as the cycle continues yet again.

EPILOGUE
Where Do We Go from Here?

We have fought for America with all her imperfections, not so
much for what she is, but for what we know she can be.
—MARY MCLEOD BETHUNE

Americans should be proud that we have elected President Barack
Obama and Vice President Kamala Harris. They were both once rising stars on their way to the top and, in so many ways, are emblematic
as global citizens, intrapreneurs, game changers, and servant leaders.
In the realm of politics and government, they are the epitome of people who get to the highest levels of the land yet make certain there are
opportunities for others to follow them. Obama, as the first Black
man to hold the title of president, and Harris, as the first woman and
first Black (and South Asian) woman to hold the title of vice president, have undeniably reached the high (and influential) places we
talk about in this book. And these victories could not have been possible without the incredible organizing, engagement, and participation of Black women!

The triumphs of Obama and Harris represent symbols of progress
for how far we have come and symbols of hope for what we can accomplish. As signature milestones in American history and Black history, their ascendancies also beg a perennial and timeless question,
which is also the title of the last book released by the Rev. Dr. Martin
Luther King Jr. before his assassination on April 4, 1968: "Where do
we go from here?"

Maya Angelou writes about modern Black achievers as being "the
hope and the dream of the slave." We know our ancestors celebrate the
many Black leaders, politicians, educators, lawyers, doctors, and businesspeople who make it to the top. We titled this book *Black Faces in
High Places* after a phrase coined by Mary McLeod Bethune, which

we shared in the introduction: "My people will never be satisfied until they see *Black faces in high places*." Building upon McCleod Bethune's wisdom, we are not *fully* satisfied by seeing Black faces in high places because being at the top is simply not enough. It is the beginning of how you can facilitate change, not the end, because long before you get "there" the need to improve the social and economic conditions of our communities becomes abundantly clear.

Being a Black face in a high place is not just about getting a seat at the table; it is about having a voice once you are at the table. Are you willing to fight for others, or instead, do you choose to forgo friend or take flight? Are you willing to expend your capital—human, cultural, social, intellectual, and financial—to effect change? Are you willing to sacrifice for future generations while recognizing that others sacrificed for you from past generations? If we reach the pinnacle of our industry, field, or sector only to forget who we are and where we come from and do not humbly seek significance by reaching back to help others, then any success we have achieved is worthless. If we get enamored with fortune, power, and fame, then all of the hard work and progress of the last four hundred years is in vain.

Success alone is worthless.

Significance alone is priceless.

The words of Dr. King reverberate today just as they did in 1968 when he wrote *Where Do We Go From Here: Chaos or Community?*:

Let us be dissatisfied until America will no longer have high blood pressure of creeds and an anemia of deeds. Let us be dissatisfied until the tragic walls that separate the outer city of wealth and comfort from the inner city of poverty and despair shall be crushed by the battering rams of the fires of justice. Let us be dissatisfied until they who live on the outskirts of hope are brought into the metropolis of daily security. Let us be dissatisfied until slums are cast into the junk heap of history and every family will live in a decent, sanitary home. Let us be dissatisfied until the dark yesterdays of segregated schools will be transformed into the bright tomorrows of quality integrated education.

If America is to respond creatively to the challenge [of achieving justice, equality, and cooperation . . .], many individuals, groups, and agencies must rise above the hypocrisies of the past and begin to take an immediate and determined part in changing the fact of their nation. If the country has not yet emerged with a massive program to end the blight surrounding the life of the Negro, one is forced to believe that the answers have not been forthcoming because there is as yet no genuine and widespread conviction that such fundamental changes are needed, and needed now.

For America (or any other nation) to change and become more inclusive, democratic, egalitarian, and just, we must have Black leaders who are not content—who are "dissatisfied"—with being the only one at the top. With the myriad problems that exist in our nation for Black, Indigenous, and People of Color (BIPOC) communities, we believe the 10 strategic actions across four levels of action—and the corresponding mindsets, skill sets, and tool sets that we have detailed in this book—are among the keys to reshaping America into "what we know she can be."

We must have broad shoulders and not see our roles of being Black faces in high places as a heavy burden but, rather, as an empowering force. We must see our culture as an asset and a competitive advantage and not as a liability and a societal disadvantage. We must stand on the shoulders of giants, while accepting our responsibility *to become giants* so that others can stand on our shoulders. We must have a burning desire to not only make things better for ourselves but for our entire community. And throughout our journey, while we may find ourselves as the first Black face in a particular high place, we must commit to making sure we are not the last.

ACKNOWLEDGMENTS

We first want to acknowledge the Creator, who has blessed us with the talents and abilities to bring this book to fruition.

We acknowledge that we are standing on the shoulders of all of our ancestors who came before; chief among them our parents, Elizabeth and Leslie Pinkett and Doreen and Ron Robinson.

When you write a book like this one, there are many people who are involved in making it happen. They say it takes a village to raise a child. In the case of this book, it took a village for us to write it.

We have had the privilege of working with two exceptional journalists for this book. Philana Patterson was instrumental in the writing of our first book, *Black Faces in White Places*. Some of the material we did not use the first time around ended up in this book, and her journalistic instincts influenced how we wrote this second book, *Black Faces in High Places*. For this book, we relied upon the expertise of Sakina Spruell Cole at Cole Media to finalize the manuscript and bring the project to a close. These Black professionals have made us better writers, and for that we are eternally grateful.

Along the way, we had some great people who provided research, creative, editorial, communications, marketing, public relations, and administrative assistance for the book, including Stacey Gatlin of Victory Concierge, David Poindexer, Bernadine Philistin, Miah Hagood, Suliman Olatunji, Briana Gilchrist, and Deborah Spigner; our friends at 3rd Edge Communications, Frankie Gonzalez and Rob Monroe, who designed another iconic graphic for the *Black Faces in High Places* "10 Strategic Actions" that we use in every chapter; Vic Carter at Lee-Com Media; Patricia Nueray and Kate Jordan at Tangelo; Renée E. Warren-Mebane, Kirsten Poe Hill, Michelle Pascal, Charles Williams, Ryan Stewart, Quamiesh McNeal, Stephanie Graves, and the entire public relations team at Noelle-Elaine Media; and Mary Brown at Cole Media, who brought her photographic artistry to the cover image of both books. We are grateful to our entire publishing team, including Tim Burgard, Mike Bzozowski, Esq., Gabrielle Reed, and Jeff James at

HarperCollins Leadership; and Jeff Farr, Beth Metrick, and Zoe Kaplan at Neuwirth & Associates. Additionally, our wonderful colleagues at BCT Partners and Rutgers Business School supported our efforts and inspired us to excellence. We offer a special shout-out to our current business partners, Lawrence Hibbert and Dallas Grundy, and our past business partners, Raqiba Bourne and Aldwyn Porter, who have labored with us over the years from Mind, Body & Soul Enterprises to MBS Educational Services & Training to BCT Partners. You inspired us years ago to go higher and farther, and you will forever be in our hearts.

While we were writing this book, we launched the Redefine the Game Institute (RTGI) with our friends and colleagues Willie Barney of the Omaha Empowerment Network and Damita Byrd at BCT Partners (formerly with the Omaha Empowerment Network). The Institute gave us a way to test some of the key ideas and material of this book with accomplished Black professionals. We are thankful for the cohorts who participated in RTGI and helped us to fine-tune the message and content of this book.

We are also thankful to all of the Black professionals we interviewed and engaged for this project, who willingly shared their stories and thoughts with us about being a Black face in a high place, including Joy Reid, Cathy Hughes, Bob Johnson, Janice Bryant-Howroyd, Bishop George Seawright, Rev. Dr. DeForest Soaries Jr., Dennis Pullin, Roland Martin, Hill Harper, Jeff Johnson, Cory Booker, Benjamin Jealous, Angela Glover-Blackwell, Kevin Powell, Don Thompson, Deborah Elam, Gabriella Morris, Dudley Benoit, Anthony Jerome Smalls, Gwen Kelly, Lawrence Jackson, Majora Carter, Dr. Cheryl Dorsey, Rey Ramsey, David Steward, Zackarie Lemelle, Rev. Otis Moss, III, Marnie McKoy, Darryl Cobb, Dr. Treena Arinzeh, Alonzo Adams, Wayne Winborne, and Ralph Smith.

And lastly, we acknowledge our families, who supported us when we needed to work on this book. Our families motivate us, inspire us, and sustain us. It is for you and future generations of Black people that we wrote this book.

Randal Pinkett, www.randalpinkett.com
Jeffrey Robinson, www.jeffreyrobinsonphd.com
Black Faces in High Places website, www.redefinethegame.com

NOTES

Introduction

1. Interview with David Steward by the authors.
2. Interview with Rodney Hunt by the authors.
3. Helen G. Edmonds, *Black Faces in High Places: Negroes in Government*, 1971.

Level I

1. Maria Popova, "Young Barack Obama on Identity, the Search for a Coherent Self, and How We Fragment Our Wholeness with Polarizing Identity Politics," Brain Pickings, https://www.brainpickings.org/2016/11/21/barack-obama-identity-race/.

Level II

1. Ronald S. Burt, *The Network Structure of Social Capital*, Graduate School of Business, University of Chicago and European Institute of Business Administration (INSEAD), Chicago, IL, 1999.
2. "Quick Facts: Hawaii, Texas, California, United States," United States Census Bureau, https://www.census.gov/quickfacts/fact/table/HI,TX,CA,US/PST045219.
3. William H. Frey, "The US Will Become 'Minority White' in 2045, Census Projects," Brookings, March 14, 2018, https://www.brookings.edu/blog/the-avenue/2018/03/14/the-us-will-become-minority-white-in-2045-census-projects/.
4. "Quick Facts: Hawaii, Texas, California, United States," United States Census Bureau.
5. D'Vera Chon, "It's Official: Minority Babies Are the Majority Among the Nation's Infants, but Only Just," Pew Research Center, June 23, 2016, https://www.pewresearch.org/fact-tank/2016/06/23/its-official-minority-babies-are-the-majority-among-the-nations-infants-but-only-just/.
6. Heather Long and Andrew Van Dam, "For the First Time, Most New Working-Age Hires in the U.S. Are People of Color," *Washington Post*, September 9, 2019, https://www.washingtonpost.com/business/economy/for-the-first-time-ever-most-new-working-age-hires-in-the-us-are-people-of-color/2019/09/09/8edc48a2-bd10-11e9-b873-63ace636af08_story.html.
7. Dave Evans, "The Internet of Things: How the Next Evolution of the Internet Is Changing Everything," Cisco, April 2011, https://www.cisco.com/c/dam/en_us/about/ac79/docs/innov/IoT_IBSG_0411FINAL.pdf.
8. "IoT Devices Outnumber Humans on Earth," Silicon Valley Innovation Center, February 9, 2018, https://siliconvalley.center/blog/iot-devices-outnumber-humans-on-earth.
9. Shelley Walsh, "The Top 10 Social Media Sites & Platforms 2021," Search Engine Journal, June 22, 2021, https://www.searchenginejournal.com/social-media/biggest-social-media-sites/.
10. Elif Shafak, "The Politics of Fiction," TED Talk, https://www.ted.com/talks/elif_shafak_the_politics_of_fiction/transcript?language=en#t-20094.

Strategic Action 4

1. Carla Harris, "How to Find the Person Who Can Help You Get Ahead at Work," TED Talk, https://www.ted.com/talks/carla_harris_how_to_find_the_person_who_can_help_you_get_ahead_at_work?language=en.

2. *The Game* was canceled by The CW network and was later picked up by cable network Black Entertainment Television.

3. "Black Shows Mean Nothing in Hollywood?" Entertainment Rundown, April 2, 2009, quoting from Rushmore Drive, http://entertainmentrundown.com/2009/04/page/37/.

4. *New York Post*, February 19, 2009.

5. *New York Post*, February 24, 2009.

Strategic Action 5

1. Kathy E. Kram and Lynn A. Isabella, "Mentoring Alternatives: The Role of Peer Relationships in Career Development," *Academy of Management Journal* 28, no. 1 (1985): 110–32.

2. Daniel Levinson (1920–1994) was a scholar in the field of adult human development.

3. Miller McPherson, Lynn Smith-Lovin, and James M. Cook, "Birds of a Feather: Homophily in Social Networks." *Annual Review of Sociology* 27, no. 1 (2001): 415–44.

Strategic Action 6

1. David Davenport and Gordon Lloyd, "Rugged Individualism: Dead or Alive," The Hoover Institute, January 10, 2017, https://www.hoover.org/research/rugged-individualism-dead-or-alive-0.

2. "Billboard Hot 100 No. 1 Songs of 2015," https://www.billboard.com/photos/6777130/billboard-hot-100-no-1-songs-2015/.

3. According to *Billboard*, the artists who reached #1 in 2015 were Taylor Swift, Mark Ronson featuring Bruno Mars, Wiz Khalifa featuring Charlie Puth, Taylor Swift featuring Kendrick Lamar, Omi, The Weeknd, Justin Bieber, and Adele.

4. "List of *Billboard* Hot 100 Number Ones of 1965," Wikipedia, https://en.wikipedia.org/wiki/List_of_Billboard_Hot_100_number_ones_of_1965.

5. "Kevin Garnett Reaffirms Team-First Reputation with Considerable Pay Cut in Reported Deal With Celtics," NESN, June 30, 2012, https://nesn.com/2012/06/kevin-garnett-reaffirms-team-first-reputation-with-considerable-pay-cut-in-reported-deal-with-celtic/.

6. Josh Wilson, "Miami Heat: How Pat Riley Got Shaq to Take Pay Cut in 2006," Fansided, https://allucanheat.com/2020/07/16/miami-heat-pat-riley-shaq/.

7. Philip Johnson, "Tim Duncan Cut His Salary in Half to Keep the Spurs Together," *Business Insider*, May 28, 2013, https://www.businessinsider.com/tim-duncan-cut-salary-half-to-keep-spurs-2013-5.

8. Duncan and Garnett were inducted to the NBA Hall of Fame together in 2021 alongside O'Neal's late teammate, Kobe Bryant.

9. "The Spirit of Ubuntu," Clinton Foundation, July 14, 2012, https://stories.clintonfoundation.org/the-spirit-of-ubuntu-6f3814ab8596.

10. Angela Thompsell, "Get the Definition of Ubuntu, a Nguni Word with Several Meanings," Thought.co, September 3, 2019, https://www.thoughtco.com/the-meaning-of-ubuntu-43307.

11. Ignacio David Acevedo, "Understanding Ethnicity: The Relation Among Ethnic Identity, Collectivism, and Individualism in African Americans and European Americans," Master's Thesis, University of Kentucky, 2003, https://uknowledge.uky.edu/cgi/viewcontent.cgi?article=1390&context=gradschool_theses.

12. Josie Pickens, "Black Wall Street and the Destruction of an Institution," Ebony, May 31, 2013, https://www.ebony.com/black-history/destruction-of-black-wall-street/.

13. Anna Menta, "Is 'The Banker' Based on a True Story? What to Know About the Real Bernard Garrett and Joe Morris," Decider, March 22, 2020, https://decider.com/2020/03/22/is-the-banker-based-on-a-true-story-apple-samuel-l-jackson/.

14. Bruce Dixon, "Black Mecca: The Death of an Illusion," The Black Commentator, October 13, 2005, https://blackcommentator.com/154/154_cover_dixon_black_mecca.html.

15. "Pastor DeForest Soaries Revisits Don Imus-Rutgers Women's Basketball Scandal Amidst Racial Injustice Conversations," CBS New York, June 8, 2020, https://newyork.cbslocal.com/2020/06/08/pastor-deforest-soaries-kristine-johnson-don-imus-rutgers-womens-basketball/.

16. Black Economic Alliance homepage, https://blackeconomicalliance.org/.

17. Elbert Hubbard was an American writer, publisher, artist, and philosopher.

18. "Transcript: Race in America: Creating Change," Washington Post, October 26, 2020, https://www.washingtonpost.com/washington-post-live/2020/10/26/transcript-race-america-creating-change/.

19. "'I Don't Believe Sandy Committed Suicide': #BlackLivesMatter Co-Founders Speak Out on Sandra Bland," Democracy Now, July 24, 2015, https://www.democracynow.org/2015/7/24/i_dont_believe_sandy_committed_suicide.

Strategic Action 7

1. "Business Lessons from American Express CEO Ken Chenault," https://neilpatel.com/blog/lessons-from-ken-chenault/.

2. Ken Chenault interview with 60 Minutes, https://youtu.be/JmMYx3X5alo.

3. Internationally there are essentially three tiers of consumers: tier one, those earning more than $20,000, 75–100 million people; tier two, those earning $1,500 to $20,000, 1.5–1.75 billion people; and tier three, those earning less than $1,500, 4 billion people (a multitrillion-dollar market).

4. The survey involved interviews with approximately one thousand people in each of twenty countries including the United States.

5. Source: DiversityInc. magazine.

6. Includes excerpts (with permission) from an article by Liz Willding for VHA's Alliance magazine, https://www.vha.com/News/Publications/Alliance/Pages/09-07_MentoringMinorityManufacturers.aspx.

Strategic Action 8

1. Karen Parker, "The African-American Entrepreneur–Crime Drop Relationship," *Urban Affairs Review* 51 (2015). 10.1177/1078087415571755.
2. Amanda Maher, "New Study Links African-American Entrepreneurship with Decline in Youth Violence," ICIC, https://icic.org/blog/new-study-links-african-american-entrepreneurship-decline-youth-violence/.
3. For more on the ten types, go to https://doblin.com/ten-types.
4. SBA Office of Advocacy.
5. "Small Business Mentor-Protégé Programs," Congressional Research Service, updated July 2, 2021, https://fas.org/sgp/crs/misc/R41722.pdf.

Strategic Action 9

1. Richard Prince, "Coalition for Diversity in Journalism May Lose Hispanic Members," The Root, October 8, 2013, https://www.theroot.com/coalition-for-diversity-in-journalism-may-lose-hispanic-1790885009.
2. http://www.mitchelltitus.com/about.html.
3. As of 2020.
4. As of 2020.

Strategic Action 10

1. Adapted from a blog by the Black Data Processors Association Education and Technology Foundation encouraging members to donate to the organization. Its suggestions are transferable to many types of giving, http://betf.blogspot.com/2009/09/things-you-can-do-to-leave-legacy.html.
2. https://drrobertbullard.com/.

INDEX

ABOUT THE AUTHORS

Randal Pinkett, PhD, MBA, has established himself as an entrepreneur, speaker, author, and scholar. He is the cofounder, chairman, and CEO of BCT Partners, a global, multimillion-dollar research, training, consulting, technology, and data analytics firm. BCT's mission is to provide insights about diverse people that lead to equity. The company has been recognized by *Forbes* as one of America's Best Management Consulting Firms, Ernst & Young as EY Entrepreneur of the Year, *Manage HR Magazine* as a Top 10 Firm for Diversity & Inclusion, the *Black Enterprise* BE 100s list of the nation's largest African American–owned businesses, and the *Inc. 5000* list of the fastest-growing private companies in America. Pinkett is an expert in several areas relating to emerging technologies, "big data" analytics, social innovation, culture, and diversity, equity, and inclusion (DEI), and is a regular contributor on MSNBC, CNN, and Fox Business News. He holds five academic degrees in electrical engineering, computer science, and business administration from Rutgers, Oxford, and MIT. Most notably, he was the first and only African American to receive the prestigious Rhodes Scholarship at Rutgers University; he was inducted into the Academic All-America Hall of Fame as a former high jumper, long jumper, sprinter, and captain of the Rutgers men's track and field team; and he was the winner of NBC's hit reality TV show *The Apprentice*. A lifetime member of Alpha Phi Alpha Fraternity Incorporated, he is happily married to Natasha Williams-Pinkett and the proud father of two daughters, Amira and Aniyah, and two sons, Jaz and Marquis.

Jeffrey A. Robinson, PhD, is an award-winning business school professor, international speaker, and entrepreneur. Since 2008, he has been a leading faculty member at Rutgers Business School, where he is an associate professor of management and entrepreneurship, the academic director of The Center for Urban Entrepreneurship & Economic Development, and a research fellow of the Rutgers Advanced

Institute for the Study of Entrepreneurship and Development. Through his research, business leadership, and community activities, he makes direct impact on corporate workplaces, entrepreneurs, and economic development policy in the state of New Jersey and beyond. Dr. Robinson has completed five degrees in the areas of engineering, urban studies, and business. He completed a Bachelor of Arts in urban studies at Rutgers College and a Bachelor of Science in civil engineering at Rutgers School of Engineering. He has a Master of Science in civil engineering management from Georgia Institute of Technology as a GEM Fellow and an MPhil and a PhD in management and organizations from Columbia University. Dr. Robinson is an active member of the community and volunteers his time with many worthy causes. He works with various community organizations to empower, educate, and encourage others.